An Awkward Truth

**The bombing
of Darwin
February 1942**

OTHER BOOKS BY PETER GROSE

A Very Rude Awakening: The night the Japanese midget subs came to Sydney Harbour

A Good Place to Hide: How one French community saved thousands of lives in World War II

An Awkward Truth

The bombing of Darwin February 1942

PETER GROSE

ALLEN&UNWIN

SYDNEY · MELBOURNE · AUCKLAND · LONDON

This edition published in 2017
First published in 2009

Allen & Unwin
83 Alexander Street
Crows Nest NSW 2065
Australia
Phone: (61 2) 8425 0100
Email: info@allenandunwin.com
Web: www.allenandunwin.com

Cataloguing-in-Publication details are available
from the National Library of Australia
www.trove.nla.gov.au

ISBN 978 1 76029 652 0

Internal design by Darian Causby
Maps by Ian Faulkner
Set in Bembo by Midland Typesetters, Australia

Printed and bound in Australia by the SOS Print + Media Group

10 9 8 7 6

*For Anouchka and Tamara, who can both write
their Dad under the table*

Bloody Darwin

This bloody town's a bloody cuss,
No bloody trams, no bloody bus,
And no one cares for bloody us,
Oh bloody, bloody Darwin.

The bloody roads are bloody bad,
The bloody folks are bloody mad,
They even say 'you bloody cad',
Oh bloody, bloody Darwin.

All bloody clouds and bloody rain,
All bloody stones, no bloody drains,
The Council's got no bloody brains,
Oh bloody, bloody Darwin.

And everything's so bloody dear,
A bloody bob for bloody beer,
And is it good? No bloody fear,
Oh bloody, bloody Darwin.

The bloody 'flicks' are bloody old,
The bloody seats are bloody cold,
And can't get in for bloody gold,
Oh bloody, bloody Darwin.

The bloody dances make me smile,
The bloody band is bloody vile,
They only cramp your bloody style,
Oh bloody, bloody Darwin.

No bloody sports, no bloody games,
No bloody fun with bloody dames,
Won't even give their bloody names,
Oh bloody, bloody Darwin.

Best bloody place is bloody bed,
With bloody ice on bloody head,
And then they say you're bloody dead,
Oh bloody, bloody Darwin.

—Anon.

(Soldiers' doggerel, circa 1941)

Contents

Contents

Introduction to
the 75th anniversary edition

The birth of Australia as a nation took place on 25 April 1915, so we are told, when Australian troops stormed ashore on the beaches of Gallipoli. For the first time, the mostly British settlers in Australia saw themselves as Australians, not as scattered British colonists in an inhospitable southern wilderness. If that is true, I would argue that Australia became an *independent* nation on 19 February 1942, when the Japanese bombed Darwin.

Consider the evidence. The first two years of the Second World War were fought exclusively in Europe, North Africa and the Middle East. Australia was then a British Dominion, part of the British Empire. When Britain and France declared war on Germany on 3 September 1939, the Australian prime minister, Robert Menzies (a lawyer), thought Australia was legally bound to join the war on Britain's side. Menzies' exact words, in a radio broadcast to the nation, were: 'Great Britain has declared war upon [Germany] and ... *as a result* [my emphasis], Australia is also at war.'

The Royal Australian Navy was simply merged into Britain's Royal Navy, under British command. In 1941 Menzies felt obliged to move to London for a few months, while he held long discussions with Churchill on the conduct of the war, and took part in some British War Cabinet meetings. In his absence, his political enemies plotted his downfall, and they lay in wait for his return. On 28 August 1941 Menzies was forced to resign. After a brief period of turmoil, on 3 October 1941 the opposition Labor Party was asked to form a government, with the untried John Curtin as the new prime minister.

Curtin saw things differently from the anglophile Menzies. Japan had entered the war on 7 December 1941, when it attacked the American Pacific Fleet at anchor in Pearl Harbor. Australia was now directly threatened. The war was no longer confined to Europe, North Africa and the Middle East; it had spread to the Pacific and Australia's doorstep. Less than three weeks after Pearl Harbor, Curtin stood Australian foreign policy on its head. In an article in the Melbourne *Herald* dated 27 December 1941, he wrote: 'The Australian government regards the Pacific struggle as primarily one in which the United States and Australia must have the fullest say in the direction of the democracies' fighting plan.' Then came the killer punch: 'Without any inhibitions of any kind, I make it quite clear that Australia looks to America, free of any pangs as to our traditional links or kinship with the United Kingdom.'

This produced a gasp of shock around Australia. In an editorial, the *Sydney Morning Herald* called the article 'deplorable' (while pinching its nose and reprinting it in full). Australia looks to America, not Britain? Free of any pangs? It sounded like madness. But Curtin's radical thinking was well vindicated seven weeks later, on 15 February 1942, when Britain's 'impregnable' Singapore base fell to the Japanese, opening a gateway to Australia. It was now clear that Britain couldn't or wouldn't—the difference was immaterial—defend Australia.

Four days later the Japanese struck directly. The same carrier force that had devastated Pearl Harbor now wreaked similar havoc on Darwin, dropping more bombs there than they had dropped on Pearl Harbor, and killing more civilians than they had killed at Pearl Harbor.

There could be only one conclusion: Curtin was right. Australia had to fight its own battles, form its own alliances, and look to its own interests. Independent Australia was born that day. The events in the pages that follow are too terrible to call for any celebration, but if Australians want to mark an anniversary of their independence as a nation, 19 February is the day to do it.

I would make one further point. I hope this book, and the television drama documentary *The Bombing of Darwin* that is based on it, have helped to change Australia's perception of events in Darwin on 19 February 1942. When I began researching this book, it quickly became apparent that there were two almost entirely unconnected stories of the Japanese air raid on Darwin. Paul Hasluck, then Australian Minister for Territories, encapsulated the first story—also the best known and the most widely believed—in a speech delivered in Darwin on 25 March 1955. Speaking to the Northern Territory Legislative Council while unveiling a plaque commemorating the civilians killed by bombs in the Darwin Post Office, Hasluck described 19 February as 'not an anniversary of national glory but one of national shame. Australians ran away because they did not know what else to do.'

However, my research led me to another story. Undoubtedly there was panic, incompetence, looting and desertion during and after the Darwin attack. But there was also a disciplined and dogged counter-attack from the Australian anti-aircraft gunners, and an exemplary display of heroism by a tiny handful of US Army Air Corps fighter pilots, blown out of the sky as they squared up to an overwhelmingly superior Japanese force. The doomed yet magnificent reply by the destroyer USS *Peary* as Japanese dive bombers swarmed around her in Darwin harbour, deserves a place in the legend books of American military history. The heroism of the Australian rescuers who braved burning oil, strafing aircraft and huge explosions to pull their comrades to safety is simply beyond praise.

In 1942 the Australian government had a commendable policy of sending only volunteers off to fight in wars overseas. Conscripts stayed behind, to defend the homeland. This led to a division of esteem. The conscripts were known as 'chockos', in other words chocolate soldiers liable to melt in the heat of battle. They were generally treated with contempt by the elite volunteers, and had to suffer inferior training, outdated weapons and poor status. The men who defended Darwin were largely 'chockos', which makes their heroic actions all the more commendable. The Australian Army has campaign medals aplenty for those who served in the Second World War in the Arctic, Africa, the Pacific, Burma, Italy, France and Germany. There is no campaign medal for those who fought in Australia, and no official recognition of their heroism and discipline.

This book has found its way into the hands of many readers. I like to think that it and its associated film have done something to correct that first perception of the Darwin story. The most frequent reaction I've had to the book and the film, either from friends or from readers and viewers, is: I never knew any of this happened. Australians have tended to treat the events in Darwin as a bit of an embarrassment, something best swept under the carpet. I sense this is changing, and Australians are now willing to face up to the worst because it is often balanced by the best. If this book and its film have played a part in that shift in attitudes, I'm delighted.

Peter Grose

December 2016

Chapter I

'Big flight of planes . . . Very high'

As the sun rose in an almost clear sky and the temperature climbed towards the regular Darwin seasonal average of 32°C, 19 February 1942 looked like an unseasonally good day. It was a Thursday and a normal working day. Nevertheless, the good weather meant there might be time after work to walk the dog, have an evening beer on the verandah or go to the open-air picture show. It would also be, if that was your fancy, a perfect day to go flying.

Like most tropical cities, Darwin has no real summer or winter. The seasons are divided into the Wet, between December and March, and the Dry, between May and September. January and February produce the heaviest rainfall, often in the form of violent tropical downpours. A single Darwin thunderstorm can produce 300 millimetres or more of rain and as many as 1600 lightning flashes in the space of two or three hours. The storms are so spectacular that the city today treats them as a tourist attraction, offering visitors and locals alike a *son et lumière* display to make up for the steamy humidity, ankle-deep water and flooded storm drains.

However, the Wet elected to take a day off on 19 February 1942. The sun rose over a few scattered white cumulus clouds and promised the tiny population of Darwin a pleasant morning. There was a sense of relief throughout the town that the evacuation of civilians, mostly women and children, had passed off relatively smoothly. The last batch of evacuees had left by plane the previous day. The two-month exodus reduced the civilian population from an original 5800 to about 2000. Of those who stayed behind, only 63 were women.

◆ ◆ ◆

The two large Tiwi Islands of Bathurst and Melville lie 80 kilometres north of Darwin. A quick glance at a map might lead a casual observer to believe they are a single island, but for the narrow and treacherous Aspley Strait which keeps them apart. Today they make a nice one- or two-day outing for visitors to Darwin looking for something else to do after the obligatory trip to Kakadu National Park. In particular, the art of the Tiwi Island Aborigines is distinctive and much sought after all over the world.

Abel Tasman first sighted the Tiwis in 1644, when he slipped past on his journey to Batavia. The British made a brief attempt in 1824 to establish a fort on Melville Island, but the Tiwi Islanders proved a tough and hostile bunch, and the fort was abandoned in 1828 after one spearing too many. There was no particular reason to settle the islands, and they remained largely untouched by Europeans until the early 20th century. In 1910 Francis Xavier Gsell set up the next European presence there in the form of a Mission of the Sacred Heart. It got off to a slow start. After 28 years Gsell had still not succeeded in converting a single Tiwi adult to Christianity. He fared better with the children, to the point where Tiwi Islanders today are almost all Catholics. Father (later Bishop) Gsell is best remembered for having 150 'wives'. This was not quite as sybaritic as it sounds: he disapproved of the Tiwis' polygamous habits and bought the wives himself to spare them from forced marriages to older men. He then sold them on to men of their own choosing. It was Christian mercy at its practical best.

In February 1942, Father John McGrath ran the Mission of the Sacred Heart at Nguiu. As well as his mission duties, Father McGrath operated as a volunteer coastwatcher. The mission was equipped with a radio transceiver linked to the Amalgamated Wireless of Australia (AWA) Darwin Coastal Station, call sign VID. These so-called aeradio stations were scattered all over Australia and operated by AWA under contract to the Australian Department of Civil Aviation. Civil aircraft used them for both ground-to-air communication and navigation. VID also acted as a voice communication station in contact with other radio transmitters as far away as Dili, in Portuguese Timor.

We can readily imagine a standard mission day for 19 February 1942, starting in the dry and sunny morning with prayer followed by breakfast, then school or work. The mission cared for 300 Tiwi Islanders, so any morning was busy. Work was well under way at 9.30 a.m., when the missionaries and the islanders were brought up short by a sight too disturbing to be ignored. Everybody downed tools to stare. Above them, and flying very high, was a huge formation of planes. They were heading south-east on a track that would take them towards Darwin.

Only 15 minutes earlier, well to the south and out of sight of the Bathurst Island mission, a group of ten American Army Air Corps P40 Kittyhawk fighters escorted by a B17 Flying Fortress bomber had taken off from Darwin's military airfield on their way to reinforce Java. However there were reports of bad weather at their first destination, Koepang, at the western end of Timor, so after less than 20 minutes in the air the Kittyhawks took the Darwin controller's advice and reluctantly turned back. Their return track would bring them well to the south of Bathurst Island and out of view of the mission.

The large formation over Bathurst Island was still highly visible, and Father McGrath switched straight to coastwatcher mode. An emergency radio frequency was kept permanently open and monitored at VID in Darwin, and the priest set off at a brisk pace to the mission's wireless room to call the Coastal Station. His radio set took an agonising time to warm up, but by 9.35 the valves were glowing and he was ready to transmit.

The mission's call sign was Eight SE. 'Eight SE to VID,' Father McGrath began. 'Big flight of planes passed over going south. Very high. Over.'

From VID the duty officer, Lou Curnock, replied: 'Eight SE from VID. Message received. Stand by.'

Father McGrath had no chance to stand by. At about that moment a Japanese aircraft screamed low over the mission on a strafing run, raking it with cannon and machine-gun fire on its way to destroying an American Beechcraft aircraft on the ground at the Bathurst Island airfield. Father McGrath abandoned the radio and raced to shelter. He had unwittingly taken part in a watershed moment in Australian history. For the first time since European settlement 154 years earlier, Australians were under attack on their own soil.

◆ ◆ ◆

Radio operating is a meticulous business, and Lou Curnock stuck by the rules. In his radio log sheet he recorded the time of Father McGrath's message—0935 local—and the readability. It came in as strength four, meaning 'readable but not perfect'. Strength five would be 'perfectly readable'. He recorded atmospherics as A3—'intermittent interference'. He then wrote down the text of the message and of his acknowledgement. His next entry is timed at 0937, two minutes later. 'Phoned R.A.A.F. Operations. 9.37 A [a.m.].'

The protocol was simple. Warning messages like this went first to RAAF Operations, located on the RAAF airfield just outside the town. It was the job of the RAAF duty officer who received the warning to raise the alarm by passing on the message to the RAAF section of Area Combined Headquarters, located at the same airfield. Next the Navy, then the Army, then the civilian air-raid wardens would be alerted, all by the RAAF.

In a situation like this, seconds count. People invariably need to go some distance to a slit trench or air-raid shelter. Fighter aircraft—had there been any—need to be given the order to scramble. Anti-aircraft gunners need to go to action stations and prepare their guns. Predictors who control the AA guns need to start looking for incoming aircraft, to establish fuse setting, height and bearing. With enough warning, ships in a harbour can start engines, cast off their moorings and prepare to take evasive action.

But at RAAF Operations there was uncertainty. The Army's AA gunners had already caused uproar two hours earlier. A group of RAAF Lockheed Hudson bombers had arrived from the north and failed to observe the established 'friendly' route inbound. They had also failed to provide proper light signal identification. Although the AA gunners were reasonably proficient at identifying Japanese aircraft, they had a legitimate worry that the Japanese might use captured Allied aircraft in a surprise attack. There was also, let it be said, some exasperation on the part of the gunners at the RAAF's persistent failure to use correct identification procedures. The Acting Gun Position Officer at Fannie Bay, Sergeant Laurie Huby, had had enough. He ordered a warning shot fired across the path of the inbound Hudsons. This led to indignation all round and a generally jumpy mood at RAAF Operations and at the AA batteries.

As well, RAAF Operations knew that the ten Kittyhawks were now on their way back to Darwin, on a reciprocal track to their westerly route to Timor. A glance at a map might have told them that the Kittyhawks' return track would be well to the south and out of sight of the Bathurst Island mission. But the possibility that the mission had seen the returning Kittyhawks could not be ruled out. Too many false alarms were bad for morale, so the decision to set off the sirens could not be taken lightly. While RAAF Operations pondered, the clocks kept ticking.

The Army maintained a series of observation posts strung out around Darwin. According to the military log: 'Post M4 reports six planes approaching from seawards flying at great height, unable identify at 0938 hours.' Post M4 had trouble getting the message through to the fixed defences. Twelve minutes later, at 0950, the message finally made it. At 0955 it reached the military barracks at Larrakeyah. The clocks kept ticking.

Lieutenant Commander James McManus was senior intelligence

officer at Navy Headquarters on The Esplanade, overlooking Port Darwin. He was chatting to the Naval Officer in Charge, Darwin, Captain Penry Thomas, when the direct-line phone rang. The signalman from RAAF Operations had a simple message: a large number of aircraft had been sighted over Bathurst Island. McManus and Thomas looked at their watches. It was 9.46. McManus spoke first. 'We have 12 minutes before they arrive.'[1]

It was the job of the RAAF to order the air-raid warning sirens to sound. In general, the first siren to go off would be at the airfield. After this, sirens spread around the town would be set off either after a message delivered by landline, or simply by troops and the air-raid wardens overhearing the airfield sirens and following suit. At this point the RAAF was by no means certain that the arriving aircraft were hostile, so no sirens sounded. However, the Navy had a separate warning system, consisting of an old foghorn mounted on the roof of Navy Headquarters. This appears to have sounded some time between 9.46 and 9.58 a.m., but it had limited range and in any case was not associated in the minds of the townspeople with an air raid. They had been told to listen for a series of air-raid siren blasts—four blasts of 30 seconds each, with five seconds in between. Nobody was going to leave their shop or desk and dive into a slit trench or air-raid shelter on the say-so of an old foghorn bleating faintly in the distance.

◆ ◆ ◆

Although the Pacific war was only ten weeks old, Captain Mitsuo Fuchida had already earned a formidable reputation. He had, after all, triggered that war by leading the Japanese aerial assault on Pearl Harbor in a Type 97 'Kate' bomber. Again flying a Kate, he now commanded a slightly larger force of 188 aircraft for the raid on Darwin. Fuchida knew what he was doing. He led his planes on a track that would take them to the north and east of the town, making them hard to see against the tropical morning sun. The huge formation tracked south-east, following the coast of Melville Island as far as Cape Gambier before crossing the narrow Clarence Strait separating Melville from the mainland. They

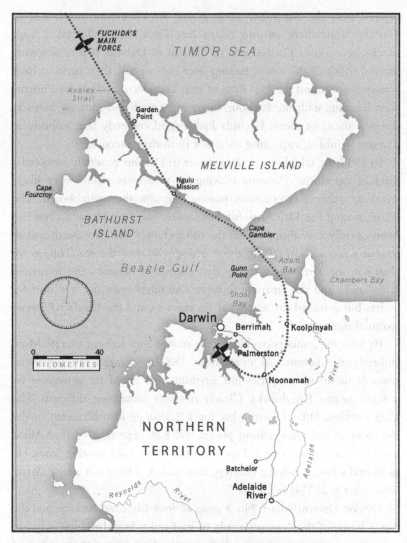

The route taken by the main attacking force of Japanese bombers. Note that the route produces a double benefit: as they cross the coast at Adam Bay, the attackers have the sun behind them when seen from Darwin; and the final line of attack is from the least likely direction, the south-east.

arrived over the Australian coast about 40 kilometres north-east of Darwin, somewhere around Adam Bay. They then followed a huge clockwise arc over Koolpinyah, to the east of Darwin, before swinging around south of the town, passing over Noonamah, then turning back somewhere around the East Arm of Port Darwin onto their final north-west heading, with the harbour, town and Larrakeyah military barracks directly ahead of them. Fuchida had judged correctly that nobody in Darwin would be expecting an attack from that direction.

In 1942 the telephone system in use in Darwin generally involved a kind of 'open line'. Anyone picking up a receiver would very likely overhear other conversations passing through the switchboard. The telephonist at the 14th Anti-Aircraft section based on Darwin Oval had been casually eavesdropping on the town chatter when he overheard an urgent voice say something about a 'dogfight' over the sea. This, as we shall see, was a reference to the first encounter between the returning Kittyhawks and the Japanese fighters. The telephonist did not wait for orders but sounded the alarm for his gunners, and the Oval's AA crews manned their guns.

By now the gunners could hear the roar of approaching aircraft. More sinisterly, the volume of noise from 188 Japanese aircraft pounding towards them was way beyond anything that could be generated by a flight of ten Kittyhawks. Clearly this was something different. The Gun Position Officer swung his Toc I (telescope identification) in the direction of the approaching planes, still half expecting to find Allied aircraft in his sights. The red spots on the wings told another story. He indicated a target, called a bearing, then yelled: 'This is not a false alarm. This is for real! This is for real!'

Out on Darwin wharf, No. 3 gang of dock labourers had opened the No. 1 hatch of the *Neptuna*, ready to start unloading the ship's cargo of explosives and depth charges. Before unloading began, they exercised their right to knock off for ten o'clock 'smoko'. They trooped off to a recreation shed on the wharf. As they did, they saw a huge wave of planes bearing down on them from the south-east. 'Yankee reinforcements at last,' one of the wharfies mocked.

Gunner Jack Mulholland remembers firing the first salvo from the Oval section's anti-aircraft guns before the air-raid sirens sounded, and well before the first bombs struck. The gunners' shells and the bombs crossed in mid-air. The first bombs detonated in the harbour, near the wharf, some time around 9.58 a.m. The same pattern of bombs swept on and caught the wharf itself. The last bomb of the stick detonated on the Oval and showered the gunners with flying rocks, stones, gravel and dirt. The roar of the first bombs merged nicely with the opening wail of the air-raid sirens.

Chapter 2

A very sinful people

Darwin has something of a history of being knocked flat. The most recent memory is of Cyclone Tracy, which struck on Christmas Eve 1974, killing 71 people and leaving the town devastated and in shock. Tracy was not the first. On 6 January 1897 a cyclone hit Darwin at the precise moment that the tide peaked in the harbour. It killed 15 people and wrecked 18 pearling luggers, three sampans and the government launch. The combination of high tide and howling wind pitched some of the wrecked boats a hundred metres or more onto the shore, giving the foreshores the appearance of a boat wrecker's yard. A local preacher proclaimed that it was 'a gentle reminder from Providence that we are a very sinful people'.

Cyclones struck again in 1917 and 1937, each time devastating the town and leaving behind more death and destruction. The local Larrakia Aboriginal people came up with an explanation much in keeping with the views of the 1897 preacher: white settlers had enraged Nunga-linya, the Dreamtime ancestor responsible for earthquakes, storms and cyclones, and Nungalinya was taking his revenge. (Nungalinya can be seen to this day in the form of Old Man Rock, off Darwin's Casuarina Beach.)

Whether the destruction was the work of Providence or Nungalinya or merely bad luck, it all gave support to the view that Darwin was no place for the quiet life. From its birth until the mid-20th century, Darwin was a hard-drinking frontier town, a last outpost, perched precariously on the far and steamy fringes of the civilised world.

◆ ◆ ◆

Lieutenant John Lort Stokes first mapped the Darwin area in 1839. He happened to be a friend of the great naturalist Charles Darwin, and he named the place in his honour. The first Europeans, who began arriving in 1869, would have none of it. They were not about to live in a town named after the man who said they were descended from monkeys. They renamed it Palmerston, after a former British prime minister.

European settlement of the area gathered momentum with the construction of the overland telegraph line. As early as the middle of the 19th century an overland and undersea cable from London terminated on the island of Java, in the Dutch East Indies. Furious competition broke out between the Australian colonies of Victoria, Queensland and South Australia (which then included what is now the Northern Territory) to complete the Australian link. South Australia won. In 1862 John McDouall Stuart, at his sixth attempt, finally crossed the continent from Adelaide and Port Augusta in South Australia to the Northern Territory coast, and returned to tell the tale.[1] He reached the sea about 80 kilometres east of the present site of Darwin, at a place he named Chambers Bay. Stuart's expedition proved that a north–south telegraph route across Australia was feasible. In 1870, a year after the arrival of the first European settlers, work began at both ends of the telegraph line, the aim being to meet in the middle. A separate company set about laying a submarine cable from Java to Palmerston. Thirty-six thousand poles and 3200 kilometres of floods and hardship later, on 22 August 1872 the lines all met, linking Java to Palmerston and Palmerston to Adelaide in South Australia. Australia was now in instant contact with the rest of the world.

Palmerston became a critical link in the chain of communication between Britain's most distant colonies and London. That would hardly have been enough to attract settlers to the otherwise swampy and hostile tropical outpost. However, in 1865 gold was discovered in modest quantities at the Finniss River, just south of Palmerston, followed by further modest finds at nearby Tumbling Waters. Gold even found its way to the surface in the diggings from an overland telegraph post hole at Yam Creek. Rumours spread. Gold fever hit hard with the discovery in 1872 of the big Priscilla reef at Pine Creek. Miners poured in, especially Chinese, to the point where Chinese gold miners at Pine Creek outnumbered Europeans 15 to 1. Towns sprang up. The Northern Territory underwent its first boom.

The overland telegraph opened the rest of Australia's eyes to the possibilities of the empty north, and a new breed of settler began to arrive. Cattle station owners from South Australia sent their sons north to claim vast tracts of land around Alice Springs. Queensland's cattle barons looked west and snapped up the cattle country of the Top End, with Palmerston as the key town. By the turn of the 20th century a pearling industry was well established along the northern and western coasts of Australia. Palmerston/Darwin never quite matched Broome, in Western Australia, for the quality and quantity of its pearls, but it was a major player in the world pearling industry. Then, just before the outbreak of the First World War, the British company Vestey built a giant meat-works in Darwin. While it lasted, the Vestey works gave new importance to Port Darwin as a distribution centre for beef as well as minerals.

The biggest losers were the Aboriginal people. Although they managed to maintain their traditional lifestyle in large areas of the Territory and continued to outnumber the European population until well into the 20th century, too many were forced off their lands by the cattlemen and by the miners and mining companies, large and small, digging for gold, copper, silver and tin. Some Aboriginals found work as stockmen on the cattle stations. Others worked in the mines. Those who found employment with the new European businesses were ruthlessly exploited, usually working for little or no pay beyond rations. Women could sometimes find domestic work in the homesteads or towns, again for little or no pay. Aboriginal camps sprang up on the edges of settlements. A few Christian missions offered rudimentary schooling and health care, and sometimes rations to lure children into the classroom. In general, the Aboriginals were marginalised, victimised and even massacred.

Throughout the 19th and early 20th centuries, there was a widespread belief that white men could not handle hard manual work in the tropics. So, whatever the White Australia policy might have dictated elsewhere, there was no squeamishness about importing non-European labour into the Territory. Rich Chinese brought some 3000 Chinese indentured labourers to work on construction of the Darwin to Pine Creek railway. At the time there were only 400 Europeans in the whole Top End. During the wet season the Chinese employers switched their labour force to the search for alluvial gold. Chinese who had came to the territory as part of the gold hunt retreated to the towns as shopkeepers and businessmen. Darwin catered to their every need, including the establishment of gambling rooms and—so went the rumour—opium dens in Cavenagh Street, known as Chinatown. The Chinese were more tolerated than liked by the minority Europeans, but as long as they provided much-needed services they could stay.

The Japanese were essential for pearling. They had a near monopoly on the necessary diving skills. Japanese luggers and their crews made Darwin their base. Non-British Europeans arrived in Darwin to swell the mixed population: Greeks in particular poured in, followed by Italians. In Darwin today there is a small but touching monument in the smart Smith Street shopping mall celebrating the link between Darwin and the Greek island of Kalymnos. More people from Kalymnos live in Darwin than anywhere else except Kalymnos.

The wild atmosphere of the tropical north of Australia in its pioneering days is beautifully caught by A.B. 'Banjo' Paterson, creator of 'Waltzing Matilda'. Two incidents from his travel diary *Happy Dispatches* paint the picture. The first took place on Thursday Island, off the northern tip of Queensland, but it might as well have been written about Darwin. On 30 July 1901 Paterson recorded:

There are more nationalities here than there were at the Tower of Babel—every Caucasian nation, local blacks, kanakas [South Sea Island indentured labourers], Chinese, Japanese, Javanese, Malays, New Guinea boys. The local white police have to be very wide awake to nip any troubles in the bud; for, when the Orientals, especially the Malays, have any grievance to avenge, they go stark staring mad. So the police here act like American police—club them first and find out about the trouble afterwards. Nobody has any rights up here; the glorious doctrine of democracy does not run north of Rockhampton. A pearler engaged two men, a Malay and a kanaka, to work on his lugger, and gave them the usual advance of ten pounds. They made a plot to stow away on our ship and get away with the tenners. The Malay billiard-marker at the local hotel gave the plot away and the kanaka was captured and locked up. The Malay evaded capture till dark. Then he went to the hotel, called out the billiard-marker and opened fire on him with a revolver. The first bullet took the ground; the second hit a bystander; and the third broke some bottles on the bar. The billiard-marker ran upstairs chattering like an ape. The barmaid lay flat on the floor among the bottles. She said: 'I guessed he would have to fire low if he wanted to lay me out.' Then the Malay decamped, and up to the time we left he was at large in Thursday Island.

The journey continued to Darwin. Paterson resumed:

Off Port Darwin. One of these violent little interludes that occasionally enliven a tropical voyage was staged to-day. The chief steward had been allowed to bring his wife with him as far as Port Darwin on their honeymoon trip, and the lady had laid out all her best clothes on the bed, intending to stagger Port Darwin when she went ashore. A Malay deckhand, washing down the decks, let a full head of water go down a ventilator into the cabin, soaking the lady and her clothes and the chief steward's papers. The chief steward ran on deck and hit the Malay; then the Malay dropped the hose and charged straight at the steward with a *kris* in his hand. The steward ran for his life with the Malay after him, round the horse-stalls and up the alley-way like a rabbit. The steward darted through the door into his cabin, and while the Malay was fumbling with the lock the second engineer arrived, hit the Malay a couple of times, took his *kris* from him, and scragged him back to his work.

◆ ◆ ◆

Rather like the Wild West of America, the Northern Territory needed an urgent dose of law and order, not to mention managed development. The system of government put in place was, however, less than ideal and well short of democratic. The Northern Territory had been part of the colony of South Australia, but this proved to be a failure, particularly when it came to development. The cattle industry in the Top End never lived up to expectations. Vesteys closed the meat-works after a mere three years. The Northern Territory historian Bob Alford summed it up: 'For almost 50 years successive South Australian administrations had encouraged and supported all manner of projects to realise the economic potential of the Territory. None of these efforts met with success and by 1910 the public debt on the Northern Territory account was nearly £4 million. Moves by SA to transfer the NT to the new Commonwealth government began in earnest in 1905 in the hope of relieving the state of the ever-mounting liabilities of its dependency.'

In 1911 the South Australians finally got their way and passed control of the Northern Territory to the new Federal Government. Prime Minister Alfred Deakin put the best face he could on it by declaring: 'To me the question has been not so much commercial as national, first, second, third and last. Either we must accomplish the peopling of the Northern Territory or submit to its transfer to some other nation.' In other words, if something was not done fast to build up the Territory, some other nation—Russia? Japan? China?—would step into the gap. As part of the Territory's fresh start under Commonwealth rule, on

18 March 1911 the governor-general, the Earl of Dudley, renamed the town of Palmerston. Darwin it was to be, monkeys notwithstanding.

Deakin and his successors governed the Northern Territory like a subject colony, rather as they administered Papua and New Guinea. The Territorians elected a single member to the House of Representatives in Canberra. Otherwise they were spared the trouble of having to vote. Their sole representative was similarly spared: at first he could neither speak nor vote in Parliament. Canberra appointed an Administrator, based in Darwin, and he ruled on Canberra's behalf, under the direction of the Minister for Territories and without the benefit of popular support.

Not to be outdone, the population of Alice Springs asked if they could have their own separate Administrator. Instead they were given a District Officer. The phrase 'District Officer' conjures up an image of a mustachioed and pith-helmeted public servant in khaki shorts dispensing justice to the fuzzy-wuzzies from a tent somewhere in the bush. It was, of course, a bit more businesslike than that. But the job titles left the local population in no doubt that they were colonial subjects with little or no say in how they were governed. In the 1930s Darwin briefly had a Town Council, but this modest experiment in democratic local government quickly collapsed, and its powers were handed back to the Administrator. The man from Canberra would see to it all.

Brough Newell, a Darwin solicitor who later became Director of First Aid in Darwin's Air Raid Precautions unit, summed it up as follows: 'We have no Government. We have two taxing authorities. We pay the ordinary Commonwealth tax, Territorial income tax, stamp duty, and we also pay the Commonwealth government, the Municipal rates, and what is called the health rate. We have no Parliamentary representative and have not got a State Parliament to decide who is to carry the baby. No one carries it in Darwin.' Yet, incredibly, this remained the system of government in the Northern Territory until 1947, when the Federal Government in Canberra finally granted limited powers to a 13-man Legislative Council. Only six of the councillors were elected: the remaining seven, who included the Administrator, were appointed by

Canberra. The Northern Territory did not have a democratically elected Parliament until 1978, when a Legislative Assembly took over the administration of the Territory for the first time.

◆ ◆ ◆

As happens in every democracy, government appointees to prestigious jobs are usually politicians who have either passed their prime or need to be got out of the way. Aubrey Abbott, appointed Northern Territory Administrator on 29 March 1937 by the conservative Menzies government, could claim a bit of both. He came from a solid political background. His two uncles had been members of the New South Wales Legislative Assembly, while two of his cousins were elected to Federal Parliament. Abbott left school at 14 and went to work on cattle stations. In 1908, at the age of 22, he joined the New South Wales Police and remained with it until the outbreak of the First World War. He served with distinction in the Army. He fought at Gallipoli, where he was commissioned, then took part in the famous Australian Light Horse charge at Beersheba. He was wounded and promoted to Captain.

On his return to Australia, his Uncle William helped him to buy Echo Hills, a sheep and cattle station near Tamworth, New South Wales. He became active in the Graziers Association and politically active in the Country Party. In 1925 he was elected to Federal Parliament for the seat of Gwydir. In 1928 he joined the government as Minister for Home Affairs. The Northern Territory became part of his responsibilities. He lost the Gwydir seat in the 1929 election.

The Great Depression now struck, with its attendant social unrest. According to the *Australian Dictionary of National Biography*, Abbott appears to have responded by becoming an organiser for the New Guard, a loony right-wing paramilitary group that was as near as Australia ever came to Britain's Blackshirts or Mosleyites. His career on the right-wing fringe ended in 1931, when he recaptured the Gwydir seat. He remained in Parliament (but not in government) until his appointment as Administrator.

The government announced that appointment three weeks to the day after the deadly 1937 cyclone struck Darwin, causing one death and leaving a trail of devastation across the town. Winds gusting up to 158 kilometres an hour sent waves breaking over the cliffs on the port foreshore. Trashed buildings littered the landscape. His Honour's first task would be to supervise the rebuilding of the town.

Administrator Abbott controlled the police and public servants and all the usual trappings of colonial power. However, he was not the only authority in the Northern Territory. The Army, Navy and Air Force all answered to their own military hierarchies. There was a third significant force: workers were heavily unionised, and trade union leaders enjoyed a level of power and influence unimaginable today. Each was elected to office, so each could claim a democratic mandate not shared by the Administrator. There was only one newspaper in Darwin at the time, the *Northern Standard*, and it was owned and controlled by the powerful North Australian Workers' Union (NAWU). The *Standard* was a captivating mish-mash of local news and shameless left-wing propaganda. Every minor Russian military success was trumpeted as though it marked a turning point in the war, while no slight to a trade unionist was too trivial to escape the *Standard*'s pitiless gaze. Within four months of his arrival in Darwin, Abbott had alienated both the NAWU and the *Northern Standard* by organising a group of civil servants as strikebreakers to intervene in an industrial dispute on the wharves. From then on, as far as the unions were concerned, he was the enemy.

Thus a picture emerges of Abbott as an old-fashioned right-winger with a strong leaning towards pastoralists and landowners. He regularly attended meetings of the executive committee of the Northern Territory Pastoral Lessees Association. While happily mixing with the 'elite' of Darwin society, he made little secret of his contempt for the rest, whom he regarded as riff-raff. His divisive personality and lack of rapport with most of those he administered would shortly cost both the Administrator and the town of Darwin dearly.

◆　◆　◆

The European war got under way on 3 September 1939. By 1941 roughly half of Australia's Army had embarked for foreign shores: two and a half infantry divisions faced Germans, Italians and Vichy French in the Middle East; a further division shipped off to Malaya, ready to defend Singapore. The Royal Australian Navy sent about half its strength to the Red Sea, Mediterranean and Atlantic to fight as part of Britain's Royal Navy. Australian airmen were assigned to British RAF squadrons in Europe, where they fought in the Battle of Britain. This was normal. Australians had never been forced to defend their own territory against foreign attack, and anyway there was no war near home to fight. They slipped seamlessly into their traditional role alongside Britain, and that meant shipping large quantities of men and military equipment to the other side of the world.

Although more than half of the RAAF's planes remained on Australian soil, that still left Australia pitifully short of any serious air defence. Even in April 1941, with the war 19 months old, the RAAF's best fighting strength at home consisted of 67 ineffectual Wirraway fighters and 60 Hudson bombers. As long as the war continued to be fought in the northern hemisphere, the RAAF's principal role was not to defend Australia but to take advantage of the more reliable flying conditions Australia offered to train pilots for the European war. This was the Empire Air Training Scheme (EATS), which relied on Canada, Australia, New Zealand and Rhodesia to maintain a steady flow of pilots to confront the Luftwaffe in Europe. EATS became Australia's key contribution to the air war.

◆   ◆   ◆

The citizens of Darwin were never in doubt that, if war did finally reach Australia, their town would be among the first to come under attack. Anyone who owned a school atlas could work that out. However they appear to have felt no obligation to do much about it. As early as September 1939, in the first month of the war, the Red Cross organised public lectures in Darwin on First Aid, Home Nursing, Air Raid Precautions (ARP), Anti-gas and Transport. Hardly anybody from the town turned up. As long as the war remained half a world away, what was the point?

Civil Defence, as its name implies, is usually a matter for the civilian administration and not a military responsibility. In June 1940 the Government Secretary, L.H.A. Giles, held a conference in his office. He invited the Chief Surveyor, a newly arrived public servant called Arthur Miller who administered land divisions throughout the Northern Territory, to take on extra duties as Chief Air Raid Warden. The Administration proved unable to deliver much by way of support for its new Civil Defence supremo. Miller wrote afterwards: 'Assistance was promised from many quarters but it was found later that little was forthcoming.' Things got worse rather than better. Darwin's citizens are not easily led at the best of times, and the division of the town into ten ARP groups under the control of a Senior Warden, with each group broken into sectors under control of a Sector Warden, produced zero result. By July 1940, Miller wrote: 'The whole organisation contained 75 per cent of Government officers and the public generally ignored its existence, at the same time holding its members up to ridicule. Volunteers for first aid squads were called for, also for fire fighting and demolition, but the response was negligible.' Two months later, in August 1940, Miller reported: 'A general appeal was issued for the construction of shelters by volunteer labour. Only two groups, Nos. 8 & 9, responded, but in a half-hearted manner. Several shelters were constructed at the workmen's camp at the R.A.A.F. aerodrome, and commencement was made on one at Parap where eight men turned up on a Saturday afternoon. Within three weeks this work was abandoned owing to lack of volunteers.'

By February 1941 the international situation had worsened. As we shall see in the next chapter, Japan looked increasingly likely to enter the war on the Axis side. If Japan declared war and struck south, the threat to Darwin from sea and air would be immense. Administrator Abbott asked Miller if the ARP organisation could be revived. Miller appears to have been more successful this time. First Aid classes were well attended; the Army, Navy and Air Force consulted with the ARP organisation to draw up Notices to Householders and Notices to Business Houses, setting out what was required of them in the event of an attack; and in May 1941 a trial blackout was held. The results, according to Miller, were 'excellent'.

At this point Miller felt the burden of two jobs was beyond him, and he recommended the appointment of a Permanent Officer in charge of ARP. He had his way. 'Mr Harrison, a draftsman in my office, was appointed to the position,' Miller wrote later. 'Working with the General Staff, an extensive programme was prepared wherein every phase of A.R.P. work was covered. This even provided for the evacuation of the female population and children, and the aged and infirm. Estimates of the requirements were prepared and forwarded. The latter covered the cost of equipment needed and the labour for certain shelters and aid posts.'

This burst of activity rapidly went the way of earlier schemes. Let Miller take up the story again:

From September [1941] onwards, apathy crept in again, and the number of wardens diminished to some extent. The attitude of the general public remained the same as ever, a laissez faire attitude mostly, and we were told that we were wasting our time, that nothing would ever happen.

Ten days before Japan declared war, a public meeting was called to take place at the Public School. This meeting was well advertised, but apart from the Wardens, only two members of the public turned up.

◆ ◆ ◆

It is ironic that communication in the form of the overland telegraph line was the making of Darwin, because communication now became its biggest headache. Until as recently as 4 February 2004 there was no railway line connecting Darwin to the rest of Australia. The main rail link from Adelaide in South Australia to the Northern Territory ended at Alice Springs, 1500 kilometres south of Darwin. This was the legendary Ghan train, a contraction of its original name, *The Afghan Express*. That, in turn, honoured the Afghan camel-train drivers who had earlier followed the same route north. Work on the Ghan railway began in 1878, but the line did not reach Alice Springs until 1929.

Another line ran from Darwin to Birdum, about 500 kilometres south, but it was both narrow gauge and poorly laid, so it could not carry much by way of heavy traffic. The local population, and later the soldiers who had the misfortune to travel on it, referred to the engine as 'Leaping Lena', and to the whole train as the 'Spirit of Protest'. Even Leaping Lena still left a yawning gap of 1000 kilometres of scrub and desert between Birdum and the railhead at Alice Springs.

Road transport could bridge the gap for an average of only eight months a year. Before war broke out, the road between Darwin and Alice Springs was little better than a dirt track. In the four months of the Wet it became a slippery, treacherous quagmire. In 1940, the states of Queensland, New South Wales and South Australia combined to resurface about 500 kilometres of the road with gravel, replacing the sand and mud. The first Army convoy made its way gingerly up the new road in March 1941. But despite the genuine efforts of the three states, in 1942 the road remained unreliable in the Wet. Without proper grounding and draining and a tarred surface, cars and trucks regularly bogged down on what the Territorians still call 'the track'.

The other land access to the Northern Territory was via the far-western railheads of Queensland, notably Cloncurry and Mt Isa. Stock routes linked cattle stations in the Northern Territory to western Queensland, but these were scarcely even tracks: they were suitable for men on horseback and for cattle on the hoof, but not for heavy trucks or even cars. In the Wet they were impassable. Until well into 1942 there was nothing linking Queensland and the Northern Territory that could decently be called a road. There were tracks through the cattle stations, but these were little more than pairs of haphazard wheel ruts dodging between the anthills. The Army found this unacceptable, and in March 1941 the government in Canberra approved construction of what is now known as the Barkly Highway, linking Camooweal in western

Queensland with Tennant Creek in the Northern Territory. Until this was built, and until the road from Darwin to Alice Springs was properly surfaced, no bulk goods or people could move reliably by road to or from Darwin for four months of the year, until the Wet ran its course.

The movement of supplies by air is a comparatively new phenomenon, largely forced on planners by the demands of the Second World War. The first serious air freighter was the Douglas DC3 whose maiden flight took place on 17 December 1935. The mass production of Dakotas did not really hit its stride until the United States entered the Second World War in late 1941. At the outbreak of war, civil aircraft in Australia were mostly light, designed to carry not much more than mail and a few passengers. The idea that a town the size of Darwin could be supplied by air would never have occurred to anybody.

That left sea transport. The only way bulk freight could reliably move into or out of Darwin all year round was by sea. So the harbour in Darwin was more than just a convenience: it was Darwin's only full-time lifeline to the outside world.

◆ ◆ ◆

If anyone had set out to design the worst possible port facility imaginable, they might easily have come up with the Darwin harbour of the first half of the 20th century.[2] Stokes Hill Wharf today is a slightly faded example of conspicuous consumption, overshadowed by the smart new Convention Centre nearby. At the end of the wharf is a collection of bars and fast-food cafés, plus an up-market seafood restaurant packed nightly with tourists and Darwin yuppies. The ships that tie up there now are often round-the-world luxury cruise liners full of well-heeled holidaymakers from Asia, Europe and the United States. The Convention Centre and wharf complex today reek of prosperity and all-purpose international good living. To put it mildly, it was not always like this.

Port Darwin has huge tides, so ships at the wharf regularly rise and fall by seven metres or more twice a day. That would have made life difficult enough, but the design of the wharf piled on more misery. The wharf itself had no cranes, so goods had to be unloaded using the ships' own derricks. These were usually lighter than a typical shore-based crane and therefore carried smaller loads in their slings. Lifting hundreds or even thousands of tons of freight in small lots from the hold of a ship bobbing up and down seven metres every 12 hours was no picnic. At low tide, when the ship dipped furthest from wharf level, the job was almost impossible. The shipboard derricks were often not tall enough to lift goods onto the wharf. The ships themselves invariably had no air conditioning in the hold, so the hard physical work of unloading in the tropical heat was both uncomfortable and exhausting.

The problems did not end there. The wharf itself was a triumph of bad design. The first Stokes Hill Wharf was built in 1885 and promptly eaten by termites. The second wharf, generally known as Town Wharf, was built on the same site in 1904 and remained Darwin's only wharf until the Japanese raid. It could take no more than two ships at a time, one berthed on the inside and one on the outside.

The design beggars belief. The railway line from Birdum in the south led ultimately to the wharf. Tracks ran along the wharf itself for about 100 metres. Then, for reasons known only to the original designer, the wharf turned a right angle, known as the 'Elbow'. On the elbow was a turntable operated by a steam-driven 'donkey engine'. A locomotive could shunt rail cars as far as the turntable but not beyond. The turntable would accommodate only two cars at a time. Once they had been shunted into place, the donkey engine then spun the turntable through 90 degrees to line the carriages up with rail tracks running along the wharf right-angle's outer arm. The carriages were then dragged two at a time *by hand* a further 100 metres to put them alongside the ships being unloaded. A maximum of five carriages at any one time could be accommodated on the loading arm of the wharf. Once a carriage was loaded it would then be pushed, again by hand, back to the turntable. Because of the added weight, the wharf labourers could push the loaded carriages only one at a time. Once two loaded carriages had been dragged to the turntable, the donkey engine would spin them through 90 degrees to line up with the original track. A locomotive then dragged the loaded trucks back to land. It was unbelievably slow, inefficient and wasteful.[3] Given that the sea route was the only reliable year-round transport serving Darwin, the Darwin wharf was not, in the management-speak of the 21st century, 'fit for purpose'.

◆ ◆ ◆

One day someone will write an honest history of the role and behaviour of Australia's trade unions during the Second World War. There is not room for it in this book, nor would it be appropriate in what is simply an account of the Darwin air raid of 19 February 1942. Nevertheless there is a story to be told, and some of it would not make pretty reading. When John Curtin's Labor government came to power on 3 October 1941, taking over from the conservative Robert Menzies, the new prime minister might have reasonably expected a better level of cooperation from his comrades in the trade union movement. After all, he had been secretary of a small trade union himself, his only public office before becoming prime minister. He shrewdly chose the firebrand Sydney left-winger Eddie Ward as his Minister for Labour and National Service, and Eddie Ward set off to talk to the unions man to man. It didn't work. In vital industries like coal mining and the wharves, union militancy was the order of the day. Coal production actually fell under Eddie Ward's stewardship. The unions might once have seen Eddie Ward as one of their own, but when it came to a choice between facilitating the war effort or downing tools, they knew where their loyalties lay. They struck, and struck again.

In Darwin the working conditions for the wharfies, as Australians call their stevedores, were undoubtedly grim. As described above, the heat was intolerable and safety levels were lamentable. As well, the abysmal workings of the Darwin wharf made for poor morale in the workforce. That having been said, the wharfies were militant to a point where the troops and the townspeople saw them as something akin to saboteurs. Wharfies loved a good strike everywhere in Australia, but in Darwin they enjoyed it more than most. Scarcely a day went by without some sort of trouble on the wharves. It became a standing joke in the town. Whenever anything ran short, it could always be explained with the phrase: 'It's on the ship.' And why was it still on the ship? 'Blame the wharfies.'

◆　◆　◆

This, then, was the scene in Darwin when the Pacific War began. It was a town still being rebuilt after a devastating cyclone four years earlier. About 5800 people lived there in mostly ramshackle wooden houses lining mostly unpaved streets. For six months of the year it was uncomfortably hot and dry. For four months it was uncomfortably hot and wet. For the remaining two months it was a bit of both. Darwin was home to a mixed population of white Australians, Europeans, Chinese, Malays, Japanese, Timorese, Filipinos and Aboriginal Australians, some 'full bloods' and some of 'mixed blood', all of them convinced they had been forgotten and abandoned at the far edge of civilisation. The town was virtually cut off from the rest of Australia except via one of the most inefficient harbours in the world. It lived on cattle, mining, fish and pearls. It had no elected government, only an appointed Administrator who held its citizens in contempt. It was hardly going to present a united front in a crisis.

Chapter 3

Horribly strained relations

The Japanese fought on the allied side in the First World War but felt cheated of a proper reward for their part in the victory over Germany. In the postwar division of spoils they were granted a mandate over the former German colonies of the Marianas and the Caroline and Marshall Islands (which they had already captured in the course of the war). This may have troubled Australia, where it was seen as bringing the Japanese too close for comfort, but it was a meagre return for a substantial contribution to the war effort in the Pacific. Worse, although Japan now saw herself as a major power, she found herself once more forced into a corner by her erstwhile allies. The Washington Naval Treaty of 1922 and the London Naval Treaty of 1930 limited Japanese sea power to 60 per cent of the sea strength of the United States and of Britain. Japan had asked for 70 per cent.

The Japanese based their demands on a fairly simple calculation. Military orthodoxy at the time said that a navy needed to be able to field 150 per cent of the enemy's strength before it could be confident of mounting a successful attack. With Japan at 70 per cent of either country's strength, Britain or America would need one-and-a-half times that to be confident of success, or 105 per cent of what they had. At

70 per cent Japan would be safe from attack. At 60 per cent it would be exposed to (likely successful) attack by 90 per cent of either the British or American navies. So the 60 per cent ruling left Japan feeling vulnerable and deeply uneasy.

Japan's foreign policy never wavered throughout the first decades of the 20th century. The Japanese felt there should be an Asian nation among the great powers of the world, and they nominated themselves for the task. By the 1930s they were hinting at plans for a Greater East Asia Co-prosperity Sphere, though they did not formally announce the project until 1 August 1940. They had in mind that the United States, Britain, France, Holland and Portugal should gracefully abandon their Asian and Pacific possessions and allow them to pass into Japan's sphere of influence. They even offered to include Australia and New Zealand in the package. The five colonial powers concerned greeted this with less than acclamation, as did the Australians and New Zealanders. In an atmosphere of mounting acrimony, Japan withdrew from both the League of Nations and the two naval treaties, and began a furious program of warship and warplane building.

Although the government of Japan came to be dominated by the military, there were wide philosophical differences between the rival armed forces. The Japanese had already fought a war with Russia in 1904–05, ending in a clear if narrow win for Japan. The Japanese Army remained convinced that Russia was the logical enemy and based its plans on a return match. The Navy, on the other hand, saw the United States and its powerful Pacific Fleet as the most likely opponent and began planning accordingly. So the Army looked west for an enemy, while the Navy faced east.

In fairness, the Imperial Japanese Navy's plans in the beginning were entirely defensive. It expected the first attack to come from the United States, not the other way round. The Japanese fleet was designed to mount an effective defence in home waters. They accepted that Japan could not match the industrial output of the United States in terms of quantity. Instead they concentrated on quality. Their ships would have less range than the American ones but would be faster, better armed, and more suited to fighting in the stormy waters near home.

Japan opened the Co-prosperity Sphere account in 1931 by seizing Manchuria, which they renamed Manchukuo, setting up a puppet government there. This move was badly received by China, and the two countries began jostling and glowering at each other in a series of 'incidents'. Full-scale war broke out after one incident too many, on 7 July 1937. The Japanese had no capacity to conquer and subdue a country with seven times their population: their only hope was to overturn the weak and corrupt nationalist government of Chiang Kai-Shek's Kuomintang and put a puppet government of their own choosing in its place. As fighting continued, Japan managed to seize and hold some Chinese territory, but the war meandered along inconclusively. There was no shortage of death and destruction, merely a shortage of clear-cut results.

Japanese expansion increasingly worried the western powers, particularly those with something to lose. France then held the Indo-Chinese colonies of Laos, Cambodia and Vietnam, plus a scattering of Pacific islands. Britain had Hong Kong, Singapore, Malaya and Burma. The Dutch had the East Indies (now Indonesia). The Portuguese had East Timor. The United States controlled the Philippines, the Hawaiian Islands and their own scattering of small Pacific islands including Wake and Midway. All were targets for the Co-prosperity Sphere, and Japan was clearly on the move.

The United States led the anti-Japanese push. In January 1940 President Franklin Roosevelt ended his country's commercial treaty with Japan. In June of the same year he imposed limited sanctions, banning exports of aviation motor fuels and lubricants and No. 1 heavy melting iron and steel scrap. He also stepped up support for China.

The Japanese were unfazed. In September 1940 they signed a deal with Vichy France, still nominally in control of France's Indo-Chinese colonies, which allowed the Japanese to station a limited number of troops in Vietnam. They justified this by saying the troops were needed to block the supply route through Vietnam to China. Having been given an inch, the Japanese took a mile. Troops poured into Vietnam, using force against any who stood in their way, including their supposed Vichy partners. The French were powerless to stop them.

Next the Japanese had a stroke of luck. On 10 January 1941 the Thais, noting the ease with which Japan had pushed back the French in Vietnam, struck at the French colonies of Laos and Cambodia, quickly capturing most of Laos. The Japanese stepped in as mediators between the Thais and the Vichy French. The upshot was agreement with the French that Japan should 'station' troops in the whole of northern Indo-China. By July 1941 some 120,000 troops had moved in, brushing aside any resistance they encountered on the way. It might not have been called an invasion, but for most observers it was hard to spot the difference.

This proved too much for the western powers. Roosevelt decided he had to crack down hard. On 26 July 1941 the United States froze all Japanese assets, effectively imposing a complete ban on trade between the two countries. For good measure Roosevelt closed the Panama Canal to Japanese shipping. A week later he specifically banned all supply of oil to Japan. The British government and the Dutch government in exile followed suit. Japan was now between a rock and a hard place. Eighty per cent of Japan's oil came from the United States. It needed an alternative source, and fast. The most promising target looked like the Dutch East Indies, particularly Java, where oil flowed in abundance.

Suddenly the creation of the Greater East Asia Co-prosperity Sphere became not a vague dream of Japanese grandeur but a matter of life and death. The Japanese saw the problem, and the likely solution, quickly and clearly. Not long after the embargo was imposed, American code-breakers intercepted a cable from Japanese Foreign Minister Teijiro Toyoda to his ambassador to the United States, Kichisaburo Nomura. Toyoda wrote: 'Commercial and economic relations between Japan and third countries, led by England and the United States, are gradually becoming so horribly strained that we cannot endure it much longer. Consequently, our Empire, to save its very life, must take measures to secure the raw materials of the South Seas.'

◆ ◆ ◆

In the 1930s Japan was fortunate to have some of the most brilliant and clear-headed military thinkers anywhere in the world, as the Allies were shortly to find to their cost. In particular, Admiral Isoroku Yamamoto, Commander in Chief of the Combined Fleet, and Admiral Osami Nagano, the Chief of the Naval General Staff, were sophisticated and able men. Both had served as naval attachés in Washington, and both knew America's strengths well.

They were supported by able younger officers capable of radical thinking. While the early focus in the shipyards was on building super-battleships, others saw a different future for naval warfare. Mitsuo Fuchida, later to lead the air attacks on Pearl Harbor and Darwin, remembers a debate at the Japanese Naval College in the late 1930s, where he took the lead by arguing: 'We must abandon the idea that all we need to do is outbuild our rivals in warships. In the future, aircraft will be the decisive factor. Conventional naval armament based on surface strength has become largely ornamental.' The Imperial Japanese Navy came to the same radical conclusion. Japanese shipyards raced to produce aircraft carriers as well as battleships. However, the emphasis remained on quality: Japanese aircraft carriers needed to be the best.

Deep divisions remained, particularly between the Army and the Navy. Whatever the frustrations of the war with China, the Army was spoiling for a fight with Russia. The easy success of the invasions of Manchuria and Indo-China (let us abandon euphemisms about 'stationing' troops there) led the Army to believe the time was ripe for further expansion on the Asian mainland. The Navy was less sure. It saw the United States as the logical enemy. Yamamoto in particular had a healthy respect for America's industrial strength. He argued that Japan could not hope to win an extended war against the United States, and he remained opposed to war.

While these arguments raged, the Navy's backroom strategists began to develop a whole new concept for the use of sea power. As we have seen, the Navy's original strategy had been to prepare itself to defend the Japanese homeland. Until well into the 1930s it was a defensive force, not an attacking force. The new situation in 1941, when oil would have to be seized by one means or another, meant that the Japanese would have to go out looking for it. They would have to cross oceans to do it, and that meant the Navy would spearhead the attack.

Before 1941, a naval attack on a land target involved warships standing off the enemy coast to pound their objective with heavy guns. This inevitably meant the attacking ships would be easily seen by the enemy and met with shore-based guns and planes, not to mention enemy ships. The Japanese Navy had a new idea. What if, they asked, the naval force stayed hundreds of miles from the target, out of sight and out of range of shore guns and shore patrols, and used ship-launched bombers instead of the ships' guns to carry out the attack? The sheer suddenness of the strike would mean that, with luck, the attackers would have the advantage of surprise. Once the target had been rendered harmless by the planes, the Army and Navy surface ships could move in as required. The planners considered all the implications. The bombers would need fighter cover if they were to do their work effectively. Clearly a large carrier force would be needed, larger than any yet seen in any battle anywhere.

A new split opened up, this time between the Combined Fleet, led by Yamamoto, and the Naval General Staff, led by Nagano. Both men agreed that Japan needed to strike south to seize the oil wealth of the Dutch East Indies. Nagano argued for a conventional strategy: an immediate thrust south to capture the oilfields straight away. This opening action would take place thousands of kilometres from the United States Pacific Fleet, based at Pearl Harbor in the Hawaiian Islands. By the time the American fleet could mobilise and counter-attack, the oilfields would already be seized, and the Japanese Navy would be ready to turn and face the Americans. It had long prepared itself for exactly this fight and would be conducting it near to home. The Americans, on the other hand, would have long supply lines and difficult sea conditions, for which they were ill prepared.

Yamamoto proposed a bolder and more radical strategy. Use aircraft to knock out the US Pacific Fleet on the first day of the war, he argued. Then, at leisure, grab the southern oilfields and anything else Japan wanted, with no risk of interference from the Americans. This would involve an attack on Pearl Harbor itself, right in the enemy's heartland and thousands of kilometres from the Japanese homeland. The Japanese Navy would be undertaking a task for which it had not prepared. It, not the Americans, would have the problem of extended supply lines and unfamiliar waters. Nevertheless, Yamamoto could see no other way to fight the war successfully.

In February 1941 Yamamoto took his plan to Rear Admiral Takijiro Onishi, Chief of Staff of the 11th Air Fleet of the Imperial Japanese Navy. Onishi liked the idea but felt his Air Fleet could not undertake the job. His aircraft were land based, and could not possibly attack from his nearest airfield on the Marshall Islands, over 3000 kilometres from Pearl Harbor. However, Onishi had a better idea: he suggested that Yamamoto talk to Commander Minoru Genda of the 1st Air Fleet.

Genda was one of the most brilliant air tacticians in the Navy. He was something of a war hero himself: in his days as a fighter pilot in the war with China his dashing air unit had been known as 'the Genda Circus'. He was called back from the China front line and sent to London as Assistant Naval Attaché for Air, where he learned the latest aerial tactical thinking. He was the author of the policy of mass fighter cover for bombers, and he supported the then radical idea of a large carrier-based striking force. Genda seized on Yamamoto's plan. His 1st Air Fleet, based on the Navy's six large aircraft carriers Zuikaku, Shokaku, Akagi, Kagi, Hiryu and Sōryu, could do the job, he said.

Genda and Yamamoto now put the plan to the Naval General Staff. At first the General Staff stuck to their argument for an initial thrust south. They were supported by Vice Admiral Chuichi Nagumo, who would lead the 1st Air Fleet in the event of the Genda's and Yamamoto's plan going ahead. Carriers were vulnerable to even a very few bomb hits, they argued. The whole thing would need complete surprise to work. How could that be achieved when so many people and ships were involved? It was too risky.

The argument became heated. Yamamoto, who remained opposed to war anyway, was adamant that the only chance of success lay with an early defeat of the US Pacific Fleet. If war broke out, however much that might have been against Yamamoto's wishes, it would be up to him as Commander-in-Chief to bring it to a successful conclusion. He threatened to resign unless he had his way and was authorised to attack Pearl Harbor first. If Admiral Nagumo was half-hearted about the plan and did not want to lead the Carrier Striking Force to Pearl Harbor, then Yamamoto would be happy to take over and do the job himself.

Faced with this ultimatum, Nagumo and the General Staff relented. Postwar records show that the last barrier to Yamamoto's plan fell at a meeting between Yamamoto and Nagumo in Tokyo on 3 November 1941, only 35 days before Pearl Harbor. Now the old defensive strategies of the Imperial Japanese Navy were gone forever. The new philosophy could be reduced to a single word: 'Attack!'

◆ ◆ ◆

It was not enough for Japan simply to build more ships if it was to match the strength of the Allied navies. If aircraft were to take the place of battleships' guns in a naval offensive, then the Japanese Navy would need a whole new breed of warplanes to do the job. An analysis of the likely requirements led them to demand a mix of dive-bombers, conventional 'horizontal' bombers, torpedo bombers, and fighters to escort them, all capable of being folded into the tight hangar space of a ship, then launched with a full load of fuel and bombs from the perilously short runway of a carrier's flight deck. It was a supreme design challenge, and the Japanese rose eagerly to meet it.

A direct comparison tells how thoroughly they succeeded. The Japanese Zero fighter first flew in 1940.* It was a stocky, agile, brutish little aircraft, with a top speed of 300 knots and a ceiling of 33,000 feet. The single pilot had at his command two 20-mm cannons and two 7.7-mm machine guns, and the option of carrying either two 30-kg

---

* That is how it got its name. Japanese aircraft design numbers derive from the last two digits of the calendar year in which the type first took to the air. The Japanese calendar began in 660 BC, so the western world's 1940 was 2600 to the Japanese. The Mitsubishi A6M first flew in the year 2600, so it became a Type 00, hence Zero.

bombs or a single 60-kg bomb. Compare this with the Wirraway fighter, then the commonest fighter in service with the Royal Australian Air Force. The Wirraway had a top speed of 191 knots and a ceiling of 23,000 feet. Its only weapon was a pair of .303 (7.7-mm) light machine guns. The Zero could out-run, out-climb and out-gun the Australian fighter every time.

Japanese carrier-borne bombers were equally impressive. The Nakajima B5N, known to the Allies as the 'Kate',[1] could carry either an 800-kg torpedo or bomb or three 250-kg bombs. It had a top speed of 199 knots and a ceiling of 27,100 feet. The three-man crew consisted of a pilot, a navigator/bombardier and a radio operator/gunner. The gunner had two rear-facing 7.7-mm machine guns to discourage any pursuing fighters. The Aichi D3A 'Val' dive-bomber was lighter but faster. It had a top speed of 232 knots and a ceiling of 35,000 feet. It could carry one 250-kg bomb slung under the fuselage and two 30-kg bombs on racks under the wings. The two-man crew consisted of a pilot and a gunner. The gunner had two forward-facing 7.7-mm light machine guns, and a rear-facing 7.7-mm heavy machine gun. The forward-facing guns could be used for strafing, while the rear-facing heavy machine gun defended the Val against pursuers.

Yamamoto decreed that the Pearl Harbor attack had to meet three essential conditions: Japan's entire large carrier force should take part, with no large carriers kept in reserve; only the best crews and commanders should be selected; and total secrecy should be preserved. Sending the entire large carrier fleet and the best crews was the equivalent of betting the farm. If the attack worked and crippled the Americans, then Japan would be free to roam the Pacific and South-East Asia with little to challenge it. If it failed and the carrier force was lost, then on the first day of the war Japan would see its key strength and fighting capability destroyed. Even a large carrier could be taken out by just two or three bombs. If the Americans got a warning, or just got lucky, Japan could lose the war in a day.

◆ ◆ ◆

On 5 November 1941, two days after the fateful meeting between Yamamoto and Nagumo in Tokyo, the Japanese government decided that if the negotiations currently taking place in Washington had not produced an acceptable result by 30 November then Japan would go to war. Essentially, the Japanese wanted all sanctions against them lifted and all assets unfrozen, while still being allowed to hold on to their current conquests and continue their program of expansion. The Americans wanted them to cease all hostile operations, withdraw from their conquered territories and generally behave themselves. The two sides were miles apart, and the chances of a deal were slim.

As soon as he heard of the 30 November deadline, Yamamoto ordered the Combined Fleet to prepare. Two days later he set the date for the attack—8 December.*

On 22 November the Japanese Task Force assembled in Tankan Bay, in the Kurile Islands, an obscure port well to the north of Japanese population centres and out of sight of prying eyes. At 6 a.m. on 26 November the fleet sailed for Pearl Harbor.

Given the scale of the job ahead of him, it is no surprise that Yamamoto put together one of the mightiest fleets ever to sail into battle. In all, 31 ships set off for the rendezvous point at 42°N, 170°W, over 2000 kilometres north-west of Pearl Harbor. Here they would receive final orders. The fleet had four sections. The Striking Force consisted of six aircraft carriers and 353 attack aircraft. A Screening Force of two battleships, two heavy cruisers, one light cruiser and nine destroyers escorted them. An Advance Patrol Unit of three submarines made sure the way ahead was clear. A Support Unit of eight tankers tagged along with reserves of fuel for the return journey.

The Washington negotiations were still stalemated when 30 November came around. The Japanese government did not hesitate. On 1 December they ordered Yamamoto to take his country to war.

◆ ◆ ◆

---

*Because of the position of the International Date Line, 7 December in the Hawaiian Islands is 8 December in Japan.

At 12.50 a.m. on 7 December (Hawaiian time), Japanese intelligence radioed the fleet with alarming news. The American aircraft carriers were not in Pearl Harbor, nor were the heavy cruisers. They had put to sea. The Japanese had been expecting to find four carriers—*Yorktown*, *Hornet*, *Lexington* and *Enterprise*—all key targets.[2] Should the attack go ahead? Nagumo pondered, then decided. The same intelligence report told him 'a full count of battleships' and plenty of lesser targets were still in Pearl Harbor. There could be no turning back now. In the early hours of the morning of 7 December 1941, the Combined Fleet arrived at a point 320 kilometres north of the target, about an hour's flying time away. The carriers turned into the 20-knot north-easterly wind. At 6 a.m. the first plane took off.

Captain Fuchida's Kate bomber took the lead. As he climbed in the pre-dawn darkness, he had to pick his way through a dense cloud layer extending upwards from 5000 feet. At the prearranged height of 10,000 feet he was in clear air, and the formation assembled behind him. In all, 183 planes made up the first wave: 89 Kates, 51 Vals and 43 Zeroes. Fuchida's own flight consisted of 49 Kates, each carrying one 800-kg armour-piercing bomb. Below and to his right flew 40 more Kates, each armed with an 800-kg torpedo. To his left and a little above him the 51 Vals took up station, each with a single 250-kg high-explosive bomb. Above them all 43 Zeroes stood ready to deal with any challenge. In strict radio silence, the giant formation growled its way towards Pearl Harbor.

The port of Pearl Harbor and the city of Honolulu are both on the southern side of the Hawaiian island of Oahu. A high mountain range runs south-east across the centre of the island, with Honolulu and Pearl Harbor in a large coastal plain beyond the mountains. Fuchida's formation was approaching from the north, so they would have to cross the range before they could attack. Fuchida noted the time. He had been airborne one hour and 40 minutes. They were still flying over thick cloud, but they must be getting close to the target.

Now the cloud broke a little. Fuchida peered down. Suddenly one of the most famous lines of surf in the world appeared beneath his wings.

Fuchida recognised it as the north coast of Oahu. The formation crossed the shoreline not far from Waimea Bay. Fuchida could now see that the air above Pearl Harbor itself was clear of cloud. He swung his formation right, away from the target towards the western end of Oahu, while he studied Pearl Harbor through his binoculars. He counted eight battleships and large numbers of other warships, all calmly at anchor. Disappointingly, he saw no aircraft carriers.

What happened next is one of the iconic moments of Second World War history. Whole movies have taken it as their title, hundreds, even thousands, of writers have solemnly repeated it, and it is now an indelible part of the legend of Pearl Harbor. According to the legend, Fuchida broke radio silence by yelling into his microphone: '*Tora! Tora! Tora!*' ('Tiger! Tiger! Tiger!'), the signal to begin the attack. So far I have found only one tiny dissenting voice from this otherwise unchallengeable narrative: Fuchida's own. If $135-million movies have to be re-shot and thousands of books and articles have to be withdrawn and rewritten as a consequence of what follows, all I can do is apologise for the incon-venience and press on with the story. In Fuchida's version, at 7.49 a.m. he ordered his radio operator to send the command: 'Attack!' The radio operator then tapped out in Morse code the prearranged signal: 'TO, TO, TO.'

The 51 Val dive-bombers now climbed and prepared to strike, while the Kate torpedo bombers dropped towards the packed lines of ships in Pearl Harbor. Fuchida's own group of bombers, armed with armour-piercing bombs, circled Barbers Point on the southern coast of Oahu and a few kilometres west of the target, waiting their turn. At 7.53 a.m. Fuchida sent a second radio message, this time to his aircraft carrier *Akagi*, saying: 'Surprise attack successful.'

The first bomb fell on Wheeler Field, a US Army Air Force base just north of Pearl Harbor, at about 7.55 a.m. Next the Vals attacked Hickam Field, near the entrance to Pearl Harbor, before moving on to the main naval base on Ford Island in mid-harbour. The torpedo bombers now joined the fray, concentrating on the battleships anchored in tightly packed rows along the eastern side of Ford Island. Fuchida watched as a series of white waterspouts in the harbour marked the sites of exploding torpedoes. A few American fighters scrambled in an attempt to offer some opposition. The Zeroes made short work of them. With no enemy aircraft to challenge them in the air, the Zeroes switched to strafing the airfields, wrecking any planes they could find on the ground.

Fuchida next led his own formation of Kates, carrying armour-piercing bombs, into the attack. By now the ships' anti-aircraft batteries had come to life, as had some of the land batteries, and Fuchida's wing did not have things all their own way. As he recalled later: 'Dark grey puffs burst all around. Suddenly my plane bounced as if struck by a club. When I looked back to see what had happened, the radio man said: "The fuselage is holed and the rudder wire damaged." We were fortunate that the plane was still under control.'

Despite his damaged aircraft and the furious barrage of anti-aircraft fire, Fuchida successfully released his bomb on his second attacking run, aiming for 'Battleship Row'. As soon as the bomb dropped clear, Fuchida lay on the cockpit floor of his aircraft and opened the vision panel to watch the result. Altogether he could see four bombs falling, and they grew smaller and smaller until he lost sight of them. Then he saw two small puffs of smoke on one of the ships. He guessed, probably correctly, that he had just hit the battleship USS *Maryland*.

The pounding from Fuchida's attack force lasted for nearly an hour. But the Imperial Japanese Navy was not finished with Pearl Harbor. A second wave of 170 attackers, led by Lieutenant Commander Shikegazu Shimazaki, had taken off from the carriers at 7.15 a.m., 75 minutes after Fuchida. At 8.54 a.m. Fuchida heard Shimazaki give them the order to attack. Shimazaki personally led a force of 54 Kates to devastate the airfields, while Lieutenant Commander Takashige Egusa led 80 Vals to mop up in the harbour. They were escorted by 36 Zeroes, but this was overkill: by now Japan had complete control of the skies over Oahu.

By 1 p.m. all surviving aircraft returned to the carriers. The Japanese had lost nine Zeroes, 15 Vals and five Kates, together with 55 aircrew, all to anti-aircraft guns on ships or ashore. Not a single US plane had successfully attacked a Japanese aircraft. Fuchida later described his force's losses as 'negligible'. The Americans lost three battleships sunk: *Arizona*, *California* and *West Virginia*; one battleship capsized, *Oklahoma*; one battleship heavily damaged, *Nevada*; three battleships damaged, *Maryland*, *Pennsylvania* and *Tennessee*; two light cruisers heavily damaged, *Helena* and *Raleigh*; one light cruiser damaged, *Honolulu*; three destroyers heavily damaged, *Cassin*, *Downes* and *Shaw*; one minelayer sunk, *Oglala*; one repair ship badly damaged, *Vestal*; one seaplane tender damaged, *Curtiss*; and one miscellaneous auxiliary vessel capsized, *Utah*. The death toll stood at 2335 military and 68 civilians.[3]

◆ ◆ ◆

There is now a fashion for saying Pearl Harbor was a disaster for the Japanese because it dragged an angry and vengeful United States into a war the Japanese could not hope to win. What is certainly true is that the attack fell far short of attaining its original objective. The returning Japanese pilots hopelessly overestimated the success of the raid. They thought they had crippled all eight battleships, as well as wreaking havoc on the rest of the fleet. While the damage and loss of life were dreadful, it was far from the knockout blow that Yamamoto set out to deliver. The US Pacific Fleet's aircraft carriers and heavy cruisers escaped entirely unscathed. So did an astonishing number of American ships in Pearl Harbor: five cruisers, 26 destroyers, nine submarines and 48 others. Even the damaged ships were not entirely lost. Many of them were quickly repaired and put back into service.

However, the Japanese concluded, with some justification, that the new naval tactic of using carrier-based bombers rather than heavy guns had proved itself and then some. If the right opportunity presented itself, it could certainly be used again. Yamamoto had bet the farm and got away with it.

Chapter 4

One suitcase, one small calico bag

The legend of Pearl Harbor endlessly requires that the Pacific War began with the first bomb falling on Wheeler Field, Oahu. Not so. The Pacific War began on 7 December 1941 Hawaiian time, all right, but not at Pearl Harbor and not even in the Hawaiian Islands. The first Japanese shots were fired not at Americans but at British and Indian troops in north-east Malaya. An amphibious landing force of the 25th Japanese Army poured ashore at Kota Bharu on the north-east coast of Malaya at about 12.45 a.m. on 8 December, 70 minutes before the first bomb hit Wheeler Field.

The Japanese attack was not confined to Malaya. They struck simultaneously on an audaciously huge front extending from Hong Kong in the north to Singapore in the south. Three hours after the landing at Kota Bharu, at 4 a.m. local time, Japanese bombs rained down on the supposedly impregnable British stronghold of Singapore, killing 61 people and injuring over 700. Next to bear the brunt of Japanese military wrath was Hong Kong. At 8 a.m. 36 Zeroes struck Kai Tak airfield, while three battalions of Japanese infantry supported by three brigades of mountain artillery swept across the Sham Chun River and poured into the colony, heading for Kowloon.

Pearl Harbor was bad enough. Next came one of the great fiascos of the Second World War. The Philippines, then an American colony, provided a home for the US Navy's Asiatic Fleet. Although the Asiatic Fleet boasted nothing like the bristling strength of the Pacific Fleet, it was nevertheless a significant force. Within 30 minutes of the first bomb falling on Pearl Harbor, American forces in the Philippines were informed that war had broken out. Herb Kriloff, Officer of the Deck on the seaplane tender USS *William B. Preston*, was anchored in Davao Gulf, off Mindanao in the southern Philippines. At about 3 a.m. the deck watch woke him to pass on a decoded message from the Commander-in-Chief, US Asiatic Fleet: 'Japan has commenced hostilities. Govern yourselves accordingly.' The *Willy B* went to battle stations, upped anchor and moved to a safer area.

Others were less zealous. The vain and vainglorious General Douglas MacArthur, commander of US forces in the Philippines, also received the warning at 3 a.m. He had just hosted a lavish party in his hotel, and his response was decisive: he chose to do nothing. At 5 a.m. Major General Lewis Brereton, commander of the Far East Air Force in the Philippines, put his crews on alert but needed MacArthur's permission to launch his aircraft against Japanese bases on their nearby colony Formosa (now Taiwan). MacArthur's Chief of Staff, Brigadier General Richard Sutherland, refused Brereton access to the general. Still nothing happened. At around dawn a group of six Japanese fighter aircraft and seven bombers attacked *Willy B* and her PBY Catalina aircraft riding at anchor nearby. A shooting war had now started in the Philippines, with US forces under direct attack. Still MacArthur did nothing.

Brereton next ordered some of his aircraft to take off and circle overhead rather than run the risk of being caught on the ground. MacArthur did nothing. At 9 a.m. Brereton again asked Sutherland for MacArthur's permission to attack Japanese targets. Sutherland again refused to put the request to the general. Nothing happened.

Finally, at 11 a.m., MacArthur agreed to a counter-attack. Brereton ordered all his planes back on the ground to rearm and refuel. That was when the Japanese struck. At 12.20 p.m., over nine hours after the first warning that war had broken out, a massive wave of some 500 aircraft swept in from Formosa and caught the Americans at their most defenceless. In the space of an hour, they destroyed half of MacArthur's Far East Air Force on the ground. The most important US power base in the Pacific region after Pearl Harbor was now incapable of defending itself successfully.

That same day the Japanese attacked American bases on Wake and Guam islands. With the notable exception of Wake Island, where the Japanese were initially beaten off, from Hong Kong to Malaya to Singapore to the Philippines to the Hawaiian Islands, the Japanese had overwhelmed Allied forces wherever they struck. Their rampaging Army and Navy could now turn their attention towards the real target of the Pacific War: the rich resources of the Dutch East Indies, particularly Java's oil and Malaya's rubber and tin. The whole eastern hemisphere seemingly lay at their feet. All in the space of a single day.

◆ ◆ ◆

In Darwin, tension was high even before news arrived of Pearl Harbor. On Friday, 5 December, troops were due to sail south on leave aboard the *Zealandia*. They had already handed in their equipment and boarded the ship when all leave was suddenly cancelled. They stomped back to barracks in a foul temper. The town braced itself for a riot. If it came, it would not be the first: the boys were given to venting their frustrations on Darwin's pubs, cafés, shops and civilians whenever things went wrong. They would be bound to tear the town to pieces, smashing whatever shop windows were still intact, or so everyone thought. The riot happily failed to materialise, but the fear of it was symptomatic of tensions between the town's military and civilian populations.

Molly Walsh, a civilian typist working for the Army, recalled how she first heard that the Pacific War had begun. Her husband Jim came home for lunch and told her Pearl Harbor had been attacked and the Americans had been taken by surprise. That was all he knew. For the next 24 hours life in Darwin continued as normal. Then the pace quickened. 'For the next week there was colossal activity,' Molly remembers.

'Our men, ordinarily clerks and such, worked like slaves carting sand, filling sand bags, building gun emplacements and learning to be efficient members of Lewis gun crews. We were fed on atrocity stories, and laughingly devised a scheme of cyanide capsules for women, on the death before dishonour principle.'

Molly's boss, an Army major, asked her bluntly: 'Well, when are you going home?'

'Home? This is my home,' she told him, 'and as far as I know I'm not going anywhere.'

'You'll be evacuated,' the major replied. 'The women will all have to go, and soldiers' wives will be first. If you're sensible you won't wait for an evacuation order. You'll go straight to town and book a passage.'

◆   ◆   ◆

When war with Japan looked likely, Britain had Asian colonies to defend and expected to play a major role in any Asian and Pacific conflict. The key British contribution would be its naval base in Singapore. Britain, India, Australia and New Zealand concentrated on making Singapore impregnable—the so-called 'Singapore strategy'—pouring in resources that might with hindsight have been better deployed elsewhere. No need to worry about Darwin, ran the thinking; the Japanese will never get near it. Singapore will stop them. Late in 1941, Churchill ordered two of his newest and most formidable battleships, HMS *Prince of Wales* and HMS *Repulse,* to reinforce the British base. Land-based bombers from Rear Admiral Onishi's 11th Air Fleet sank them both on 10 December 1941, when the war was two days old. That same day the Japanese captured Guam from the Americans.

◆   ◆   ◆

The gallant cry 'women and children first' was, in Darwin's case, rather less chivalrous than it sounds. The women and children were certainly seen as vulnerable and in need of protection. But, more to the point, they drank and ate. The adults enjoyed a beer, smoked cigarettes, and drove cars that needed parts and petrol. Women and children required doctors and dentists and hospitals and schools and teachers and what were delicately referred to as sanitary services (Darwin had no sewerage system). All of this put pressure on the already stretched supply routes and on local resources. The war had just moved much closer to Darwin, and the ships might have to run a gauntlet of submarines to bring in essential supplies for a town with a population of almost 6000. The ships would need to be escorted and to travel in convoys. Even more crucially, they would need to make room for increasing quantities of military equipment. That left less capacity for civilian needs. The fewer non-military mouths to feed in Darwin the better. If that meant packing the women and children off south, so be it.

Edgar Harrison, the Permanent Officer in charge of Air Raid Precautions, drew up a plan for the evacuation. It took him months and involved cooperation with the Army, which would be charged with the task of actually moving the evacuees out. On 5 December 1941 he handed the plan over to the Darwin Defence Coordination Committee, consisting of the heads of the three services. They approved and passed the plan on to the Administrator, who also agreed. Three days later, the Pacific War began.

On 9 December, the day after the Japanese entered the war, the air-raid wardens met to discuss next steps. The evacuation of Darwin's civilians was at the top of the agenda. There is some debate over exactly what happened next. After the Darwin raid, the government appointed a Royal Commissioner, Charles Lowe, to investigate the circumstances surrounding the attack. The Administrator, Aubrey Abbott, gave both written and verbal evidence to the Lowe Commission. The Chief Warden, Arthur Miller, prepared a written report, which was taken in evidence by Lowe. The Permanent Officer, Edgar Harrison, and the Acting Government Secretary, G.V. Carrington, both gave contradictory verbal evidence to Lowe. Talking afterwards to the author Douglas Lockwood, both Abbott and Miller told a story that was often at variance with their evidence to Commissioner Lowe. This leaves the researcher with six different versions of what took place. Abbott's evidence to the Royal Commission does not match his version in

Lockwood's book *Australia Under Attack*. The same could be said of Miller. In the face of all these memory lapses, I have simply done my best to piece the story together in a way that makes most sense.

In his evidence to the Royal Commission, Edgar Harrison recalled that he attended a meeting with Administrator Abbott on 10 December at 10 a.m. Accompanying him were Arthur Miller, the Chief Air Raid Warden; Miller's Deputy, E.V. White; W.A. Hughes, Director of Demolitions; and Brough Newell, Director of First Aid. Abbott's account omits this meeting altogether, though he discussed with author Lockwood a meeting on 12 December with a slightly different cast list. My own view favours two meetings, on 10 and 12 December. Whatever the timing or number of meetings, the delegation told Abbott that the evacuation of women and children from Darwin should begin as soon as possible. Abbott promised to consult Canberra.

At 11 p.m. on Thursday 11 December, three days into the Pacific War, Darwin's air-raid sirens wailed in earnest for the first time. Revellers at a party in the smart New Darwin Hotel abandoned their glasses and headed for the shelters. Orderlies at the hospital carried patients down to the beach. The citizens of the town headed for open ground, as they had been briefed to do, and waited for the all-clear, which came through 90 minutes later. The next day Berlin Radio announced that Darwin had been wiped off the map. This turned out to be a little premature, though it caused some anxiety among short-wave listeners in other parts of Australia. Darwin had survived its first false alarm, and its citizens had a good laugh at the expense of the over-excitable Hun.

Nevertheless, all did not go smoothly. Someone had left a light burning in the ladies' underwear shop window at C.J. Cashman & Co. A passing soldier hurled a brick through the plate glass and shattered the light. Lights had been left on at the Soldiers' Hall: someone broke in and smashed the offending electrical fittings. At Young's Garage a light had been left burning on a battery charger: someone forced the door and put it out.

The following day, 12 December, the air-raid wardens were seriously jumpy. It was a Friday morning, and the four most senior wardens descended on Administrator Abbott's office again. Arthur Miller arrived with Edgar Harrison and two of his zone wardens, Eric Wilmott and W.J.E. White. They were in mutinous mood. They demanded two things: an evacuation of Darwin's civilians straight away, and an end to their ambiguous legal status as air-raid wardens. The military already had statutory powers under the National Security Act, but these powers were limited to enforcing a blackout and regulating road traffic. No one had taken the trouble to delegate power to the civilian air-raid wardens. As things stood, they could not enforce their orders. Statutory powers might require the declaration of a State of Emergency, which would in turn involve the Federal Government in Canberra and a gazetted notice under the National Security regulations.

Abbott resisted. His Honour argued that a declaration of a State of Emergency would cause unnecessary panic. The four wardens refused to accept this. They eventually persuaded Abbott to cable Prime Minister Curtin in Canberra and ask for a decision. Curtin sent an encrypted reply to Abbott on the afternoon of Friday 12 December. The War Cabinet had decided, Curtin wrote, to evacuate compulsorily all women and children from Darwin with the exception of nurses and the wives of missionaries. The first group of evacuees should leave the following Thursday on the *Zealandia*, which had just been used to bring troops to Darwin. His Honour had just six days to get the evacuation organised and under way.

◆ ◆ ◆

Darwin's defences came in for a lot of scrutiny at the Royal Commission. In particular, Commissioner Lowe spent a lot of time looking at 'gun density'. How many heavy anti-aircraft guns did Darwin need? The ideal answer seemed to be 36. But it was hardly negligent of the defences to deploy a smaller number. There weren't 36 heavy AA guns to spare in the whole of Australia.

Similarly, with fighter aircraft, Commissioner Lowe was told Darwin needed 250 front-line fighters to be effective against a bomber force of the size that struck on 19 February 1942. This was a pipe dream. The

RAAF didn't have 250 fighters to its name. Most of the few it had in Australia were spread thinly around the large cities in the south. Others were in Malaya and Timor. Still more were in the Western Desert, facing the Luftwaffe rather than the Imperial Japanese Navy. In 1942 the RAAF's only possible response to a call to station 250 fighters in Darwin could be to shake its collective head and say: I wish.

The Royal Australian Navy had built a boom net, the longest of its kind in the world, sealing off Port Darwin. The net gave the harbour some protection against submarine attack but not much else. There were heavy guns mounted around the foreshores and facing the sea, particularly at East Point. So a seaborne invader might have faced a tougher time than an attacker from the air. However, there were no fighting ships of any consequence permanently based in Darwin, for the simple reason that they were all needed elsewhere. The Army, Navy and Air Force all faced accusations of failure to provide adequate defences for Darwin. The hard truth is that in those desperate days there were no resources available, and all three services provided Darwin with as much as they felt they could spare at the time.

However, the defenders could reasonably face a different set of charges. The defence planners made elementary mistakes. Rather than keep important resources like hospitals and reinforcements away from the likely first line of attack, they piled everything into the front row. The civil hospital at Cullen Bay was right next to the Larrakeyah Army barracks.[1] Both were on the shore, about a kilometre from the harbour and town. They could expect to be caught up in the first wave of any attack. The new military hospital at Berrimah was further inland but barely 1500 metres from the runway threshold at the RAAF airfield. There could be no question of moving the wounded to safety at the rear, and no question of keeping troops in the barracks and back from the fight until they were needed.

The positioning of the new RAAF airfield just a few kilometres inland from the coast showed the same lack of foresight. Rather than place aircraft, hangars, fuel dumps, workshops and ammunition stores well back from the opening onslaught of any attack, the defence planners had put them in the most exposed area of all. To cap it all, the nerve centre of any coordinated response by Army, Navy and Air Force, known as Area Combined Headquarters, was part of the administration complex at the RAAF airfield. If the airfield came under attack, so would ACH.

◆ ◆ ◆

The Army rather than the RAAF provided Darwin's most potent defence against air attack. By late 1941 four sections of heavy anti-aircraft guns, each consisting of four QF 3.7-inch guns, stood at sites on the Oval in central Darwin, at Fannie Bay just north of the town centre, at Berrimah to the east of the town, and at McMillans, well outside the town to the north of the RAAF airfield. Each gun fired 28-pound (12.7-kg) shells, and each gun could launch between ten and 20 rounds a minute, depending on the skill of the gunners. They were serious weapons. The shells could reach a height of 29,500 feet (9000 metres) and had a maximum horizontal range of 11.7 miles (18.8 kilometres). However, as late as mid-February 1942, the sites were far from complete. The revetments—earthworks mounded up around the guns to protect the gunners—were still unfinished. The cables linking the guns to their command post still ran above the ground, making them a very likely first casualty of any direct hit. Nevertheless, the guns were in place and ready. In addition to the four sections of 3.7-inch guns, two 3-inch anti-aircraft guns were mounted at Elliott Point near the Quarantine Station, five kilometres south-east of the town centre.

Jack Mulholland, a gunner with the 14th Heavy Anti-Aircraft Battery, remembers the training he and his fellow soldiers received on the 3.7-inch guns. 'All the training was with dummy rounds against slow-moving targets. Even the Flying Doctor came in for our attention. He would be returning from one of his missions and as he flew over our site, he would cut his motor and yell out: "Don't shoot, you bastards." He had no worries because the one thing we did not do was waste ammunition in practice shoots. There were none.' Mulholland's unit arrived in Darwin at the end of 1940. By the time the Japanese arrived over

Darwin 14 months later, he and his comrades had fired just a single live round from their guns (a warning shot across the nose of a 'friendly' incoming plane that failed to observe the correct approach procedures). The deafening noise, heat, smoke, shouting and confusion of a full-blooded barrage would all have to be discovered in action on the day.

The big 3.7-inch AA guns, often referred to as HA (High-Angle) guns, were designed to tackle high-flying 'horizontal' bombers. They were less useful against low-level strafing fighters, dive-bombers or torpedo bombers. The height and bearing of a dive-bomber or any low-flying attacker are both changing rapidly all the time, and it is difficult for the heavy guns to track them. To meet this type of attack, the Army used a handful of Lewis machine guns. The 14th AA Battery had a group of about eight Lewis guns on top of the oil tanks at the harbour, for instance, and a single Lewis gun was assigned to each of the four AA sections to defend against strafing aircraft. The Lewis guns were largely useless. Each magazine held only 50 rounds of light .303 ammunition, so there was no chance of sustained, heavy fire. Darwin desperately needed the heavier punch of rapid-firing pom-poms, or Bofors guns, to repulse dive-bombers or strafing fighters. There were none.

A shortage of Lewis guns led to more problems. At Mulholland's battery, he recalls: 'It was necessary to share our Lewis gun with a searchlight unit. At dusk of an evening a truck would arrive, pick up the Lewis gun and take it to the searchlights for the unit's protection during the night.'

Improvisation was the order of the day. Mulholland again: 'The Lewis machine gun was originally an infantry weapon in the Great War. To adapt the gun to anti-aircraft defence, a length of sapling was embedded in the ground. On top of the sapling a piece of pipe allowed the gun to be mounted and the gun could be traversed through 360 degrees. Anti-aircraft mountings were not provided.' So a handful of First World War light machine guns mounted on bits of old pipe that spun around a sapling jammed in the ground provided Darwin's main protection against Japan's notoriously effective strafing fighters and dive-bombers.

◆   ◆   ◆

Ground-based anti-aircraft guns are one thing. The best defence against air attack comes not from the ground but from fighter planes, which can mix it with the bombers and challenge them in their own element. When the Pacific War broke out, Darwin was home to two RAAF squadrons. The brand new RAAF airfield north-east of the town played host to the Hudson bombers of 13 Squadron, while the Wirraway fighters of 12 Squadron were based at the smaller civil airfield at Parap.[2]

12 Squadron began its life at Laverton Air Base in Victoria, under the command of Squadron Leader, later Wing Commander, Charles 'Moth' Eaton. Eaton is one of the legendary characters of Australian aviation. Born in London, he flew with the Royal Flying Corps on the Western Front in the First World War. He crashed behind German lines, was taken prisoner, and repeatedly escaped, finally making it back to his own side in the last few days of the war. Eaton flew on the first regular passenger service between London and Paris, ferrying delegates to the Paris Peace Conference. After marrying, he moved to Australia and worked as an instructor for the RAAF, training some of Australia's best pilots. He was a stickler for discipline and he trained his pilots well. In September 1941, Wing Commander, later Air Marshal, Sir Frederick Scherger, took over from Eaton as Station Commander in Darwin.

12 Squadron was originally equipped with four Avro Anson and four Hawker Demon fighters. The Avro Anson was generally used as a trainer rather than a front-line fighter, while the Hawker Demon was a slow, under-armed two-seater 'fighter' adapted from a 1928 bomber design. Happily for 12 Squadron, the Ansons and Demons were replaced by Wirraways. As we have seen, the Wirraway was no match for any of its likely Japanese opponents, but it was an improvement on the Anson and the Demon. I have found it impossible to establish with any certainty how many Wirraways 12 Squadron had at its disposal either at the time the Pacific War broke out or when the first Japanese raid on Darwin took place, but the most likely number is 14, of which as many as nine were not in Darwin but dispersed to Batchelor airfield, 75 kilometres to the south. So if the Japanese arrived unexpectedly in the skies over Darwin, the town could not expect much protection from the RAAF.

Chapter 5

No place and no time for argument

Japanese troops poured into Thailand and down the Malay Peninsula, swatting British, Indian and Australian defenders aside. On 11 December they attacked the British colony of Burma and headed for the capital, Rangoon. On 18 December Hong Kong surrendered. Two of the returning aircraft carriers from the Japanese Pearl Harbor force detached themselves and diverted to join the attack on Wake Island, begun on 8 December. After a 15-day siege, Wake Island fell. The sheer speed and ruthlessness of the Japanese advance left the Allies reeling. They had hopelessly underestimated Japanese strength and military prowess. Now they knew better. Anyone with a map could see what was afoot. The Japanese were being denied oil and other essentials by the Allies. They clearly intended to bulldoze their way south and grab it for themselves.

◆　◆　◆

As the pace of war quickened, Darwin found itself playing a major role as both a staging post and a maintenance base for aircraft. The Hudson bombers of 13 Squadron had moved north to the island of Ambon, in the Dutch East Indies. They were quickly followed by the Hudson bombers of the RAAF's 2 Squadron, who staged through Darwin on their way to Penfoie in Timor. However, the forward bases on Timor and in the Dutch East Indies had poor maintenance facilities, and the aircraft had to be rotated back to Darwin whenever they needed attention.

On 22 December 1941 General George C. Marshall, Chief of Staff of the US Army Air Corps, directed that Darwin be used as an American Army and Navy base. The Americans had previously been wary of Darwin after two of their four-engine B17 Flying Fortress bombers were damaged breaking through the unpaved surface of the new RAAF field's runway. They preferred to use the stronger (if narrower and shorter) runway to the south, at Batchelor. However, the Darwin strip was strong enough to handle the Air Corps' P40 Kittyhawk fighters as well as the lighter Hudson bombers of the RAAF, and a steady stream of aircraft swept into Darwin on their way to the Dutch East Indies to confront the Japanese advance.

The Curtiss P40 Kittyhawk was no slouch as a fighter aircraft. It had a maximum speed of 310 knots, which made it a whisker faster than the Japanese Zero. It was manoeuvrable and tough, and its six M2 Browning 50-mm guns gave it plenty of punch. It could not match the Zero at high altitude, but low down it could compete on something like equal terms, especially if it used its speed advantage. It was never quite as agile as the Zero, but it was more robust because it had armour protection for the pilot and self-sealing fuel tanks, which could survive a few bullet strikes. The Zero had no such shielding and tended to succumb to comparatively light damage. A skilful and experienced pilot in a Kittyhawk could expect to meet a Zero and survive. The problem was the almost total lack of Kittyhawk pilots who could be classified as skilful and experienced.[1]

The Kittyhawks were shipped in from the United States in kit form. Usually they were unloaded at either Brisbane or Townsville. They were then assembled and flown to the front line, using Darwin as a final refuelling point before beginning the perilous journey over water to Timor and Java. Outback airfields in Queensland, including Charleville, Winton and Cloncurry, and Daly Waters in the Northern Territory, suddenly found themselves vital links in the supply chain. Other aircraft flew to Darwin from bases in New South Wales and Victoria, staging through the same airfields.

The Kittyhawk pilots were pitifully inexperienced. All were unfamiliar with Australia and the special problems of Outback flying, particularly navigation. They began the multi-stage trip to Darwin armed with the barest of briefings. It was not an easy journey. One pilot recalled asking about finding his way. 'Simple,' he was told. 'Just follow the trail of crashed Kittyhawks.'[2]

◆   ◆   ◆

Inexperienced pilots from the United States were not the only problem. On 27 December 1941, Prime Minister Curtin published in the Melbourne *Herald* his famous declaration that Australia 'looks to America' (and, by implication, away from Britain) for protection in the face of the Japanese threat. This turned out to have unforeseen consequences. For one thing, the Americans sent black troops to Australia. When the first convoy arrived in Melbourne in January 1942, Australian Customs refused the desperately needed troops permission to land. The Australian Minister for the Army rapidly countermanded the order and referred the whole issue to the External Affairs Minister, Dr. H.V. Evatt. Evatt grumpily agreed that there was not much choice but to let in black troops if that's what the Americans sent. However, he thought the Americans might be persuaded to go a bit easy. He cabled his Minister in Washington, Dick Casey, on 21 January 1942 with 'guiding instructions on the subject of coloured troops'.

Under the heading MOST SECRET IMMEDIATE, Evatt wrote:

> Whilst the Advisory War Council decided that the Australian reaction to the despatch of negro troops to Australia would not be favourable, the composition of the forces that the U.S.A. government might decide to despatch is a matter for that Government to determine.
>
> If the U.S.A. Authorities find it necessary to include certain coloured labour units as a proportion of coloured troops to their

forces it is not the desire of the Commonwealth Government to make any stipulation which might destroy the nature of the organisation of the Army formation.

Nevertheless it is assumed that the U.S.A. Authorities, being aware of our view, will have regard to Australian susceptibilities in the numbers they decide to despatch.

The Americans, quite rightly, took not a blind bit of notice.[3]

◆ ◆ ◆

With Darwin now a major supply base for the defence of the Dutch East Indies, the situation on the wharves became critical. The combination of the desperately inefficient wharf and the bloody-mindedness of the wharfies ensured that the harbour was a serious bottleneck blocking the flow of men and military equipment northwards to the fight. The Americans found it intolerable and decided something had to be done. When a convoy including the *Holbrook* arrived in Darwin on 5 January 1942, the wharfies saw something akin to a job for life arrayed invitingly before them. Unloading the *Holbrook* alone would be good for three weeks. The whole convoy might, with luck, take forever.

Colonel John Robenson, the US base commander in Darwin, had enough. Despite pleas from Administrator Abbott, he posted guards with machine guns along the wharf and told his own men to get on with unloading. The guards held back the fuming wharfies while the troops started unloading the ship. The political explosion is thought to have rumbled as far as Washington before a compromise was reached: the wharfies could work one small hold of the ship while the troops worked the other nine. Robenson had made his point: the convoy now unloaded at normal speed, using a mixture of troops and wharfies to do the job.

The situation on the wharves clearly could not go on. Eddie Ward, the Minister for Labour, had appealed to the Darwin wharfies on 11 December to speed up the job. It is only fair to acknowledge that the wharfies responded by increasing the length of their working day, but it was not enough. Ward flew to Darwin and negotiated a new deal: he would increase the workforce by 160 men brought in from other ports around Australia. They began arriving a few days later, on planes from the south, and were generally known as the 'Flying Wharfies'. The Darwin workforce accepted them grudgingly, and not without cause. Port Darwin was not exactly a workers' paradise, and the volunteers who arrived were not exactly the pick of the crop. No doubt the Darwin wharfies' motives in resisting the infusion of extra workers were entirely selfless, and the fact that the new arrivals meant less overtime pay for them never entered their heads.

The combination of Flying Wharfies, longer hours and the intervention of troops speeded work at the wharf a little, but the situation remained profoundly unsatisfactory. Large convoys took weeks to load and unload, and ships piled up in the harbour while the whole creaking system failed to deal with them. Meanwhile, they made an inviting target for the Japanese.

◆ ◆ ◆

The Northern Territory administration's first task, in the wake of the prime minister's cable directing them to evacuate Darwin's women and children, was to decide who should go and who should stay, and in what order those leaving Darwin should depart. The air-raid wardens had already drawn up a comprehensive survey of Darwin residents, dividing them into women and children, the elderly, essential workers and so on. Administrator Abbott was not satisfied. A month earlier, in November, he had asked Edgar Harrison, the Permanent Officer in charge of ARP, to conduct a census of the civilian population. By coincidence, the census was set for 12 December, the day of the air-raid wardens' confrontation with Abbott in his office. As the wardens all had other jobs, they could undertake census work only in their spare time in the evening. Abbott felt they would not be able to do the job quickly enough, and switched the task to the police.

In his nine-page report on 'Plans for Air Raid Precautions and Evacuation of Civilians, Darwin' (one of the exhibits at the Royal

Commission on the Darwin attack), Abbott wrote: 'The Police started upon this job [the census] on Sunday, 13th December and completed it on Monday, 14th. The Police Return gave the number of women and children as 1,066 women and 900-odd children.[4] Advice was received from the Army that 822 women and children could be embarked upon the "Zealandia" which was an Army transport and under Army control.'

On Sunday afternoon Harrison and other wardens were working on evacuation plans in their office. Harrison wanted to challenge some points, and rang the Administrator. Abbott now dropped his bombshell. This was no place and no time for argument, he told Harrison. The air-raid wardens' plans for the evacuation were scrapped. From now on His Honour would issue such instructions as he considered necessary. Administration of the evacuation would be taken over forthwith by the Acting Government Secretary, Mr Carrington. The wardens' plan had divided Darwin's population into women, children, the sick and so on, and had assigned priorities for evacuation. Carrington's plan, based on the police survey, simply divided the population by street. Darwin's evacuation priorities would be determined by address, not by need.

It is hard to like Charles Lydiard Aubrey Abbott. Most writers have tended to spring to his defence, believing that the Royal Commission treated him harshly. Yet, when his words are read all these years later, not the least of his misdemeanours is that he is often economical with the truth. In the report quoted above he sets out to create the impression that he was simply following orders sent peremptorily from Canberra. He makes no mention of any meeting with the air-raid wardens and no mention of scrapping their evacuation plan. He describes Curtin's telegram ordering the evacuation as though it arrived out of the blue, rather than in response to a request from him. He is quick to blame others. In the report quoted above, he wrote: 'I visited the A.R.P. headquarters and saw that matters were becoming chaotic. Whilst Mr Harrison, the Permanent Officer, had done a very good job in fixing up preliminary organisation in connection with evacuation, Army assistance and other matters, his temperament was such that he rapidly lost his head and I was overwhelmed by complaints from

the public regarding his manner.' Harrison was an ex-Sergeant Major in
the Army, so Abbott may have had a point there. Others certainly agreed
that he was officious and excitable. Nevertheless, Abbott's report was
hardly loyal to his staff, and in fact many of the public's complaints were
directed not at Harrison but at Abbott himself. His Honour's minor
carelessness also suggests an untidy mind: 14 December 1941 was a
Sunday, not a Monday.

Curtin's telegram to Abbott did not give the ARP wardens anything
like what they wanted. It did not include the promise of a declaration of
a State of Emergency in Darwin, nor was any measure gazetted to give
the wardens statutory powers. Furthermore, although the wardens were
no longer in charge of the evacuation, it would nevertheless be their job
to bluff the public into complying.

On Monday 15 December the Administrator issued 2500 printed
notices to be delivered to every household in Darwin. The full text is
reproduced in Appendix I. This first notice did not actually order the
evacuation. It merely told everybody what to expect if the order came.
Each evacuee could take personal belongings including a small calico
bag containing hair and tooth brushes, a towel and toilet soap, and a
suitcase of clothing weighing not more than 35 pounds. In addition each
person could take two blankets, eating and drinking utensils, and a two-
gallon (eight-litre) water bag per family.

No pets were allowed. 'Any pets owned by Evacuees should be
destroyed before the Evacuation,' the notice declared. The order did not
apply to the chooks. 'Domestic Poultry,' it continued, 'would be an
Auxiliary Food Supply for those remaining in Darwin, and as such will
not be destroyed under any circumstances.' So Darwin's chooks suddenly
found themselves in the unusual position of being a better life insurance
risk than its cats and dogs.

On the day the first notice was issued, Darwin residents packed the
local school where they were told they would receive instructions and
the latest information. There they learned that the evacuation would be
overland, by road, though how this was to be achieved remained a
mystery. They left the meeting little the wiser about anything.

The actual order to evacuate took the form of a notice published in the *Northern Standard* on Tuesday 16 December 1942. It betrayed no nervousness over the dubious legality of the evacuation order. Instead it told the citizens of Darwin that they had been ordered to leave by no less august a body than the War Cabinet, and pleaded with them to go willingly. The notice read:

COMMONWEALTH OF AUSTRALIA
NORTHERN TERRITORY ADMINISTRATION
PROCLAMATION
EVACUATION ORDER

CITIZENS OF DARWIN

The Federal War Cabinet has decided that women and children must be compulsorily evacuated from Darwin as soon as possible, except women required for essential services.

Arrangements have been completed and the first party will leave within the next 48 hours.

This party will include sick in hospital, expectant mothers, aged and infirm and women with young children.

You have all been issued with printed notices advising you what may be taken and this must be strictly adhered to. Personal effects must not exceed 35 lbs.

The staff dealing with evacuation is at the Native Affairs Branch in Mitchell Street and will be on duty day and night continuously.

The personnel who will make up the first party will be advised during the next few hours and it will be the duty of all citizens to comply at once with the instructions given by responsible authorities.

Remember what your Prime Minister, Mr Curtin, said recently. 'The time has gone by for argument. The instructions of the Federal Government must be carried out.'

The Federal Government has made all arrangements for the comfort and welfare of your families in the South.

Darwin citizens will greatly assist the war effort by cheerfully carrying out all requests. There will be hardship and sacrifice, but the war situation demands these, and I am sure Darwin will set the rest of Australia a magnificent example to follow.

(Sgd.) C.L.A. ABBOTT
Administrator of the Northern Territory

The first group of evacuees, 225 women and children, left Darwin on 19 December 1941 not by road but by sea, aboard the *Koolinda*. They could count themselves lucky, certainly luckier than the next batch of 530 evacuees, who left on 20 December aboard the *Zealandia*. Their trip was a nightmare. Some had been given only one hour's notice to leave their houses and board the ship. The journey began with the guards throwing overboard any bags weighing more than 35 pounds. *Zealandia* had been used for transporting troops to Darwin from the south and had not been cleaned for months. Food and water ran short. Toilet and washing facilities were a calamity. Some cabins designed for four people were occupied by 11 instead. The ship called in at Thursday Island and collected 200 Japanese internees, who were kept in the hold under armed guard. Chinese families were made to travel on the open deck rather than in cabins. The stories the evacuees sent home did nothing to improve morale in Darwin or boost confidence in the authorities' assurances about comfort and welfare. The *Adelaide News* got hold of the story and had its entire report blocked by the censors.

Others were more fortunate. The remaining women and children of Darwin might have waited another three weeks for the next ship if it had not been for a stroke of luck. The 12,000-ton American luxury passenger liner *President Grant* had been tied up in Manila harbour when the Japanese invasion of the Philippines looked likely. The captain received orders to sail for the nearest friendly port. Armed only with a chart torn out of a *National Geographic* magazine, he set off for Darwin and, against all the odds, made it there safely. On 23 December the *President Grant* left Darwin for Brisbane, carrying better charts and a further 222 evacuees. All but 20 were placed in first-class cabins, and the crew treated them royally, including giving everyone a small present on Christmas Day. There were 166 adults conveyed at full fare of £18 each, 38 half fares, three quarter fares and 15 infants travelling free. On 8 July 1942, almost seven months later, the Department of the Interior wrote to the ship's agents, Wills Gilchrist and Sanderson Pty Ltd, in Brisbane, to say that the government's long-overdue cheque for £3,343.10.0 was in the post.

There can be no doubt that the evacuation was chaotic. The neatly typed passenger lists, on file at the National Archive in Darwin, have been converted to a maze of arrows and scribblings and marginal notes, with endless revisions and crossings-out. Nobody seemed able to agree on who had sailed on which ship, or where they disembarked, or what happened to them afterwards. Short words tell long stories: 'missing', or 'plane', or, in one sad case, 'Died in raid 19/2/42'. It was a bureaucratic nightmare, and the people of Darwin were not impressed. They blamed the administration, and the Administrator.

Some of Administrator Abbott's personal style is caught in his account of the row over the legal status of the air-raid wardens. In the report quoted above, Abbott gives his version of how he first heard that there might be a problem. He chooses to ignore the wardens' delegations on 10 and 12 December and instead cites an approach from the hated trade unions. 'This was first brought up to me by a Committee of what was then known as the "People's Party",' he wrote. He is vague about the date, putting his meeting with them 'between the 12th and the 21st December, 1941'. The actual delegation was made up of 'a Mr Ward, a local solicitor, Mr Ryan, the Secretary of the North Australian Workers' Union, Mr Ming Ket, a local Chinese and another whose name I am unable to remember'.

The committee he refers to was the worthy-sounding Citizens' War Effort Committee, which had been set up by the trade unions in an attempt to shore up their weakening authority in what was increasingly a military town. The fact that Abbott could not remember either the date of the meeting or the names of the delegates is a fair indication of the seriousness with which he treated their submission. This high-handed approach was shortly to cost him dearly. His report continues: 'The Committee stated that there was no legal authority to remove people from Darwin and that there was no legal authority for the A.R.P. organisation to function. I told the Committee that I had a direct and definite instruction from the Prime Minister and the War Cabinet to evacuate women and children from Darwin.' This was not the point, and the delegation retreated, unsatisfied.

◆ ◆ ◆

The Japanese continued their push south. They streamed down the eastern and western coasts of the narrow Malay peninsula, brushing aside any resistance. They quickly occupied the whole of Thailand. On 16 December they captured Miri in Sarawak, part of the island of Borneo. Brunei's and Borneo's vital oilfields were now within their grasp. The Pacific War was a mere eight days old.

◆ ◆ ◆

Admiral Nagumo's carrier task force met with a rapturous reception when it returned from Pearl Harbor to the Japanese mainland on 23 December. The failure to knock out the American aircraft carriers was forgotten in the general back-slapping and congratulations. The war was going well on every front, and Nagumo Force had led the way. Mitsuo Fuchida recalled: 'Both the Naval General Staff and Combined Fleet were fully satisfied with the results achieved at Pearl Harbor and saw no need for further neutralising action against the US Pacific Fleet.' Instead they ordered Nagumo's force, now reduced by the Wake Island attack from six to four carriers, to support the impending invasions of Rabaul and Kavieng, on large islands north-east of New Guinea. Nagumo Force left Kure Naval Base on 5 January 1942 and headed south for the staging post of Truk Lagoon and the next phase of the war.

Chapter 6

The judge sums up

There is a noisy orthodoxy that says the Japanese never had any intention of invading Australia in 1941, 1942 or any other time. Whoever proclaims this usually follows up with a paragraph or two mocking the large number of Australians, mostly of older generations, who are convinced a Japanese invasion was once imminent.

These historians are, of course, correct. The Japanese never seriously set about an invasion of Australia. However, this orthodoxy leaves out two important facts. First, Australians didn't know it at the time. And second, the decision not to invade Australia was closer run than many historians care to admit.

◆ ◆ ◆

By the end of December 1941, with the Pacific War only three weeks old, Darwin was increasingly a military town. Civilian women and children had moved out in large numbers. The military had moved in to take their place. Ships of the American Asiatic Fleet retreated from the Philippines to Darwin. By 23 January, Port Darwin was briefly home to eight submarines, three cruisers and eight destroyers, all from the Asiatic Fleet. Kittyhawk fighters and Douglas A24 dive-bombers of the US

Army Air Force staged through Darwin on their way to the Dutch East Indies. RAAF Hudson bombers flew back to Darwin from Ambon and Timor for refitting and repair. Australian, British, Dutch and American ships used Darwin as a fuelling and supply stop.

On 11 January 1942, the Japanese began their long-awaited attack on the Dutch East Indies. Rather than tackle Java first, they struck at Tarakan Island, off the north-east coast of Borneo, near the town of Tanjungselor. Tarakan was a major oilfield. The Dutch defenders were quickly overwhelmed—and brutally massacred. Given that oil was Japan's principal goal of the war, this was an important victory for them. However, Java remained the ultimate prize, and Japanese forces were now closing on it in a pincer movement. Their surging army swept down the Malay peninsula towards Singapore, threatening Java from the north-west, while their victory at Tarakan gave them an important base to the north-east of the target island.

On 20 January, Nagumo Force took up station off Rabaul, on the northern tip of New Britain. Again Mitsuo Fuchida led the way. With a force of 90 bombers and fighters, he swept in to attack Rabaul harbour and the defending airfields at Vanakanau and Lakunai. To his disappointment, his fliers found little worthy of their attention. 'I saw just two enemy planes,' Fuchida recalled. 'They were attempting to take off from one of the two airfields and were promptly disposed of by our fighters. The second airfield was empty.'

Fuchida's Val dive-bombers sank a lone cargo ship in the harbour while his Kate bombers, 'for lack of any more worthwhile target', dropped their 800-kg high-explosive bombs on the coastal guns at the harbour entrance. To Fuchida the whole sorry affair was a waste of the superb talents of Nagumo Force. 'If ever a sledgehammer had been used to crack an egg, this was the time,' he wrote afterwards.

The despair felt by Allied forces as the Japanese inexorably closed in on them is caught in a cable sent by Wing Commander J.M. Lerew from the RAAF base at Vanakanau, one of the two airfields defending Rabaul. Lerew had sent up the two aircraft so quickly dispatched by Fuchida's fighters. The Wing Commander was originally told to use his discretion in deciding whether to withdraw his forces if Rabaul came under attack. On 21 January, the day after Fuchida's bombers struck, he was ordered to hold on rather than withdraw. RAAF Command in Australia cabled him: 'Begins. Rabaul not yet fallen. Assist Army in keeping aerodrome open. Maintain communications as long as possible. Ends.' The cipher staff in Melbourne at first had trouble with Lerew's reply, which they unscrambled as: 'Nos morituri te salutamus.' It took them a while to realise it was in Latin, and even longer to translate it. Lerew had replied with the Roman gladiator's traditional nod to the emperor before mortal combat began: 'We who are about to die salute you.'

Fuchida's bombers returned to Rabaul on 22 January, but their attack was hardly worth the trouble. Next day the Japanese captured Rabaul without a struggle.

The various RAAF and Dutch forward bases, in such places as Ambon in the Moluccas and Koepang in south-west Timor, became increasingly untenable. Japanese raiders attacked them with land-based bombers and fighters. The Japanese methodically destroyed aircraft on the ground and shot them down in the air. As the British, Australian, Dutch and American forces withdrew or were captured, the airfields at Darwin and Batchelor assumed new importance. They were a safe haven for the retreating troops. And they were a base from which the Allies could counter-attack the new Japanese positions. Such was the speed of the Japanese advance that, far from being remote from the war, by the end of January 1942 Darwin was on the front line. In eight short weeks the Japanese had redrawn the map of Asia and the Pacific.

◆ ◆ ◆

There can be little doubt that the speed of their advance took even the Japanese by surprise. Their first objective was to capture oilfields, and in less than five weeks from the start of the war they had taken Tarakan and had the major prize of Java in their sights. Where to next?

The Imperial Japanese Navy, anxious to dominate the strategic planning of the war, considered three major new policy directions. It came down to a choice of three targets. They could go for Australia.

They could go for India. Or they could go for the Hawaiian Islands. Whichever they chose, they would need to move quickly. The one luxury they could not afford was to give the Americans time to regroup and rearm.

The argument for invasion of Australia was straightforward. The Allies, particularly the Americans, were bound to counter-attack at some point. American mass-production methods would soon generate a formidable bomber force, so the counter-attack would probably be delivered from the air. Australia was the logical land base from which to mount it. So Australia would have to be placed under Japanese control or, at the very least, cut off from the United States.

Thus the Navy reasoned. However, the Japanese Army would have none of it. Its commanders judged that the occupation of even part of Australia would require ten of their best combat divisions, and they could not spare them. The Navy suspected that the Army had another, unstated reason for rejecting the Australian option. The Army had not lost sight of Russia as a major target. It believed that Germany would attack in the Caucasus in the Northern Hemisphere spring of 1942. If that happened, Japan might profitably attack Russia from the east. The Army preferred to keep that juicy possibility on the table. Australia could wait.

The Army had similar reservations about India. Any attack in this direction would need to be coordinated with the Germans, and Hitler was not as forthcoming as he might have been in cooperating with his Japanese ally. Best not to rely on the Germans but instead focus on Japan's immediate Pacific neighbourhood. That meant looking east, rather than west or south, for new fields to conquer. The ultimate target would have to be the Hawaiian Islands, probably after an invasion of Midway.

Nevertheless Australia could not be ignored. If a land invasion of that vast country was out, the question remained: What could the Japanese do to seal off and neutralise an increasingly dangerous Allied sanctuary?

◆ ◆ ◆

Thomas Alexander Wells, Judge of the Northern Territory, was something of a maverick. He particularly enjoyed ruling against the government, usually in the person of the Administrator. Mr Justice Wells had little time for the Territory's Aboriginal people, either. Whenever they appeared before him, he was inclined to dismiss their evidence as worthless. The death sentence he imposed on an Aboriginal man named Dhakiyarr, after accepting the very flimsy case against him, made world headlines. It was overturned on appeal.

On 22 December 1941 Wells put aside his judicial robes and waded into the row over air-raid precautions in Darwin. In a five-page letter to the Chief Air Raid Warden Arthur Miller, he quietly demolished the plans already in place to protect the town's citizens in the event of an air raid. His letter makes total sense: in short, he was right.

The printed instructions issued to householders advised them that in the event of an air raid they should 'leave the house or building immediately and proceed without delay to your slit trench or refuge area'. The judge dispatched this with a single sentence: 'As everyone is well aware, there are no "slit trenches"—or "refuge areas" either, in the proper sense of the term—available anywhere in Darwin.' There were slit trenches aplenty for the military, of course. But Darwin's householders would have to take their chances.

As had happened on the night of 11 December, when the air-raid sirens sounded, Darwin's citizens understood that their best option was to leave their houses and proceed to any open spaces in the neighbourhood. This was bad advice, the judge argued. It meant people would take to the roads, where they would be 'in very serious danger of being run down by military vehicles and ambulances which must continue to use the roads without lights, or with dimmed lights'. The judge's advice, heavily underlined in the typewritten letter, required less of Darwin's civilians: 'The proper course for people to follow is to simply turn out all lights and remain quietly in their homes. Let them get into bed, or, if they wish, under the bed.' The judge noted that the houses of Darwin were not packed tightly together but spread out. By remaining in their homes, he said, people would automatically disperse themselves, reducing the risk of mass casualties from a single direct hit.

The judge warmed to his theme.

I notice that in the last issue of the *Northern Standard* volunteers have been asked to come forward for the purpose of digging refuge trenches. It has apparently been completely overlooked that it is quite impossible to dig trenches without extensive blasting in most places in Darwin—including the places particularly mentioned in the advertisement; it has also apparently been overlooked that in the wet season, due to commence any moment now, refuge trenches would be not only useless but definitely dangerous—unless in rare cases where drainage could be arranged.

Last but not least, the judge dismissed as irrelevant the preparations made by the civil defence forces. They had put too much effort into fire-fighting, he said, when it was very unlikely that the Japanese would use incendiary bombs. 'The purpose of a bombing raid on Darwin would be the destruction of the oil fuel tanks, aerodromes, wharf, ammunition dumps and other similar objectives,' Wells wrote. 'All these can be dealt with much more effectively with high explosive bombs, either delayed action or percussion, than with incendiary bombs. The latter are effective against large city buildings and factories, and large congested areas of buildings—none of which exist in Darwin.'

The judge had his own simple plan. Like most tropical towns in Australia, Darwin's houses were often built on pillars to allow air to flow freely beneath them. People should be encouraged to build sand-bag shelters, where possible under their houses, he wrote. After all, there was no shortage of sand, or bags.

Having dealt with the practical details, Wells moved on to the legal status of the air-raid wardens. As things stood, the wardens had none, the judge opined. If they issued an order, the citizens of Darwin were under no legal obligation to obey it. Furthermore, the wardens risked criminal prosecution if they damaged property or caused injury while trying to enforce their orders. The judge cited the breaking of the shop window at C.J. Cashman & Co., the smashing of electrical fittings at Soldiers' Hall and the break-in at Young's Garage during the last air-raid alert. All three acts were criminal. Judge Wells concluded: 'Steps should be taken by A.R.P. officials to ensure that there is no recurrence of such unreasonable officiousness, which is not at all likely to secure the cooperation of the public.'

The letter, far from disturbing the wardens, was music to their ears. Here was confirmation from no less a person than the Judge of the Northern Territory that their lack of any legal framework left them dangerously exposed. Two days later, on 24 December, a delegation of four wardens, led by Arthur Miller and Edgar Harrison, descended on Wells. Three of the four were the same men who had confronted Administrator Abbott in his office 12 days earlier. Essentially, they told Wells they were fed up with lack of support from the Administrator. How could the judge help?

The trade unions, who also had no love for Abbott, had their Citizens' War Effort Committee. On 27 December the judge sent a copy of his letter to the committee. He left its members in no doubt whom to blame for the debacle. The final sentence of Wells's covering letter to the committee read: 'If the information given to me by the A.R.P. officials is correct, it would appear to be quite useless to approach the local Administration authorities.' The trade unions owned the only newspaper, the *Northern Standard*. On 30 December the *Standard* gleefully published on its front page the parts of the letter that set out the inadequacies of the present civil defence arrangements, under the headline 'Judge Attacks A.R.P. Lack.' It also published the judge's confirmation of the wardens' lack of legal status.

The cat was now out of the bag. Darwin's citizens had been told, on no less authority than that of the Judge of the Northern Territory, that they were not being properly protected against Japanese attack. Furthermore, they were under no obligation to obey any order issued by an air-raid warden. If they were told to leave their homes and evacuate to Adelaide or Sydney or Alice Springs or anywhere, they could say no. The evacuation was never popular, so there was a real possibility people would rebel. Even if all they were told was to put out a light, they could still say no if the order came from a civilian air-raid warden. Not only that, they now had confirmation of what was obvious to one and all, that the air-raid precautions for Darwin were seriously misconceived and largely ineffectual.

The Citizens' War Effort Committee called a public meeting on 7 January 1942. There is no record of how many of Darwin's citizens turned up—it may have been as few as seven or eight—but they were certainly of one mind. The meeting voted unanimously for the Administrator to be sacked. The motion passed read:

This meeting of the people of Darwin demands the removal of Mr Abbott from the post of Administrator in view of:—

1. Reports received from the wives of the people of Darwin of despicable treatment accorded to them and their children during evacuation, for the arrangements for which the Administrator admits full responsibility.

2. General handling by the Administrator of the war effort in Darwin.

3. The complete neglect of the welfare of the town and territory during his administration.

The *Northern Standard* splashed the story across its front page on 9 January 1942, under the headline 'Abbott's Removal Urged: Public Meeting Alleges Bungling of Evacuation, War Effort'. The *Standard* shyly failed to mention how many had actually attended the mutinous meeting, but it published the full text of the motion and noted that it had passed unanimously. Administrator Abbott was now publicly on the rack.

◆ ◆ ◆

After the judge's comments became public knowledge, the wardens found their job difficult, if not impossible, to carry out. They responded in the only way they could, by staging a mutiny of their own. First to depart was Brough Newell, the Director of First Aid. On 22 January he wrote to Chief Warden Miller, saying he was resigning with effect from noon next day, and quoting public apathy as the reason. He concluded his resignation letter: 'I therefore recommend that . . . the public of Darwin be advised through the press that in the event of their being wounded in an air (or other) attack, they must either walk to the New Civil Hospital or die on the spot.' On 23 January the wardens held a meeting and informed Administrator Abbott that unless they were granted proper legal authority within three days, they would resign in a body. When the 26 January deadline passed without the grant, or indeed any move at all by His Honour, they resigned. Officially, Darwin now had no air-raid wardens. (In fact the wardens did a secret deal with the Army, promising to turn out if needed. They kept their word.)

◆ ◆ ◆

With Rabaul in Japanese hands, Nagumo Force's four giant aircraft carriers, together with their escorting ships, returned to the Japanese naval base at Truk, in the Caroline Islands north of New Guinea. Here they were told to prepare to support 'south-west operations', meaning the conquest of the Dutch East Indies and the Portuguese colony of East Timor. The Navy calculated that the only obstacle to Japanese plans would be a counter-attack by American and other Allied forces operating from bases in northern Australia.

Yamamoto's Combined Fleet headquarters proposed an amphibious invasion of Port Darwin to forestall any problems from that direction. Both the Naval General Staff and the Army responded with a flat 'no'. Combined Fleet then decided there was only one solution to the problem of Darwin. Nagumo Force had proven its ability to strike effectively with its Pearl Harbor attack, followed by its effortless humbling of Rabaul. So Nagumo Force would settle this problem too: on 15 February 1942 the aircraft carriers *Akagi*, *Kaga*, *Sôryu* and *Hiryu* left Palau and headed south for the Banda Sea and Darwin. They were escorted by the battleships *Hiei* and *Kirishima*, two heavy cruisers, *Tone* and *Chikuma*, the light cruiser *Abukuma*, and nine destroyers. This was essentially the same force that had attacked Pearl Harbor, reduced only by the absence of two of the aircraft carriers, *Zuikaku* and *Shokaku*. Nevertheless it was a formidable battle group, capable of doing formidable damage. It proposed to do just that.

Chapter 7

Convoy for Koepang to return to Darwin

On 20 January 1942, the Japanese mine-laying submarine I-124 attacked three US Navy ships off Cape Fourcroy on Bathurst Island, about 110 kilometres north-west of Darwin. The I-124's torpedoes missed USS *Trinity* and its two destroyer escorts, USS *Alden* and USS *Edsell*. *Alden* replied with depth charges. Three Australian corvettes, HMAS *Deloraine*, *Katoomba* and *Lithgow*, raced to join the fray. The hunt lasted two days. At the end, I-124 and her 46 crew lay at the bottom of the Timor Sea in 45 metres of water. *Deloraine* received most of the credit for the kill. It was a rare victory, but it highlighted the fact that the waters around Darwin were now a Japanese hunting ground.

On 10 February 1942, a Japanese spy plane from the 3rd Reconnaissance Squadron, based on Ambon, flew high over Darwin. The crew counted about 30 aircraft on the ground at the two airfields. They photographed an 'aircraft carrier' and five destroyers in Port Darwin, together with 21 merchant ships. Given that American aircraft carriers remained the Imperial Japanese Navy's highest priority target, the discovery of the USS *Langley* must have caused a frisson of excitement in the Japanese high command.

The *Langley* was an old collier, converted to an aircraft carrier in 1922 by plating a flight deck above the collier superstructure. She was the first ever aircraft carrier in the US Navy, and was known affectionately as the 'Covered Wagon'. By 1937 she had been well superseded by newer, larger carriers, and the US Navy decided to convert her to a seaplane tender. Some of the plating of the forward flight deck was removed, leaving slightly more than half the flight deck in place. The surviving portion was used to transport fully assembled aircraft by sea. *Langley*'s flight deck could not be used for take-off or landing, but from a high-flying Japanese reconnaissance plane she must still have looked for all the world like a slightly peculiar aircraft carrier.

Ironically, the *Langley* was the last ship of the American Asiatic Fleet to leave Darwin. She sailed next day, 11 February, for Fremantle in Western Australia, to pick up a load of Kittyhawks. That left the seaplane tender USS *William B. Preston* as Darwin's only remaining warship from the Asiatic Fleet. The *Willy B* stayed in Darwin to support her clutch of PBY Catalina aircraft operating reconnaissance missions from Port Darwin.

◆ ◆ ◆

The evacuation of Darwin's women and children continued apace. On 10 January, 187 sailed south on the *Montoro*. A further 173 left on 26 January aboard the *Koolama*. On 15 February, the final shipload of 77 left on the *Koolinda*.

Not everybody left by sea. The planes that brought the 'Flying Wharfies' to Darwin returned south with women and children evacuees on board. Others left by train for Birdum and Larrimah, then rode in Army trucks to Alice Springs. Some of the Alice Springs contingent then caught the Ghan train south to Adelaide. Others chose to stay in Alice Springs, to the fury of the local administration. As early as 23 December 1941 Police Superintendent A.V. Stretton, the Acting District Officer in Alice Springs, wrote to Administrator Abbott to say: 'A large number of additional troops are likely to be stationed here which will considerably tax our services, particularly water and sanitary. Might I respectfully suggest that public attention be directed to the fact that evacuees will not be permitted to remain at Alice Springs.' He was told firmly that he could not force them to move on. Anybody who arrived from Darwin to Alice Springs had every right to stay there.

Nor was everybody who left Darwin a woman or a child. Audrey Kennon worked as a clerk for the State Shipping Company. She drew up the passenger lists. 'At holiday time,' she remembers, 'there were a lot of men on the ship and it was my job to take them off and book women and children on.' Not all of them accepted Audrey's ruling. 'There was one man in particular who threw a wad of notes on the counter and said: "You get me on the ship." I said: "Don't you think the women and children should go first?" He said: "I've made my money here and I don't want to lose it here." I had to say to him: "I'm sorry."'

Men paid for seats on commercial flights, to the disapproval of those who thought their places should have been occupied by women and children. There was a strong suggestion that those who fled were foreigners, not regular Aussies. Lieutenant Commander McManus, the senior Naval Intelligence officer in Darwin, set out the widespread suspicion when he reported: 'A few Australians, many Italians and Greeks are distinctly "windy", the Italians and Greeks are besieging the Airlines for accommodation on south-bound planes and many have gone by rail to Larrimah and Birdum in the hope that they will be given passages on the military convoys proceeding to Alice Springs.'

◆ ◆ ◆

Aircraft continued to stage through Darwin on their way to reinforce the Dutch East Indies, particularly Java. The fate of the 3rd Pursuit Squadron illustrates the perils of the journey.[1] Eleven Kittyhawks flew into Darwin, with Timor as their next stop. Two of the planes, flown by Lieutenant Robert Oestreicher and Lieutenant Robert Buel, stayed grounded in Darwin with engine trouble. The remaining nine set off on 9 February 1942 for Koepang. One turned back; the rest became lost in poor weather trying to find Penfoie airstrip in Timor and ran low on fuel. The pilots either bailed out or crash-landed on the Timor coast. Seven were rescued by the RAAF, but the eighth was killed. That left Darwin with just two fighter aircraft, both unserviceable.

The military situation to the town's north and west grew increasingly tense. At the beginning of 1942 the Allies had formed the short-lived and ill-fated joint command ABDA (American, British, Dutch and Australian forces), led by the British General Sir Archibald Wavell. On 15 February 1942 the unimaginable happened: Singapore fell. It remains the worst military disaster in Australian history. The Australians lost 1789 dead and 1306 wounded in a vain defence of the 'impregnable' British base. Worse, the Japanese captured 15,395 Australian troops, the Australian Imperial Forces' entire 8th Division. The catastrophe numbed the Australian population at home. What more terrible news would the future hold? Would Australia itself be next, put to the sword by the all-conquering Japanese?

As the British, Australians and Indians crumbled in Malaya and Singapore, Wavell became increasingly desperate for reinforcements and supplies to keep some sort of grip on the Dutch prize of Java. With no air cover and no control of the sea, Java was probably a lost cause from day one, but Wavell piled on pressure. The Australian War Cabinet relented on 5 February 1942.

Port Darwin was giving shelter to three American transports—*Meigs*, *Mauna Loa* and *Port Mar*—and the Australian transport *Tulagi*. Fighting ships in Darwin included the Australian sloops HMAS *Swan* and *Warrego*. The American heavy cruiser USS *Houston* and the destroyer USS *Peary* were not far away and could be diverted to Darwin for escort duty. It was agreed that they should form up as a convoy to carry troops and military equipment to reinforce the Dutch East Indies. The transports loaded the Australian 2/4th Pioneers and an Australian anti-tank troop, together with the 148th US Field Artillery Regiment, and all their equipment. On 15 February 1942, the day Singapore fell, the convoy, escorted by *Houston*, *Peary*, *Swan* and *Warrego*, set off for Koepang.

By 10.30 a.m. on the first day, the convoy was in trouble. The ships were spotted by a patrolling Japanese Kawanishi H6K 'Mavis' flying boat, probably based at Ambon. *Houston* sent an urgent radio call to Darwin for fighter support. The two Kittyhawks, now repaired and serviceable, were the only fighters available. When the call for fighter support came in, Oestreicher was already in the air and could not be reached, so Buel set off alone to tackle the intruding flying boat. What happened next is one of those extraordinary stories of war. As the two aircraft met over the Timor Sea, each managed to shoot the other down in flames. Buel died alone, his fate a mystery to his comrades for more than 40 years. Five of the nine Japanese crew of the Mavis survived. They drifted for five days in a life-raft before reaching shore on Melville Island, where local people handed them over to the Australian Army. The Japanese prisoners succeeded in persuading everyone that they were survivors of a wrecked fishing boat, and stuck to their story throughout the war, which they spent in Cowra prisoner-of-war camp. (One of the repatriated prisoners, Marekuni Takahara, eventually broke silence in 1985 and told the true story. Only then did Buel's fate become known.) Oestreicher returned to Darwin, refuelled, and flew out to look for his buddy. He found nothing: no convoy, and no trace of Buel. He returned alone.

That evening more Kittyhawks arrived in Darwin. Major Floyd Pell's 33rd Pursuit Squadron had intended to fly from Amberley near Brisbane to Port Pirie in South Australia, then on to Perth in Western Australia to meet the USS *Langley*, which would have transported the aircraft as deck cargo to Java. However, ABDA needed fighter cover urgently for the Darwin convoy, so Pell's squadron was ordered directly north from Port Pirie. Again, the perils of the journey are well illustrated by the planes' fate. Twenty-five Kittyhawks had left Amberley air base. Only 15 reached Port Pirie. Of the 15, only ten made it to Darwin. One Kittyhawk crashed at Port Pirie, killing the pilot. Four others experienced engine trouble. The exhausted survivors arrived at the RAAF base on the afternoon of 15 February. Despite the long journey, Pell took off in the late afternoon with five other Kittyhawks and flew over the convoy.

With no enemy in sight, the planes returned to Darwin. All now needed servicing before the long flight to Timor and Java.

◆ ◆ ◆

After the convoy had been spotted by the Mavis, Area Combined Headquarters in Darwin felt it was unsafe for them to continue. At 17.18 p.m. Darwin time on 15 February, they cabled ABDA Command, with copies to South West Pacific Command in Melbourne: 'In view of enemy knowledge of convoy return to Darwin appears advisable.' They were quickly proved right. Next morning a force of 35 Japanese land-based bombers and nine flying boats struck the convoy. The cruiser USS *Houston* led the counter-attack with a furious anti-aircraft barrage, which proved highly effective According to an Australian eyewitness on one of the troop ships: 'She spun on her heel, every gun was blazing. She kept the Japs right up in the sky and they could not get down to bomb us.' The Japanese were beaten off, more or less single-handedly by *Houston*. The Japanese claimed afterwards that three transports had been badly damaged, but in fact the convoy suffered not a single direct hit and emerged largely unscathed. Nevertheless, ABDA Command agreed that it was too dangerous for the convoy to continue and on the afternoon of 16 February it cabled Area Command Headquarters in Darwin with a simple message: 'On review of situation today have ordered convoy for Koepang to return to Darwin.' The ships arrived back in Port Darwin on 18 February.

The two American escorts returning with the convoy, *Houston* and *Peary*, did not hang about. They refuelled, then set off the same day to link up with the Allied fleet at Tjilatjap (now usually referred to as Cilacap) on the south coast of Java. They had barely left Darwin when *Peary* broke off to chase a submarine contact, while *Houston* continued towards Java. *Peary* burned up a huge amount of fuel racing after the submarine, and her captain decided it would be prudent to return to Darwin to refuel. She anchored in Port Darwin at about 2.30 a.m. on the morning of 19 February.

The harbour was now packed with ships. As well as the usual clutter of merchantmen and transports waiting to load or unload, there were fighting ships from the Royal Australian Navy and the US Navy. The grand total came to 45 ships. They were anchored in a comparatively confined part of the harbour, with two tied up at the wharf for unloading. The fighting ships were corvettes HMAS *Deloraine* and *Katoomba*, sloop HMAS *Swan*, auxiliary minesweeper HMAS *Tolga*, patrol boat HMAS *Coongoola*, destroyer USS *Peary*, and seaplane tender USS *William B. Preston*. *Katoomba* was trapped inside the floating dock and incapable of manoeuvring, though she could still use her machine guns. The rest could fight. Other Australian Navy ships in the harbour were boom-net ships HMAS *Karangi*, *Kara Kara*, *Koala* and *Kangaroo*, auxiliary minesweeper HMAS *Gunbar*, depot ship HMAS *Platypus*, lugger HMAS *Mavie*, and examination steamer HMAS *Southern Cross*.

The two merchant ships waiting at the wharf to unload were MV *Neptuna* on the outer berth and SS *Barossa* on the inner berth. *Neptuna* was packed with depth charges and other explosives. HMAS *Swan* tied up alongside her, hoping to transfer *Neptuna*'s explosives directly from ship to ship. Out in the harbour stood the troop-ship SS *Zealandia*, the hospital ship SS *Manunda*, the three American transports from the convoy, USS *Port Mar*, *Meigs* and *Mauna Loa*, the American freighter USS *Admiral Halstead*, the transport MV *Tulagi* (also from the convoy), the British oil tanker *British Motorist*, the Norwegian oil tanker *Benjamin Franklin* and the coal hulk *Kelat*. There were 19 other small ships. In addition to the ships in Port Darwin, two US supply ships, *Don Isidro* and *Florence D*, were en route to the Philippines. On the morning of 19 February they were off Bathurst Island, not far away.

Darwin was now an ideal target. The reconnaissance flight on 10 February told the Japanese they could expect to find as many as 30 aircraft on the ground, while the harbour very likely contained ships from the convoy as well as the usual complement of warships and transports. With luck they might even find an aircraft carrier. There was a clinching argument, unknown to Darwin's defenders. The Japanese planned to invade Timor the next day, 20 February. Timor was only 700 kilometres from Darwin, so any counter-attack would very likely come from Darwin. To protect the Timor invasion, Darwin would have to be taken out of the war.

The Darwin defenders may not have known about the Timor attack, but they were very clear about the threat posed by the convoy's presence in the harbour. Captain Penry Thomas, the Naval Officer in Charge, Darwin, told the Royal Commission: 'As soon as ABDACOM [ABDA Command] ordered the return of the convoy I spoke to Group Captain Scherger and told him I thought we should have visitors the following day, and he quite agreed. It is very obvious, is it not?'

That night Arthur Wellington, a postal worker, wrote to his wife and daughter, who had been evacuated south:

My Dear Nin and Aldyth,
It is after midnight, and have been on the paysheets, but hope to get them cleaned up tomorrow with a bit of luck. A hammering with the overtime, as usual.

Our blackout is OK. People are not worrying overmuch about it. The blue paint they put on the light globes soon burns off, and then there is as much light as before.

Sent down three parcels last night, and they should be there Saturday week with a bit of luck. I sent down all the cutlery and silverware and your cottons that you had to leave behind.

Today I insured all our belongings against war risk for 150 pounds, and it cost twelve shillings, so that is not too bad. There is always a chance that we will have to clear out and leave the rest of the furniture behind, and 150 pounds would help us re-furnish.

You asked me to send you down some blue for the washing. There is plenty up here, even if you can't get it in Adelaide. Jolly's are on the short side, but I got some from Yam Yeans, some from Fong Yuen Kee, and nine nobs of it from Fang Chong Loong.

Things are not getting any easier. Business and work is increasing all the time, and there is no doubt the Darwin post office is paying its way.

Mr. Bald hasn't been too good the last few days, and I have been trying to give him a bit of extra help with the trench at the back of his house. It is going to be a very substantial job. It's 13 feet long and about 3 feet wide, with two railway irons the full length for reinforcement for the sand bags. The depth is about 5 ft. We have galvanised iron across the top and hope to get another three layers of sand bags. Everyone says it will be safe from anything but a direct hit. It's where I'll be going if there is a raid.

You mustn't worry about that possibility. A lot of ships came into the harbour late today, they were the same ones that sailed a few days ago. They were bound for Timor. The talk all around town is that the Japs forced them to turn back. If that's right, the enemy can't be far from here, but I can't see that any of the higher ups seem to be too concerned about it.

Sorry that Aldyth is having trouble with her teeth. They are a worry for grownups, let alone nippers. Do hope the worst is soon over.

Now, my dear, it is one a.m. and have just had a ring from the airways mob, Qantas, to say that all their plane arrangements have been altered and we have got to get the mails out early.

Sweet dreams my sweethearts, and loads and loads of kisses and hugs to you both,

From your loving husband and Daddy,
Arthur.

◆　◆　◆

It is worth standing back at this point and looking at the overall picture of Darwin's defences. Darwin could and did expect an attack from land, sea or air, or a combination of any or all of them. In general, a well-organised defence would consist of a hard front line backed up by supplies, support and reinforcement kept well to the south and out of reach of the initial onslaught. Darwin, as we have seen, had the opposite. The hospitals were right on the front line, offering no sanctuary to the inevitable influx of military and civilian wounded in the event of an attack.

Port Darwin is large. Its deep water, huge tides and dodgy sea bed make anchoring difficult in some parts. Nevertheless, scattering the ships in the harbour would seem an elementary precaution against air and sea attack. Instead, the 45 ships packed into a comparatively small area in the centre. Sitting ducks generally display more common sense and more instinct for self-preservation.

The RAAF cannot be held responsible for the lack of fighter aircraft. There were none to be had. However, putting the new RAAF airfield so close to the coast, with no working radar to give advance warning, meant an attacking enemy would be on top of the base before anybody had time to call 'Scramble!'

As a result of internal tensions and poor administration, an official civil defence was nonexistent. The air-raid wardens had resigned *en masse*. They had made a secret pact with the Army to turn out if needed, but they would not be operating at full efficiency when they did, and the citizens of Darwin could expect to pay the price for any shortfall.

◆ ◆ ◆

Around dawn on 19 February Nagumo Force reached 9°S, 129°E, the prearranged launch point in the Timor Sea south of Maluku Island. The ever-cautious Nagumo sent off a weather-watch plane to check that Darwin was clear of cloud. It reached Darwin just after dawn, at about 7.30 a.m., but the crew's radio failed, and no message came back. Nagumo decided not to wait. They were now about 350 kilometres north-west of Darwin. The four aircraft carriers turned away from the town and into the north-west wind. The flight decks became a turmoil of blue smoke and bellowing engines as 36 Zero fighters, 71 Val dive-bombers and 81 Kate horizontal bombers manoeuvred onto the launch catapults. A total of 188 aircraft took to the skies, five more than in the first wave that attacked Pearl Harbor, and more than twice the force that had attacked Rabaul. The Pearl Harbor force included 43 Zeroes but only 51 Vals. The Japanese could afford to cut down on fighters this time and concentrate on bombers. If Darwin proved to be as poorly defended as Rabaul, fighters would hardly be needed, while a few extra bombers might come in handy. By 8.45 a.m. the entire force was in the air and in prearranged formation. The planes set a course of 148 degrees, a track that would take them a little to the east of Darwin. Mitsuo Fuchida led the way.

Chapter 8

'Zeroes! Zeroes! Zeroes!'

As day dawned on 19 February 1942, the skies above Darwin were far from empty. At that time of year, the sun rises at about 6.45 a.m. At 3.30 a.m. six Hudsons from RAAF 2 Squadron took off from Penfoie on Timor, evacuating all but 23 RAAF men (who had volunteered to stay behind) from the last vestiges of their base. The Japanese had been dropping leaflets all over the island warning the native population against helping the Dutch or taking part in demolition operations. Clearly an invasion was imminent. The Hudsons set course for Darwin, estimating they would arrive at about 8 a.m.

The Hudsons, as we have seen, enjoyed the distinction of being the first to be shot at, in this case by their own side. Instead of arriving via the 'friendly' corridor and flashing the correct light signal, they chose to track in over Fannie Bay without the benefit of a signal and without lowering their wheels, the other way of indicating that they were 'friendly'. The Fannie Bay AA guns fired a single warning shot, leading to all-round recriminations over trigger-happy Army gunners who couldn't tell the difference between a Hudson and a hand-moulded sushi, and RAAF pilots who could not be bothered to follow proper procedures. The day was off to a bad start.

At about 8 a.m. two of the five Catalinas of the US Navy's 22nd Patrol Squadron took off from Port Darwin and headed north on their separate ways to check the seas and skies for intruders. They were particularly on the lookout for enemy submarines. One of the US Navy's best pilots, Lieutenant Thomas Moorer, flew the Catalina assigned to patrol off the coast of Bathurst Island. Moorer had been one of the first pilots to take off from Pearl Harbor on 7 December 1941. He was no stranger to combat or to Japanese attack. However, his main job now was to check the sea below. If he had looked up, he might have seen the nine Zero fighters detach themselves from Fuchida's inbound flight and swoop down on him.

The slow-flying twin-engined Catalina didn't stand a chance against a single Zero, let alone nine of them. Moorer recalled the Zeroes 'setting my plane afire, destroying the port engine and shooting large holes in the fuel tanks and fuselage'. Before anyone had time to radio an alarm, the Catalina and its crew of eight crash-landed on the sea. Four of the crew were wounded in the attack, but the rest escaped unscathed. They piled into the Catalina's rubber dinghy and were picked up about half an hour later, not far from Bathurst Island, by the freighter *Florence D*. Darwin had missed its first chance of an early warning of inbound raiders. The Japanese had been too quick.

◆ ◆ ◆

By 18 February 1942 there were 252 wharfies registered in Darwin. They were broken up into 18 gangs of 14 men apiece. The gangs regularly worked around the clock in three eight-hour shifts of six gangs each. For no clear reason, when the roster was posted on 18 February for work next day, only five gangs were called for the first day shift. They were 1, 2, 3, 17 and 18, a total of 70 men. No. 4 gang was told it would not be required until the next shift. The postings listed only the gang number, not the names of the men.

When the wharfies clocked on, the most urgent task was to unload *Neptuna*, on the outer berth, with her hold full of depth charges and explosives. *Barossa*, on the inner berth, was not quite such a high priority.

She was carrying mostly wooden piles to repair and improve the wharf. The wharfies began the weary task of dragging railway trucks out to the berths and started unloading.

◆ ◆ ◆

The Wirraway fighters of RAAF 12 Squadron had split up as part of an entirely sensible dispersal plan. Most were at Batchelor. Five Wirraways remained in Darwin, but on 19 February all were on the ground and unserviceable, awaiting mechanical work. Darwin's only serviceable fighter aircraft were ten Kittyhawks of the US Army Air Corps' 33rd Pursuit Squadron, and they were due to take off at dawn for Timor, on their way to Java. As it happened, engine trouble delayed the take-off. At 9.15 a.m. they were finally on their way, escorted by a B17 Flying Fortress giving them navigation support. Led by Major Floyd 'Slugger' Pell, but this time including the experienced Lieutenant Robert Oestreicher, the flight set off for their first Timor staging point of Koepang on the long and dangerous route to Java. The Japanese were already attacking all over the Dutch East Indies, and there was no certainty that the landing fields would be safe or even under Allied control. Most of the pilots were raw beginners with fewer than 20 hours at the controls of a fighter. None had ever fired their guns in anger. It was a desperate situation.

The timing could not have been worse. At about 9.35 a.m., US Army Air Corps Operations in Darwin called the flight by radio. Captain Connelly told Pell that Koepang reported low cloud down to 600 feet with scattered heavy rainstorms. He advised Pell to return to Darwin. Conscious of his pilots' inexperience, Pell ordered the flight to turn back. He wanted no repetition of the fate of the 3rd Pursuit Squadron ten days earlier, when all eight aircraft were lost in bad weather. Reluctantly the P40s wheeled around and headed towards Darwin, while the B17 continued to Timor.

◆ ◆ ◆

The Royal Australian Navy stationed two coastwatchers on the Tiwi Islands to guard the approaches to Darwin. Father John McGrath kept watch from the mission station at Nguiu on the south-east corner of Bathurst Island. At Garden Point, on the northern tip of Melville Island, John Gribble, a Navy officer, also maintained a lookout, supported by Tiwi Islanders. Given the direction from which Fuchida's raiding party was arriving, the Japanese planes must have come into Gribble's view first.

We will never know with certainty what happened next. Both Douglas Lockwood and Professor Alan Powell report that at 9.15 a.m. Gribble radioed a warning of 'a large number of aircraft' sighted. Both Powell and Lockwood agree that the message was received at the shore-based naval communication station HMAS *Coonawarra*. Lockwood names the signal officer from *Coonawarra*—Warrant Officer Bill Phaup —who telephoned Lieutenant Commander J.C.B. McManus, Naval Intelligence Staff Officer, in Darwin, to pass on the message. Gribble had given no details of the planes' identification or direction. McManus telephoned his counterpart at RAAF Intelligence and passed on the warning. The RAAF officer told him the planes were probably the ten Kittyhawks en route to Timor (which a glance at a map would have told him was impossible). McManus, as reported by Lockwood, was unconvinced. He told Lockwood later: 'I was confident that Gribble must have seen something unusual. I wanted to sound the alarm at once but was overruled. There had been a series of earlier false alarms which it was undesirable to repeat.' Both Lockwood and Powell then remark on the fact that this first warning is nowhere mentioned in the Lowe Commission report, although McManus gave detailed evidence to Lowe less than two weeks after the event. In particular, McManus gave a detailed account of how the coastwatcher system worked.

There is another version of this story, which did not emerge until 2001. In 2000, two Northern Territory historians, Peter and Sheila Forrest, interviewed Brother Edward Bennett as part of the research for their book *Federation Frontline: A people's history of World War II in the Northern Territory.* Bennett had been with Gribble on the day. In his version, he urged Gribble to radio a warning but Gribble refused.

He said the message would have to be sent in code, and he didn't have the necessary code books. Bennett told the Forrests no message was sent.

Readers will have to make up their own mind about which story to believe. My instinct is to trust Bennett. Phaup makes no mention of the Gribble sighting in his written report of 25 February 1942, submitted to the Naval Board. I have combed through the evidence given under oath to the Lowe Commission by both McManus and Captain Penry Thomas. If the Gribble warning had come through to McManus, who was with Thomas at Navy Headquarters at the relevant time, then failure to disclose it to Lowe would have gone pretty close to perjury by both men. They both had every opportunity to reveal the message, and every reason to do so. The Gribble warning does not appear in any log book or record. There is no mention of it in the Official History, nor in the Lowe Report, nor anywhere in the verbal or written evidence on which Lowe based his findings. Only two things are reasonably certain: Gribble saw the Japanese aircraft on their way south, and at some point the warning process broke down. Darwin had missed its second chance. It is no more than a cliché to say that the memory sometimes plays strange tricks. It seems to have worked its magic pretty heavily on Gribble's sighting.

Gribble's alert may not have got through. Father John McGrath's certainly did. As we have seen, his terse call, 'Eight SE to VID. Big flight of planes passed over going south. Very high. Over,' was received loud and clear by civilian aeradio station VID in Darwin, which telephoned the message to RAAF Operations at 9.37 a.m. By 9.37 Darwin's defenders had their third and best chance to go to action stations.

Pilot Officer Saxton at RAAF Operations passed the VID message on to the Operations Controller, Flight Lieutenant C.G. Fenton. 'I went downstairs and spoke to the Commanding Officer,' Fenton recalled:

I discussed the matter with him because I had other information which did not confirm that any enemy was approaching. I was aware that a formation of P40s and a B24 [in fact it was a B17] had taken off for Koepang, and shortly after they left I was aware they had got a meteorological report when they left. I was told they were ordered to return. As soon as I got the message I plotted the position where they would have been, and it more or less corresponded with the report received from Bathurst.

This, frankly, is tosh. The outbound track from Darwin to Koepang is about 280 degrees magnetic, ten degrees north of west. An aircraft flying low along this track would pass 35 kilometres south of Bathurst Island, well out of sight of McGrath. When the ten Kittyhawks turned back, their inbound track would still have kept them 35 kilometres from the island, flying more or less due east. McGrath's message referred to a large formation flying south. To suggest that a 'big flight of planes' heading south and very high over Bathurst Island could plausibly match the plotted position of ten Kittyhawks flying east and low over the ocean 35 kilometres away stretches credulity too far.

In Fenton's version of events, Wing Commander Sturt Griffith, the Commanding Officer at the RAAF station, accepted Fenton's analysis and declined to order the air-raid sirens to sound.[1] About the only relevant fact that emerges from all this nonsense is that Pell's ten Kittyhawks were returning to Darwin from the west at about the same time as Fuchida's 188 Zeroes, Kates and Vals were arriving from the north.

◆ ◆ ◆

The nine Zeroes that had broken off from Fuchida's group to tackle Moorer's Catalina did not simply rejoin the main formation, which, as far as they were concerned, was now way ahead of them. Instead they continued separately towards Darwin. However, Fuchida led his flight off to the east in preparation for his huge clockwise circle around the town, so the nine Zeroes actually got to Darwin first. They arrived from the north, over the harbour.

Floyd Pell, commanding the flight of ten Kittyhawks, was no beginner. He was an experienced pilot who had once worked on the staff of General Brereton's US Far East Air Force in the Philippines, so he was familiar with Japanese surprise attacks. Instead of simply leading his entire formation back to the airfield, he ordered Oestreicher and four others to climb to 15,000 feet and mount a protective patrol overhead while the remaining five planes landed.

Oestreicher, the most experienced pilot, took the role of 'weaver'. He climbed above his four companions and rolled his aircraft from side to side, checking above and below as well as all around him. As they clawed their way through 8000 feet, Oestreicher's throat suddenly went dry. In his eight o'clock position (just behind his left shoulder) and 2000 feet above him he saw what was obviously a Zero on an attack dive towards the formation. He just had time to shout 'Zeroes! Zeroes! Zeroes!' into his microphone before the first Zero barged through the formation, breaking it up. Oestreicher dropped his belly tank to give his Kittyhawk more speed. Let him continue the story: 'Climbing into the sun I was able to get a small burst into one Zero, who rolled in his climb and shot me. I spun out, regaining control at 4000 feet. I again climbed and around 12,000 feet I counted 18 more enemy planes in a lazy circle at what I would judge to be 20,000 feet. I called 'B' Flight [Oestreicher's own flight] on the radio and advised heading for the clouds about five miles south of Darwin that were at an altitude of 2000 to 2500 feet.' Oestreicher wasted no time taking his own advice, and buried himself in the nearest cloud.

His warning shout and his excellent advice to hide in the clouds came too late for Lieutenant Jack Peres, part of Oestreicher's group of five Kittyhawks. Peres was shot down and killed over Gunn Point, 15 kilometres north of Darwin, becoming the first airman to die in Australian skies as a result of enemy action.

Yamamoto had insisted that Nagumo Force should include the best and most experienced pilots available. Most had fought in the war with China and were aerial combat veterans. The five patrolling Kittyhawk pilots, with the exception of Oestreicher, were absolute beginners. It was about as even a contest as a boxing match between four Muhammed Alis and a lone schoolboy flyweight champion.

Lieutenant Elton Perry's Kittyhawk followed Peres. He was shot down and killed. Lieutenant William Walker was attacked and badly wounded in the left shoulder. Landing a plane one-handed is no mean feat, but Walker managed it. He put his Kittyhawk down safely at the RAAF field, scrambled clear, and watched as his plane was strafed and burned by the wheeling Zeroes. Lieutenant Max Wiecks had his plane badly shot up, and parachuted to safety. He landed in the harbour, was swept out to sea by the huge Darwin tide, and did not reach land until after dark—a feat in itself. That left Oestreicher's Kittyhawk alone to face 36 Zeroes, 71 Vals and 81 Kates.

◆　◆　◆

The 14th Anti-Aircraft battery in Darwin consisted of twelve 3.7-inch guns grouped in sections at the Oval, Fannie Bay and McMillans. The battery also had two 3-inch guns at Elliott Point and a section of Lewis guns on top of the oil tanks on the foreshores of Port Darwin. There was a fourth section of four 3.7-inch guns of the 2nd AA battery at Berrimah. Each 3.7-inch section's four guns were arranged in a U shape, with a command post at the centre of the U.

Getting a group of heavy anti-aircraft guns into action is far from simple, but it nevertheless has to be done in a tearing hurry. Once the alarm is raised, the Gun Position Officer in the command post races for the Toc I telescope identification and confirms the presence of enemy aircraft. He then calls a bearing. Next, the three-man crew of the height finder, technical name UB7, use the bearing supplied by telescope identification to lock onto the target. The UB7 operator can see two images of the target through his viewfinder, one of them upside down, and he twiddles his knobs and dials until the images line up opposite each other. He then calls: 'Read'. This gives the plane's height. This number—on the day it was 14,000 feet—is called out to the predictor unit inside the command post, who call: '14,000 set.'

The predictor is a kind of mechanical calculator, about a metre square, standing on metal legs. It has telescopes and adjusting wheels for calculating the bearing, elevation and fuse setting for the guns. This information is relayed electrically to the four guns. On each gun, two gun layers sit with their backs to the target. They each turn their handles until the pointer on their dials matches the bearing and elevation information fed in electrically by the predictor. Meanwhile, the shell to be fired is first passed through a fuse setter, also using information fed in from the predictor. This sets the time—and therefore the height—at which the shell will detonate. The shell can then be locked into the breech of the gun. If all has gone according to plan, the gun is now pointing in the direction and at the angle ordered by the predictor unit, and the shell fuse has been set separately to detonate at the height supplied by the height finder. The gun is now ready to fire. As the target changes height or bearing, new information is fed to the predictor unit and then to the gunners, who adjust accordingly.

Heavy anti-aircraft shells are not looking for a direct hit. The idea is to fill the air around the planes with lethal explosions and thereby disrupt them from attacking their target. It goes without saying, however, that the most effective disruption is to shoot them down. So the gunners aim to have their shells explode as close as possible to a target plane or formation, and have the blast and flying shrapnel do the damage, ideally destroying a couple of bombers with a single well-placed shot. With a skilful predictor crew working closely with a radar unit, the 3.7-inch AA guns could be very effective against high-flying 'horizontal' bombers. On 19 February 1942, Darwin had no functioning radar unit.

Jack Mulholland, part of the Oval group, remembers an ordinary start to the day. The crews serviced the guns at 'dawn manning', then stood down for breakfast. ('Powdered eggs, most likely,' Mulholland remembers gloomily.) The gunners could still hear the engine noise of the patrolling Kittyhawks overhead. This masked any sound of Fuchida's bombers, still miles away to the south. However, there were other eyes watching and other ears listening. As we have seen, the telephonist in the command post at the Oval was casually eavesdropping on the town chatter when he heard an urgent voice refer to a 'dogfight' out to sea. This was almost certainly a reference to the shooting down of Wiecks'

Kittyhawk. The telephonist quickly alerted his Gun Position Officer, who ordered his Oval gun crews to action stations. At this point there was still no official alert. Mulholland grabbed a pack of Craven 'A' cigarettes left over from Christmas, and a cowboy novel, *Gun Whipped*, and headed for his gun. A book and a fag would relieve the boredom during the inevitable false alarm.

As they listened and watched, the gunners gradually became aware of a new, deeper, more menacing sound, bearing down on them from an unexpected direction, the south-east. On one of the gun positions—not Mulholland's—the crews were training by using the five patrolling Kittyhawks as an imaginary target. As the noise of Fuchida's approaching bombers grew louder, the instructor decided to switch the training drill to the new source of aircraft noise. A gunner swung his telescope to the new target, then yelled: 'Hell, they've got bloody red spots on their wings!'

At the Oval, the Gun Position Officer saw Fuchida's Kate bombers bearing down on the town. His gunners were already alert. He set the predictor process into motion, shouting as he did: 'This is not a false alarm! This is for real! This is for real!'

♦ ♦ ♦

At the RAAF airfield, Floyd Pell was standing near his aircraft, where he could still hear the radio. He heard Robert Oestreicher's shout of 'Zeroes! Zeroes! Zeroes!' and ordered his five Kittyhawks to ditch their belly tanks and get back into the air. Pell was first to take off. At about 80 feet above the runway, he was attacked by three Zeroes who instantly crippled his plane. He bailed out and miraculously survived the parachute descent. A Zero casually machine-gunned and killed him on the ground as he attempted to crawl to safety.

Next to scramble was his No. 2, Lieutenant Charles Hughes. He was almost certainly dead before his wheels had left the ground, killed on his take-off run by a strafing Zero. Hughes's plane continued into the air, now with a dead man at the controls. Next to take off was Lieutenant Robert McMahon, whose first sight as he lifted off was a fireball on the ground some 2000 yards ahead of him, undoubtedly Hughes' aircraft crashing and exploding on impact.[2]

McMahon escaped Hughes's fate. As he clawed his way into the air he managed to get onto the tail of a Zero. He then fell for the oldest sucker punch in the fighter pilot's handbook: at about 600 feet the Zero he was chasing pulled up hard into a loop, which reversed their positions, putting the Japanese pilot on McMahon's tail. The Zero calmly poured machine-gun fire into the exposed Kittyhawk. Although his plane was heavily shot up, McMahon managed to stay in the fight until he ran out of ammunition. He parachuted into the mangroves surrounding Port Darwin and found his way to the water's edge, where a launch picked him up.

Next to take off was Lieutenant Burt Rice, quickly followed by Lieutenant John Glover. Rice climbed to 5000 feet before three Zeroes pounced. Eyewitnesses saw him diving and zooming and actually outrunning his pursuers, who continued to fire at him. From a position ahead of the three Zeroes, Rice slammed his plane into what he hoped would be a steep left turn, wheeling him around behind his attackers. He was too late. His plane had already taken too much damage: as he tried to enter the turn, the controls stopped responding and Rice bailed out, knocking himself unconscious as he left the cockpit.

By whatever instinct, Rice pulled the rip cord and was floating down inert while the Japanese pilots set about finishing him off with their machine guns. Glover stormed into the fray, firing at and hitting one of the Zeroes. With staggering courage Glover then broke through the ring of attacking Zeroes and put his Kittyhawk into a tight spiralling dive, circling the dangling figure of Rice as they both descended. The Zeroes continued to machine-gun Glover's already damaged aircraft until at 3000 feet his dive threatened to become uncontrollable. Glover fought to get his Kittyhawk level, managing to do so just before he hit the ground. The plane cartwheeled and disintegrated, some of the wreckage flying as far as 100 metres from the crash site. Miraculously, Glover crawled clear of the wreckage. An Australian ran and grabbed him, dragging him to a slit trench before the Japanese could machine-gun him, too. Meanwhile Rice's parachute lowered him safely into a swamp, where he was rescued a few hours later.

With all the Wirraways on the ground and unserviceable, and nine of the ten Kittyhawks blown out of the sky, Darwin's defences against Fuchida's 188-aircraft armada were now reduced to the Army's 16 3.7-inch heavy AA guns and their untested gunners, some largely useless Lewis guns tied to saplings, the AA guns on the small handful of fighting ships in the harbour, a few makeshift machine guns at the RAAF base, and Robert Oestreicher's lone Kittyhawk, lurking in the clouds five miles south of the town.

As the sound of the first explosions rocked Darwin, the ever-meticulous Lou Curnock, at aeradio station VID, noted the time in his log book. It was 9.58 a.m.

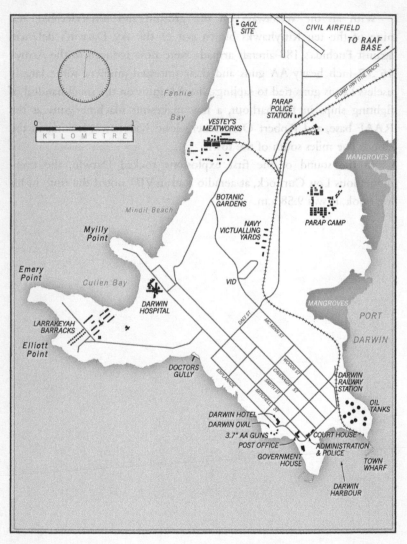

The city of Darwin on 19 February 1942, showing the principal targets.

Chapter 9

QQQ QQQ QQQ de VZDN

Mitsuo Fuchida's attack plan was nothing if not methodical. The 81 Kate high-flying 'horizontal' bombers divided into two groups, one to attack the port while the other set about the RAAF airfield. 'I led the main strength of my level bombers in an attack on the harbour installations and a nearby cluster of oil tanks,' Fuchida recalled. 'The rest of the bombers went to destroy the airfield hangars. While the fighter group went after the enemy planes, I detailed the dive bombers to attack ships in the harbour.'

The terror and devastation these matter-of-fact words conceal are almost beyond description. Herb Kriloff, whom we first met as officer of the deck on the USS *William B. Preston* when it was under attack from Japanese aircraft in Davao Gulf, and who went on to serve on escort convoys in the Battle of the Atlantic, wrote: 'No single incident in my life has affected me more than that raid, a disaster of a magnitude and ferocity that is hard to describe. When it was over, had anyone told me that the war was to last another three and a half years, I would never have expected to see it end.'

Fuchida's Kate bombers arrived in tight formation, worthy of an air display fly-past. They flew in carefully calculated giant V formations. The three leading aircraft arranged themselves in the first V; two more Vs, each of three aircraft, formed up close behind them to produce a compact group of nine aircraft. This group of nine then became the apex of a bigger V, with two more groups of nine flying behind them, one on their left and the other on their right. The 27 aircraft were now in a perfect position to pattern bomb a broad swathe of the target area. The first group arrived on an attack line that began at the port, passed over the town, and led on to the Larrakeyah military barracks and the nearby civil hospital.

There is universal agreement that the first bombs from Fuchida's opening salvo fell into the harbour, missing the wharf by 20 or 30 metres. But the next ones slammed into the wharf, ripping out a huge section, cutting off the wharfies unloading *Neptuna* and *Barossa*, and damaging both ships. A bomb fell on the recreation shed near the wharf elbow, blasting it out of existence and killing instantly a group of wharfies who had knocked off for a smoko a few minutes earlier.

The first explosion flicked a locomotive and six railway trucks into the harbour, together with some bystanders on the wharf. Surviving wharfies and ships' crew dived into the harbour, reckoning they would be safer in the water away from the obvious targets.

The first blasts fractured and scattered oil lines running along the wharf. The flowing oil pumped into the harbour and soon caught fire. Oil enveloped the men struggling in the water, blackening them all over and making breathing difficult. Those attempting to swim had to pick their way through the flames. The ebbing tide swept up some of the pools of burning oil and dragged them towards the centre of the harbour and the main anchorage full of ships.

◆ ◆ ◆

Edgar Harrison, the permanent air-raid warden officer, had just left the Post Office when the first bomb fell. He had covered about 150 yards on his way back to his office in the Native Affairs Department. The first blast mingled with the opening wail of the first air-raid siren, sited on a water tower in the town. The big occasion turned out to be more than the siren could handle. It wheezed and died before it could complete its two-minute warning.

Harrison's first instinct was to drop to the ground. Then he realised he had work to do. Although the wardens had in theory disbanded on 26 January, they had made a pact with the Army to do their jobs if the need arose. Clearly it had just arisen. Harrison recalled: 'I picked myself up on [sic] the road and galloped down to my own office a couple of hundred yards away and started the air raid siren. At the time the Army telephone was ringing.'

Harrison's office was understandably deserted: officially, there were no air-raid wardens to staff it, and in any case the wardens were all at their day-job desks. It did not take them long to work out that the long-awaited raid had begun. They could hear bombs falling and Harrison's siren howling its confirmation. Around the town the sirens took up the call.

◆ ◆ ◆

Darwin town lay just beyond the port, on the extended line of Fuchida's opening attack run. There is no proof that the Japanese bombers set out deliberately to attack civilian targets in the town— Fuchida denied it in postwar interviews—but any bomb that failed to find the port would inevitably strike the civilian buildings beyond it. There is universal agreement that accuracy was a hallmark of the bombing attack that day. It is hard to avoid the conclusion, when so many bombs hit civilian targets, that at least some of the Kates deliberately went for the town, concentrating on the administration buildings along The Esplanade.

Darwin's communications centre was on the southern edge of the town, close to the harbour. It occupied a whole block between The Esplanade and Mitchell Street, and housed the Post Office, telephone exchange and cable office—virtually the town's entire civilian communications system. Of the 67 women still in Darwin after the evacuation, six worked in this building, in the telephone exchange and at the Post Office.

Two minutes after the alarm sounded, the staff packed into the shelter in postmaster Hurtle Bald's garden. As we have seen, it was regarded as one of the safest in Darwin, vulnerable only to a direct hit. That was exactly what it took—a direct hit from a 250-kg high-explosive bomb dropped from a Kate. It instantly killed Bald, his wife Alice, his daughter Iris, sisters Eileen and Jean Mullen, Emily Young, Freda Stasinowsky, Archie Halls and Arthur Wellington (the writer of the late-night letter to his wife and daughter quoted in Chapter 7). Police later ripped down curtains from the Balds' living room to cover the women's bodies: the blast had stripped off all their clothing. One of the more horrific sights of the day was the bloodied body of one of the postal staff hanging a metre and a half above the ground in the fork of a nearby tree. He had clearly been thrown high in the air before crashing to his final resting place.

The same salvo wrecked the telephone exchange and cable office, effectively destroying all civilian and most military communication in the town. Four kilometres above the carnage, Fuchida's Kate bombers continued on their serene way. The raid was now perhaps four minutes old.

◆ ◆ ◆

There can be no doubt that Administrator Abbott suffered one of the worst and most terrifying experiences of those who survived the day, but His Honour was an experienced soldier and knew what it was like to be under bombardment. The same could not be said for his wife and his staff.

Government House stood on sloping land near the harbour, right in the main line of the attack. The building, including the Administrator's office, had a concrete floor supported by reinforced-concrete pillars. Below Abbott's office was a concrete strongroom with a heavy iron door, tough enough to hold out against anything but a direct hit. Abbott, his wife Hilda, and their staff piled into the strongroom shelter as soon as the sirens sounded.

Government House took the feared direct hit. A bomb of at least

250 kg landed in the grounds about 15 metres from the shelter. The blast smashed in the iron door and the shock wave lifted the concrete ceiling as the wind might lift a sail. The ceiling crashed back down, snapping the reinforced-concrete pillars. Everybody in the shelter might have been killed on the spot by falling concrete but for the caved-in iron door, which proved strong enough to support parts of the roof. Dust and tons of masonry showered into the strongroom, wrecking half of it.

Abbott's account of this is modest and understated. He set out his version of events in a six-page report, tendered as evidence to the Royal Commission and entitled *Japanese Air Raid, Darwin, 19th February 1942—Movements and Actions of the Administrator Upon That and Following Days.* He wrote:

> The raid by Japanese bombers commenced about 10 a.m. on the 19th February. I took shelter under the Office which sustained an almost direct hit and collapsed, killing a half-caste servant girl, and almost burying another half-caste girl and an aboriginal boy.
>
> With the help of Kamper, my driver and messenger, we procured crowbars, which were with other garden tools near by and freed these two people. As the raid went on, we again took shelter until about 11.15.

The girl killed by the falling roof was 18-year-old Daisy Martin. Abbott says she died instantly, crushed under tons of falling masonry, and that is almost certainly the truth. However, as we shall see in Chapter 11, an altogether more terrible version of this event soon began circulating in Darwin, supported by the police. It is a measure of Abbott's unpopularity with the people of Darwin that the counter-story was widely believed. It did nothing to improve Abbott's standing with them in the aftermath of the raid.

The bomb that crashed into Abbot's garden left a crater ten metres wide and six metres deep. The raid was now five minutes old.

◆ ◆ ◆

Constable Leo Law was in the police barracks in town when the raid began. 'I was in the bathroom. I'd had a shave and was about to have a shower,' he later recalled. 'I was under the shower when the alert went. I immediately ran outside with nothing but a towel on. I dived into a slit trench a foot deep and approximately 18 inches wide. The next thing I looked up—almost simultaneously this happened—and I saw these planes. I didn't count them, but I should say there would be 18 that I saw. Very shortly afterwards—a matter of a minute—there was a terrific explosion. I was covered with three feet of clay. There was a Government Office official in the trench ahead of me. His body was entirely covered. We had to dig him out.'

Constable Robert 'Bob' Darken was standing at the rear of the police station when the raid began. He heard no sirens. 'The first thing I knew of the air raid was when I heard the drone of the planes,' he recalled. 'I looked over the roof of the Police Station and saw a formation of nine bombers. I ran across to the barracks to wake up Constable Mofflin, who was asleep in bed.'

Dave Mofflin had worked the night shift and was dead to the world. Darken waited impatiently as his notoriously slow-waking mate dragged his boots on. The barracks was no place to be. As the two policemen reached the back door, a bomb tore into the ground immediately in front of the barracks, throwing Darken and Mofflin off their feet and hurling them under a concrete water tank. 'There was no shelter for us to take,' Darken explained later. 'There were trenches in the yard but they were all occupied.' They crawled under a car.

The first wave of Kates continued past the town towards the military barracks at Larrakeyah. The barracks had been partly camouflaged with paint and might have been hard to identify from 14,000 feet. The same could not be said for the new civil hospital at Cullen Bay, only a few hundred metres away. It had been painted white and clearly marked with a red cross. It is generally accepted that the Japanese did not deliberately target it, and it may be that the high-flying Kates mistook it for the barracks. Hospitals and barracks can look alike from the air. All that can be said with certainty is that six bombs landed close to the hospital and none went near the barracks.

The hospital had a well-planned air-raid drill. Patients who were reasonably mobile abandoned their beds and headed for shelter under the nearby cliffs at Cullen Bay. Less mobile patients who could nevertheless fend for themselves slid under their beds, with the mattress as their only protection. The staff lifted the least mobile patients and placed them under their beds before heading off to find shelter for themselves. Some doctors and nurses dived into the few available trenches in the grounds, others simply hid among the rocks.

Although none of the bombs hit the hospital directly, the six massive blasts showered the buildings with rocks, glass and other heavy debris. Rocks smashed through the thin roof, crashing onto beds and mattresses vacated only minutes earlier. Three wards and some outbuildings were damaged, and one naval ward was totally wrecked. Incredibly, no one was killed.

◆ ◆ ◆

At the Oval, Jack Mulholland's 3.7-inch anti-aircraft guns began firing even before the first bombs struck. The thunder of their own artillery was almost as devastating for the gunners as anything delivered by the Japanese. The dozen 3.7-inch guns of the 14th Heavy AA Battery had between them fired a total of *two* live rounds in their entire 14 months' training in Darwin. Both were warning shots fired across the path of 'friendly' bombers. The gunners had no experience of the full fury of an anti-aircraft barrage, when between 40 and 80 deafening rounds a minute are fired by the four-gun section.

An anti-aircraft section fires its first salvo from all guns simultaneously, aiming for maximum surprise. After that each gun fires independently, as fast as it can. To the inexperienced gunners, the first shattering roar of four guns firing at once might have heralded Armageddon. No one had prepared them for this. Gunners could not look up as they worked, so it was impossible to know what was going on around them. All they could do was keep firing. As the barrage continued, the roar of the guns was every bit as intimidating as the thunder of exploding bombs. At times it was hard to tell which was which. 'There was the ever-present wonder as to whether the adjoining gun had fired or a bomb had burst nearby,' Jack Mulholland wrote later.

The spent shells from each round were ejected automatically from the breech of the gun. They were heavy enough to break the leg of an unwary gunner. They were also blisteringly hot and had to be heaved over the revetment wall with gloved hands. There was a real risk the hot shell cases might set fire to the camouflage netting over the guns. The combination of gun noise, smoke, hot shell casings, deafening bomb explosions, Lewis machine-gun fire, plus swarming dive-bombers and fighters screaming low overhead must have seemed to the gunners like a vision of the apocalypse.

In the face of this onslaught, the gunners kept firing. However, lack of practice with live rounds sabotaged their disciplined efforts. Until 19 February 1942 nobody had a chance to discover that tropical heat plays tricks with fuse timers on anti-aircraft shells. As the command post crew watched in impotent fury, the shells burst below and behind the bombers.

◆ ◆ ◆

There are as many accounts of the tactics of Fuchida's 81 Kates as there were eyewitnesses. No two match exactly. However, there are some common threads, of which the most widely repeated is the grouping of the bombers in three waves. From the dozens of fragmentary eyewitness reports, the most likely scenario is that two waves of 27 Kates attacked the port, the town and the military barracks, while a third wave peeled off and headed for the civil airfield and RAAF base to the north and north-east of the town respectively.

The planes passed over the civil airfield first. As they did, the staff heard the anti-aircraft batteries open up. This was the first indication they had that the aircraft were hostile. Bruce Acland, one of the operations staff, raced to his radio and broadcast the coded message: 'QQQ QQQ QQQ de VZDN', telling the world Darwin was under air attack. Acland waited for confirmation that the message had been received by Daly Waters and other centres before cutting off all electric power, locking the code books in the safe, and heading for a slit trench.

At the RAAF field, the officers and men in the RAAF Operations Room could see the smoke and hear the thud of bombs already blasting the town. Many sprinted for slit trenches and shelters, while others manned the makeshift anti-aircraft machine-gun posts. Group Captain Sturt Griffith, the station commander, noted the time the first bomb struck his base. It was 10.08, ten minutes after the first salvo hit the harbour.

The machine guns could not reach the Kates. With no fighter aircraft to challenge them, the Japanese continued on their leisurely path of destruction. Bombs poured down on the hangars and workshops at the RAAF base, wrecking them all, together with any aircraft inside. Fires broke out at the ammunition dump and stores. When the high-flying bombers had finished their work, the dive-bombers moved in.

Zeroes and Vals flashed across the airfield, strafing and bombing. They flew low enough for the defenders to see the faces of the pilots. The machine guns did their best, but there was no stopping the smiling pilots as they roared effortlessly overhead.

At one of the machine-gun posts, Wing Commander Archie Tindal sat exposed on the lip of a trench, firing his Vickers gun at the swarming attackers. A single bullet, very likely from a cannon, passed through his throat, killing him instantly. He was the first Australian airman to die in combat on Australian soil.[1]

The Vals and Zeroes now spread the attack to the civil airfield, using incendiaries and anti-personnel 'daisy-cutter' bombs as well as high explosives. The daisy-cutters blasted lethal shrapnel in a flat pattern close to the ground, designed to kill and maim anybody caught in the open. The Japanese machine-gunned buildings, set the oil store on fire, and destroyed a light plane owned by a Flying Doctor pilot. They smashed vital radio sets in the administration building, and the emergency power generator. The fire-fighting tender caught fire and was rendered unusable. An ammunition store was soon ablaze, exploding hundreds of .303 machine-gun rounds. The noise of wind, fires and explosions was so great that people could hardly make themselves heard when they spoke.

◆　◆　◆

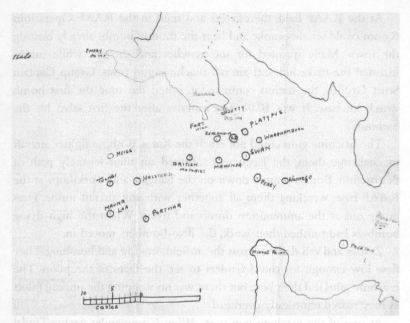

Original sketch map of Port Darwin showing key ships' positions at the beginning of the raid. The map was drawn by Lieutenant John S. Bell RAN, Darwin's harbourmaster on the day.

Over Port Darwin, the dive-bombers worked in pairs.

Darwin may have been packed with ships, but its defenders had no battle plan, no prearranged strategy, no inkling of who should do what in the event of an attack. It was simply every man for himself.

Six fighting ships in the harbour carried anti-aircraft guns: the destroyer USS *Peary*, the seaplane tender USS *William B. Preston*, the corvettes HMAS *Deloraine* and *Katoomba*, the sloop HMAS *Swan*, and the depot ship HMAS *Platypus*. Some others, such as the auxiliary minesweeper HMAS *Gunbar*, carried a single Lewis gun.

Gunbar was the first to come under attack, from the nine Zeroes fresh from dispatching the Catalina and the Kittyhawks. At 9.57 a.m., one minute before the first bombs fell, *Gunbar* was just passing through the boom gate guarding the harbour entrance when the Zeroes swooped.

Lieutenant D.H. Davies, aboard the minesweeper, described what happened. 'Nine fighter aircraft attacked giving in all 18 separate attacks from ahead, astern, port, starboard and the four quarters,' he wrote in his report. 'The attackers used a mixture of armour piercing, tracer and common ammunition of about .303 calibre. The first run hit our single Lewis gun in the magazine, rendering the ship defenceless. Including the Captain, nine men were injured, one of whom, Able Seaman Sheppard F.3384, has since died of wounds received during the attack.' The crew still had a few single–shot Lee–Enfield .303 rifles and the captain's Webley revolver to hand, and they fired away to no effect. The captain, Lieutenant Norman Muzzell, later described the defence of his ship as 'like throwing peanuts at a tiger'.

Even as the first bombs hit the wharf, ships in the harbour struggled to get under way. HMAS *Swan*, tied up alongside *Neptuna*, quickly cast off and headed for more open water. USS *Peary* and *William B. Preston* slipped, followed by HMAS *Warrego*. The depot ship HMAS *Platypus*, which had been one of the first to see the bombers, sounded the alarm and began a furious anti–aircraft barrage. HMAS *Katoomba*, trapped in the floating dock but nevertheless able to use her guns, joined the fray. Between them the ships did not have anything like enough anti–aircraft firepower to beat off the Vals and Zeroes, but they now erupted in a roar of smoke, flame and high explosives.

For the Japanese dive–bombers surveying the target area, the most valuable prize was the *Peary*. She was no stranger to Japanese aircraft. With the Pacific war only three days old, Japanese bombers had attacked the destroyer in a raid on Cavite Navy Yard, in the Philippines. In that raid, a direct hit killed eight of *Peary*'s crew and set her on fire. The Japanese attacked her again on 26 December, this time at sea. On 28 December she was bombed and damaged by 'friendly' aircraft. Next day the Japanese resumed where the friendlies had left off, attacking with bombs and torpedoes. By the time *Peary* limped into Darwin on 3 January 1942, she had already had a tough war.

Peary returned to Port Darwin in the early hours of 19 February to pick up fuel. When the bombers arrived, her skipper, Lieutenant

Commander John Bermingham, was pacing the bridge, desperate to collect his fuel and get away. He ordered engines started and anchor up, and was barely under way when the planes struck. The first direct hit from a dive-bomber caught *Peary*'s stern and destroyed her steering-gear engine. An incendiary ripped into the galley and started the first of several fires. A third bomb failed to explode. *Peary* kept fighting. All over her decks, anti-aircraft guns poured fire in the direction of the swarming dive-bombers, until the ship was almost enveloped in the smoke of her own guns. It was too late. A fourth bomb sliced its way into the ammunition store, triggering a catastrophic explosion that utterly wrecked the destroyer. A fifth incendiary exploded in the engine-room, but it needn't have bothered.

Herb Kriloff, on the bridge of the seaplane tender USS *William B. Preston*, watched from about 300 metres away. He recalled: 'The explosion was blindingly bright. When you opened your eyes, it took time to adjust so you could see again. We were dressed in shorts with short-sleeved shirts. The *Peary* blast made us feel as if every uncovered part of our bodies was on fire.'

Peary was now like a dying animal, dragging painfully along, with her stern gradually sinking. Her guns kept firing to the bitter end. More than one eyewitness reported that the forward guns were still firing as she slid under the burning waters of Port Darwin.

◆　◆　◆

The *William B Preston* got under way at about the same time as the *Peary*. *Willy B* had anchored in splendid isolation at the eastern end of Port Darwin, well clear of other ships. That left her dangerously exposed and furthest from the comparative safety of the open sea. Her captain, Lieutenant Commander Etheridge 'Jimmy' Grant, had gone ashore at 8 a.m. to chase up a delivery of aviation fuel and some desperately needed food. The ship's executive officer, Lieutenant Lester Wood, realising he had no time to lose, took command. *Willy B* always kept one boiler going, so the engines were immediately usable. Wood ordered her under way, and she was on the move within five minutes of the first alarm.

Willy B was a converted destroyer with a good turn of speed. She rapidly built up to 20 knots. Suddenly Wood heard a shout of 'Bombers overhead!' He heeled *Willy B* hard right to put the bombers off their aim. No bombs fell, but this new course was taking him straight for the shoals outside Port Darwin's East Arm. Wood slewed *Willy B* hard left. Now he was headed for a buoy marking a second set of shoals. Hard right again. This put him on what looked like a collision course with *Peary*, just under way and yet to be hit by the bombers. Wood judged that, with enough speed, he would just clear *Peary*. He left *Willy B* on full ahead, and scraped past.

While all this violent manoeuvring was taking place, the crew had cause to be grateful for some casual 'souveniring' over previous weeks. Whenever one of *Willy B*'s Catalinas had to be scrapped, the crew made sure they kept any serviceable machine guns or cannons. They improvised mounts on railings, on decks, wherever they could. As a result, *Willy B* was fairly bristling. She had nine .50 and five .30 medium-calibre anti-aircraft machine guns, and she now set about pouring this wholly unexpected fire at the startled Japanese dive-bombers, who responded by treating her with caution.

The luck could not last. After a series of near misses, and at about the same time as *Peary* came under attack, *Willy B* took a direct hit. The bomb triggered a deadly secondary explosion. In his action report, Les Wood wrote: 'At 1010 the ship was struck by probably a one hundred pound bomb [given that it came from a Val, it was probably 60 kg] a few inches aft of frame 137 main deck port. This bomb detonated fourteen 4-inch projectiles stored within four to five feet in an ammunition rack for the after gun. Fire immediately broke out and steering control was lost.'

The scene on *Willy B*'s deck was appalling. Herb Kriloff recalled: 'Aft of the deckhouse lay several bodies, in pieces. One man had been cut in half at the waist, and the area was covered with blood, so much that it was difficult to keep one's footing.'

Willy B was still going flat out. She was now on fire, her steering gear crippled, and desperately difficult to control. She threatened to collide with the Australian hospital ship MV *Manunda*, about 500 metres ahead. Wood needed to come left. 'With no steering control (the fire was so strong aft men could not reach the steering engine room) this was achieved by using the engines,' Wood wrote in his action report. He was now steering by altering the thrust on his two propellers, all the time trying to avoid the bombs and other ships twisting and turning in the harbour.

At about 10.15, in the midst of all this mayhem, *Willy B*'s second patrolling Catalina radioed in with an urgent message. The first Catalina, piloted by Thomas Moorer, had been shot down by nine Zeroes before it had time to broadcast a warning. The second Catalina's crew told *Willy B* they could see one aircraft carrier, four cruisers and three destroyers about 150 miles north of Bathurst Island. This vital message did not reach the RAAF (which, at this point, had three serviceable Hudson bombers at its disposal and might have used them to launch a counter-strike) until the next day. The collapse of military communications in Darwin saw to that.

Willy B's crew had pressing problems of their own. They assessed the damage: no steering control; flooding aft; large fires not under control; large holes below the waterline aft; heavy casualties killed and wounded. They could still manoeuvre using the engines, and they continued towards the harbour entrance. As they tried to escape, they faced a threat even deadlier than secondary explosions of stacked shells. *Willy B* was still carrying fifty 500-lb bombs and 30,000 gallons of aviation fuel for its Catalinas. Kriloff again: 'Should a strafing aircraft pierce our side, we might go up in one puff, making *Peary*'s loss look like a minor incident.'

There was, however, a far worse explosion threatening. *Neptuna*, tied up on the outside berth at the wharf, had taken only light damage from the first wave of Kates. After the first blasts, the crew moved to the forward saloon for shelter. When the Val dive-bombers moved in, a bomb sliced through *Neptuna*'s bridge and exploded in the saloon, killing as many as 45 of the sheltering crew. A second bomb slammed into the timber-filled No. 1 hold, setting it on fire. Captain William Michie quickly ordered any wharfies and crew still alive to abandon ship.

Michie knew two of *Neptuna's* other holds were filled with TNT and 200 tons of depth charges, all of which could go up at any moment.

◆ ◆ ◆

Everywhere there were remarkable escapes. The crew of the sloop HMAS *Katoomba*, trapped immobile in the floating dock, watched transfixed as a Val roared towards their port side. The crew opened fire with rifles and a Vickers machine gun. The pilot pressed on, taking a hail of bullets, until he was within 300 metres of the ship. Then he thought better of it, swerved off the attack line, and dropped his bomb in the harbour.

The second Val now attacked from starboard. *Katoomba* had a 12-pound anti-aircraft gun, not something to be challenged lightly. Captain Cousin ordered the gun crew to use a short fuse. As the plane pulled out of its dive and began its final horizontal run towards them, with no chance of missing, the gun crew fired a single shell that burst in front of the Val. The panicked pilot pulled into a vertical climb and disappeared, never to return.

The Lewis gunners stationed on top of the oil tanks around the harbour's edge kept pouring fire at any Zero or Val with the temerity to come within range. Despite their puny weapons, they managed to disrupt the bombers sufficiently to save the tanks. At the end of the raid the tanks had taken some damage but no direct hits.

Nevertheless, no amount of courage and tenacity from the gunners could prevail against the overwhelming force of Fuchida's attack. The harbour was now a howling, screaming, smoke-filled tumult of dive-bombers, swooping, strafing Zero fighters, exploding bombs, bursting shrapnel, spreading oil (some of it on fire), crippled or sinking ships, and men trying to stay afloat in the oily water.

For those still alive in the wharf area, there was an ominous new development. It began as a low rumbling sound that grew steadily more insistent. It came from the direction of *Neptuna*. The fire lit by the dive-bombers was spreading through the ship towards the TNT and the depth charges.

Of the three services, the RAAF emerges from the Darwin raid least well. The Army gunners put up a spirited fight. The ships of the US Navy and the Royal Australian Navy did their best with limited resources. The RAAF had next to nothing to fight with, and it showed.

Although the RAAF base was technically home to the Hudson bombers of 13 Squadron, these planes had spent most of their time at Ambon, in the Molucca Islands. Darwin was not an air base at all in the usual sense of the word: no aircraft were kept there permanently. Instead it was a maintenance facility, a fuel and ammunition store, and a staging point on the route to the besieged Dutch East Indies.

That might not have mattered were it not for a further handicap. The RAAF personnel permanently stationed at the base were mostly technicians and maintenance crew, and did not see themselves as front-line fighters. They had not drilled with even the handful of old Lee-Enfield rifles at their disposal. They had set up a few makeshift machine-gun posts, using guns cannibalised from unserviceable aircraft, but they had no serious anti-aircraft batteries. In the event of an attack they could do little more than jump into slit trenches and hope to survive whatever was thrown at them. To compound the problem, the RAAF usually promoted people for technical competence rather than managerial and leadership skills. The most senior officer in the maintenance section, for instance, would invariably be the best mechanic and not necessarily the best officer.

On 19 February 1942, Group Captain Frederick Scherger, an experienced pilot and natural leader (later, as Air Marshal Sir Frederick Scherger, he became head of the RAAF) was the most senior air-force officer at Area Combined Headquarters at the RAAF base. As the Japanese bombers arrived, he was on his way into town by car to meet the former Chief of Air Staff, Air Marshall Sir Richard Williams, who happened to be staging through Darwin on his way back to Melbourne from London. Scherger recalled: 'When I reached the corner of the main road to Darwin and The Esplanade I heard AA guns firing. I stopped the car, looked out, and saw they were firing at a formation of 27 aircraft which appeared flying at a height of approximately 20,000 feet.'

Scherger quickly judged that the bombers were about to deliver 'a pattern of bombs commencing, as I thought, about the oil tanks and spreading right through to Larrakeyah'. This had one serious implication: the bombs would fall about where he was standing. He jumped back into the car and raced towards the civil airfield. He could hear the thud of bombs exploding behind him, catching up with him as he drove.

At the airfield he stepped out of the car, looked around, and saw smoke rising from the direction of the RAAF base. He jumped back into the car and headed there. 'As I approached I could see it was being dive-bombed and machine gunned, and I realised that anything moving on the station would immediately be fired at,' Scherger remembered. 'I stopped about 300 yards outside the main gate and when there was a lull in the attack I drew onto the station.

'Unfortunately I was only about 150 yards inside the gate when a fighter shooting at a machine gun post nearly hit the car, or his machine gun fire nearly hit the car. I stopped the car, got out, and as there was no shelter trench in the immediate vicinity I lay down in the long grass and remained there until the attack was over.'

◆ ◆ ◆

In Port Darwin, the carnage mounted. *Peary* suffered worst: 91 dead. After that came *Willy B*: 15 dead. The sloop HMAS *Swan*, having detached herself from the ominously rumbling *Neptuna*, was caught in the harbour and brutally attacked, with three killed. The depot ship HMAS *Platypus* took only moderate damage. Nevertheless, two men died. The lugger HMAS *Marie*, tied up alongside *Platypus*, was sunk by a dive-bomber. *Platypus*'s crew were close enough to see the pilot smile and wave at them as he swept past. Dive-bombers sank the oil tanker *British Motorist*: two dead. The troop transport USS *Port Mar* was towed off her mooring and beached, not before she took heavy damage and one man was killed. *Mauna Loa*, *Port Mar*'s fellow transport from the ill-fated convoy, was sunk: five dead. The biggest transport of all, USS *Meigs*, was bombed and machine-gunned: two dead. The troopship MV *Tulagi* was beached. The boom-net vessels HMAS *Kangaroo*, *Kara Kara*, *Karangi* and *Koala* were all machine-gunned. On *Kara Kara*: two dead. On

Kangaroo: one dead. The *Zealandia*, which had given the women and children evacuees such an uncomfortable trip south two months earlier, would trouble them no more. It was sunk: three dead. The coal hulk *Kelat* was also sunk. Two of *Willy B*'s Catalina aircraft were sunk at anchor.

Of all the destruction, the most bitterly resented involved the hospital ship MV *Manunda*. She was anchored in mid-harbour about 1500 metres due south of the wharf, with the oil tanker *British Motorist* about a kilometre to her west and the destroyer USS *Peary* a similar distance to the south-east. Other ships were not far away, including *Zealandia*, *Katoomba* (trapped inside the floating dock) and *Platypus*. So *Manunda* was certainly surrounded by legitimate targets. She was painted white, with three large red crosses on each side of her hull and large red crosses on her funnel to indicate her status as a hospital ship.

Peary, with her steering-gear engine destroyed, was both under way and out of control in the first few minutes of the attack. Some eye-witnesses said *Peary* passed close to *Manunda* and the hospital ship was hit by accident by aircraft attacking *Peary*. Others say no, *Peary* was already burning and sinking, and was not even close to *Manunda* when the bombers struck the hospital ship. For these witnesses, it was a deliberate and unforgivable assault on a sacrosanct target.

Charles Stewart was Third Officer on the *Zealandia*. When the *Peary* was hit, some of her crew dived overboard. Stewart volunteered to man one of *Zealandia*'s lifeboats to try to rescue *Peary* crew members struggling in the harbour. He was emphatic that *Peary* was never close to *Manunda*. He recalled: 'When we were returning from picking up men from the oily water, one of the dive-bombers made an attack on the *Manunda*. From my position in the boat I do not think that she [*Peary*] was that close. It did not appear to me to be very close. We were close to the *Manunda*.'

So was the attack on the *Manunda* deliberate? 'Yes, because the same plane came back and machine-gunned when over our boat.' Stewart was about 150 metres from *Manunda* at the time of the attack and, having just rescued some of *Peary*'s crew, was in a good position to judge her distance from *Peary*. If he says the attack was deliberate, his view deserves respect.

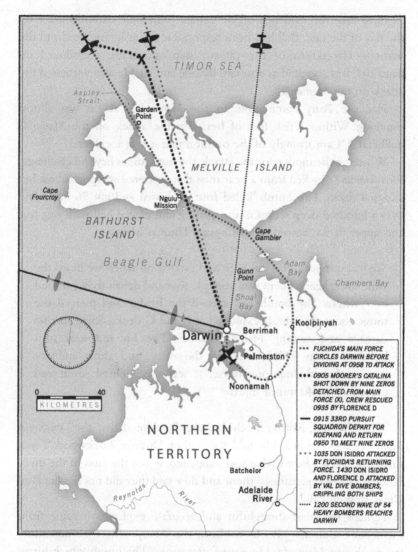

Chronology of the attack, beginning at 0905 with the shooting down of Moorer's Catalina and ending at 1200 with the arrival of the heavy bombers in the second wave. Note the wide gap between Pell's Kittyhawks on their track to Koepang and Fuchida's inbound attackers overflying Nguiu Mission.

Now take the evidence of Lieutenant John Bell, harbourmaster on the day of the raid. Bell had been responsible for assigning berths in the harbour. His sketch of the various ships' positions, reproduced on page 104, was accepted as accurate by one and all. He also witnessed the attack on the *Manunda*.

Had the *Peary* come close to the *Manunda*? 'Yes, it was almost touching. Within a few feet of her.' Was the attack on the *Manunda* deliberate? 'I am strongly of the opinion that it was accidental.'

Whatever the motive for the attack, the outcome is beyond challenge. First *Manunda* rocked from a near miss that spattered shrapnel across her exposed decks. This bomb 'killed four on board and cut 76 holes and over a hundred deep scores in our plating and played hell with our rear and upper decks,' according to Captain Thomas Minto.

> We had just got our wind back and carried on when we heard the same thing again. There was a terrific roar and debris flying around everywhere. The bomb had missed the bridge and pierced the music room skylight. It exploded at B and C decks, doing terrific damage and causing many casualties. The hit and near miss between them killed nine of the crew and three military personnel, including one nurse. It seriously injured seven and caused about 40 minor injuries.

After the war, Mitsuo Fuchida heatedly denied that the attack on *Manunda* was planned. He told the author Douglas Lockwood: 'I was surprised when I heard what had happened. It was the fault of the dive-bomber crews. I questioned them and they said they did not see the Red Cross, though I did.'

Perhaps the most thoughtful and accurate explanation came from Lieutenant Colonel J.R. Donaldson, the Army officer commanding troops aboard *Manunda*. He wrote afterwards: 'The bomb which hit us was apparently deliberate but though one or two dive bomber pilots may have lost their heads during the excitement the remainder left us well alone and if it had been the enemy's intention to destroy us he could easily have done so as the bombing was extremely accurate.'

Tragedy struck again at the new military hospital at Berrimah. As we have seen, the hospital was about 1500 metres from the end of runway 29 at the RAAF base. A machine-gun post close to the hospital had been exchanging fire with the strafing Zeroes. Whether by accident or design, the low-flying Zeroes raked the hospital with machine-gun fire, damaging four wards. As at the civilian hospital, immobile patients had been placed under beds. The mattresses might have given some protection against the odd piece of falling timber, but they were no shield against machine-gun bullets. One patient died from his wounds.

Tokyo radio's English-language broadcast later apologised for the damage to *Manunda*, and for damage to the hospitals at Cullen Bay and Berrimah. Ironically, Major General D.V. Blake, the military commandant in Darwin, saw a glimmer of light in this tragedy. In a secret report to Lieutenant General Vernon Sturdee, the Australian Chief of General Staff, he wrote: 'This attack on Australian soil, combined with its ferocity in attacking hospitals, both military, civil and waterborne, has had much to do with the stiffening of morale of the Forces.' The morale of Army troops in Darwin needed no stiffening. However, as we shall see, the Australian government, under pressure from the military Chiefs of Staff, failed to take this opportunity to do a bit of civilian morale-stiffening instead.

◆ ◆ ◆

Although the death and destruction inflicted on both civilian and military targets was by now horrific, the Japanese did not have it all their own way. A Lewis gunner in 2nd AA Battery, 'Darky' Hudson, brought down the first enemy aircraft ever destroyed on Australian soil, a Zero fighter. It crashed near HMAS *Coonawarra*, the Navy shore base about ten kilometres west of the town. Hudson was awarded a Military Medal.

Robert Oestreicher's Kittyhawk had been threading in and out of clouds ever since the first attacking Zero had broken up his formation. 'After flying among the clouds for about half an hour,' he recalled, 'I spotted two Series 97 [Val] dive bombers with fixed landing gear on a course for Batchelor Field. Intercepting them at about fifteen hundred feet I fired and saw one definitely burst into flame and go down. The other was smoking slightly as he headed for the clouds.' Oestreicher chased the second Val but lost him before he could witness the result. The next day a coastal battery found both Japanese aircraft crashed within a mile of each other. They were the first confirmed aerial victories in the skies over Australia.

Four Zeroes had been duelling with four machine-gun posts at the Army camp at Winnellie, just to the east of the RAAF field. The Zeroes raked the area with strafing fire while the gunners replied with their Hotchkiss light machine guns, producing not much result either way. The Japanese pilots flew close enough for the gunners to see 'rude finger gestures' delivered from the cockpit, doubling their fury. Then one of the Zeroes swooped over a gun manned by Trooper Max Grant, who managed to track it through 180 degrees as it swept overhead. As the Zero roared away, Grant's fellow gunner Allan Weidner yelled: 'Up his arse! Up his arse!' Grant did as he was bid. To the delight of the gunners, a thick cloud of smoke poured from the Zero. It crashed in flames about a mile away, killing the pilot.

Jack Mulholland's 3.7-inch anti-aircraft section on the Oval had a clear view of the harbour. The big guns employed a different tactic when dealing with low-flying planes. Instead of the complicated predictor unit giving target information, each of the four guns was assigned a 90-degree sector and left to do its own aiming and firing using open sights. Mulholland's sector faced the harbour.

The gunners had a delicate decision to make. If they fired low at the swarming dive-bombers, they risked pouring shrapnel onto their own ships. If they did nothing, the Japanese pilots would have the skies to themselves. In the end, the balance of advantage seemed to be to fire away and try to disrupt the attacking Vals by placing a shield of bursting shells over the ships.

Mulholland's gunners set their fuses to the highly unconventional one and a half seconds (regulations said two seconds was the safe minimum) and began pouring fire low over the harbour. They had their reward as a Val pulled out of its dive. A shell burst near the aircraft's nose.

Mulholland recounted, with his usual modesty: 'It was not a matter of accurate shooting. To be fair it would be more likely the plane ran into the shell. I saw the plane crash into the sea.'

◆ ◆ ◆

The Japanese pilots were not content merely to bomb Government House. The Zero fighters took offence at the Australian flag still fluttering in the grounds, and set about machine-gunning it with furious enthusiasm. The flag held out gamely, though one of the stars and bits of the Union Jack were blown away. The battered flag can be seen today in the Australian War Memorial in Canberra.

◆ ◆ ◆

At the height of the raid, Police Sergeant William McKinnon found himself taking shelter with a Chinese man in a trench at the police barracks. 'During the whole of the time he was there,' Sergeant McKinnon recalled, 'he was saying: "What for aeroplanes? What way our planes? What for not at 'em? Shoot 'em down Japanese planes."' He might have spoken for the whole of Darwin.

After 42 minutes, at about 10.40 a.m., the last Japanese plane from Fuchida's aircraft-carrier group had left the skies over Darwin. The all-clear sounded.

Chapter 10

Between the raids: Can anyone drive?

Darwin was now a smoking shambles. Some 15 heavy bombs had destroyed civilian targets in the town's administration area, smashing buildings and killing and maiming people. The remaining bombs found targets in a huge killing zone extending over 40 square kilometres. The path of destruction began at the port, steamrollered over the town as far as the civil hospital, swung north-east to the two airfields, and then spread its remaining fury over the 45 ships. Black smoke billowed from burning ships, buildings, oil stores, wrecked aircraft and oil floating on the harbour. The air was foul with the smell of oil, smoke, cordite, burnt flesh and charred wooden wreckage. Darwin's dazed citizens, grateful and mildly surprised to find themselves still alive, crawled from their shelters and basements and hiding places and surveyed the ruins of their homes, shops and workplaces.

◆ ◆ ◆

There had been no shortage of heroism during the attack. Apart from the Army, Navy and Air Force anti-aircraft gunners who stood their ground in the face of overwhelming odds, the rescue workers set a standard of selfless courage of which any nation might be proud. As the dive-bombers sank ships, the burning, oil-smeared waters of Port Darwin filled with sailors forced to abandon their vessels and swim for it. A makeshift armada of lifeboats, boom-net vessels, tugs and larger ships now set about rescuing them.

As we have seen, when the USS *Peary* took five direct hits from the dive-bombers, the hospital ship *Manunda* lowered lifeboats that headed straight into the danger zone around the burning destroyer. The 298-ton examination vessel HMAS *Southern Cross* unhesitatingly joined in, lowering her own lifeboats to pick up sailors from *Peary* who were struggling in the oily water. The boom-net vessels *Kangaroo*, *Kara Kara*, *Karangi*, *Kiara* and *Kookaburra* hurled themselves into the turmoil, scooping up sailors, first from *Peary*, then from *British Motorist*. Approaching a blazing oil tanker, which might have exploded at any moment, took more than ordinary courage.

The Department of Civil Aviation maintained a small flotilla of launches on the harbour to ferry passengers to and from the Qantas flying boats. The tender CA22, manned by a civilian, John Waldie, is credited with rescuing more than 100 sailors from the harbour. A second flying-boat tender, CA2, commandeered by Naval Reserve officer Lieutenant Ian McRoberts and a volunteer crew, saved the lives of dozens of struggling seamen.

The most unlikely rescuers took to the water. At Talc Point, on the far side of Port Darwin, a section of four men from the Army's 54th Searchlight battery watched as a rowboat pulled into shore, clearly manned by crew from one of the stricken ships. The crewmen jumped out and fled, abandoning the boat. Phillip Herring and his three mates, Vince Highland, Tommy Reynolds and Sam Langwich, got in the abandoned rowboat and put to sea. They picked up eight swimmers. While their courage was undoubted, their rowing skills left a lot to be desired. One of the rescued, thought to be the purser of the *Tulagi*, spent his journey to shore standing up in the boat calling 'row, row, row' in an attempt to synchronise the landlubbers' efforts with the oars. The searchlighters made repeated trips into the harbour until they were worn out. Seamen from *Tulagi* and *Port Mar* can thank them for their lives.

The Japanese were not in the business of chivalrously standing back to allow the rescue of drowning sailors. Bombs continued to rain down throughout the rescue operation, while the dive-bombers and fighters kept up a murderous hail of machine-gun fire, targeting anything that moved in the port. Ivan Sinclair, who later cleared many of the bodies from the beaches and the mangroves, reported that most had been killed by machine-gun fire in the back. In the midst of this non-stop bombing and machine-gunning, the rescue boats threaded their way through patches of blazing oil to gather desperate sailors from the water. The oil left faces and bodies blackened, to the point where close friends who had been working together for months and even years failed to recognise each other when they met in the water. The oil temporarily blinded some of the victims. For weeks after the raid, the foul taste of oily seawater lingered in the throat and haunted those unfortunate enough to have swallowed some.

Oil and the Japanese were not the only threats. Shrapnel from friendly anti-aircraft shells exploding overhead could be equally deadly. Even when the planes finally departed, the burning oil and dangerously unstable burning ships combined with the regular hazards of Darwin harbour—raging tides, sharks, crocodiles and deadly box jellyfish—to make the rescue operation almost as dangerous after the all-clear as it had been during the attack.[1]

On a day when good fortune was not much in evidence, both rescuers and rescued took comfort from the presence of the hospital ship *Manunda* in mid-harbour. *Manunda* had taken a fearful beating from the bombers, with 12 dead and more wounded, one of the worst casualty lists of the day. Her crew found themselves fighting seven separate fires on board, one of which kept burning for an hour. Nevertheless *Manunda* stood ready and able to accept casualties, with doctors and nurses on the spot to offer treatment to the injured and comfort to the dying. On the day of the raid *Manunda* took aboard 76 patients, and would take on another 190 the next day.

◆ ◆ ◆

At the RAAF base, Group Captain Scherger gingerly got to his feet amidst the long grass near the airfield entrance and set out to assess the damage. There was instant good news. As Scherger recounted: 'Immediately the raid was over I got back into the car, drove round the buildings and the aerodrome, found that three Hudsons were undamaged, and realising that some of the aircraft must have come off an aircraft carrier I ordered these Hudsons on a preliminary search to northward.' Ground crews were told to prepare the aircraft for an extensive search mission.

Scherger did not stop there. 'I also ordered all Wirraways and A24s [American Douglas A24 dive-bombers] to be bombed up, in the case of the Wirraways with two 500 lb semi armour piercing bombs. The A24s were already bombed up.'[2] The Hudsons' job would be to find the aircraft carriers. The dive-bombers would then sink them. Now the Japanese might get a taste of their own medicine.

It was not to be. The Wirraways were all at Batchelor airfield, 75 kilometres to the south. With the Darwin telephone exchange and cable office wrecked in the first few minutes of the raid, there was no way to pass the order to Batchelor except by sending a dispatch rider on a two-hour ride on a motorbike. Nor was there any ground-to-air radio operating at the RAAF base. Even the Hudsons on the base had to receive their orders by dispatch rider. Without ground-to-air the Hudsons would be useless: they would have no way of sending target locations back to the dive-bombers once they had located the carriers. Scherger fumed while he tried to get some ground-to-air communications working. Meanwhile, the Hudsons sat impotent in their camouflaged dispersal bays.

◆ ◆ ◆

The two ships still tied up at the wharf represented a special problem. *Neptuna* and *Barossa* were both on fire within minutes of the start of the raid and surrounded by burning oil from the burst oil pipes on the wharf. *Neptuna*, carrying 200 tons of depth charges and additional TNT below her decks, might explode at any moment. With luck, *Barossa* could be saved.

Barossa was tied up on the inner side of the wharf and hemmed in by an oil lighter whose hoses had fractured and whose oil was feeding the spreading fire. The Navy tug HMAS *Wato* managed to get a line onto the lighter and drag her out of the way, leaving a path clear to pull *Barossa* to safety. Although the rumbling from *Neptuna*'s fires was now ominously loud, *Wato*'s commander, Warrant Officer Andrew Gibson, and his crew, with extraordinary courage, returned to the wharf and managed to get a line onto *Barossa*. They had just managed to pull her clear of the wharf when their worst fears were realised.

Of all the terrible memories of Darwin that morning, the most terrible for those who saw and heard it was the death of *Neptuna*. No sooner had *Wato*'s lifeline begun to pull *Barossa* clear than the biggest explosion of the day rocked Darwin. Author Douglas Lockwood wrote graphically afterwards:

> I was driving my car along The Esplanade half a mile away and believed the explosion meant another raid had begun. I stopped and ran for the gutter but while doing so saw the column of smoke and flames dwarfing all the other smouldering fires from burning ships and buildings that were blacking out the town. I will never forget that on top of it all, rolling slowly over and over as though it were a dumb-bell tossed by a giant juggler, there was what I took to be, and now know to have been, *Neptuna*'s main mast.

The blast could be heard beyond the RAAF airfield seven kilometres away. A gigantic mushroom cloud blossomed over the ship, which promptly rolled over and sank. It is simply impossible to know how many crew, wharfies and rescuers died in the blast. By now the waters around the wharf were littered with injured, dead and dying from the earlier bombs, and the precise cause and timing of their final agony cannot be stated with certainty.

Incredibly, *Wato* and *Barossa* survived the blast. With *Barossa* well and truly on fire, the auxiliary minesweeper HMAS *Tolga* took over the towing job from *Wato*. *Tolga's* crew put out *Barossa's* fires, then dragged her to a nearby beach. *Wato* meanwhile nosed her way back into Port Darwin to look for sailors in need of rescue.

◆ ◆ ◆

When the raid began, John Wilkshire and Don Bergin had been loading sand into Wilkshire's truck at Mindil Beach, north-west of Darwin and outside the target area. As the bombs started falling, they both realised sand might be needed to fight fires. Heedless of their own safety, they drove straight for the danger zone, towards the oil tanks on the edge of the port. The bombing was still going on when they arrived at the wharf. Wharfies and sailors, some wounded, were struggling to get ashore while others remained in the water, cut off by the burning oil.

Wilkshire sized up the situation quickly. He called: 'Can anyone here drive a truck?' A wharfie volunteered. Okay, Wilkshire told him, use the truck as an ambulance to get the wounded to hospital. Meanwhile, Wilkshire plunged into the harbour and started dragging the wounded to shore, then handing them over to Bergin. He could see the splashes of the machine-gun bullets crawling towards him as the Japanese pilots kept up their strafing attack. When Wilkshire and Bergin had finished hauling the wounded to safety, the two civilians heard a naval officer ask for volunteers to man a launch. They agreed at once. Gathering up Lieutenant Jimmy Grant, the captain of the USS *William B. Preston*, they formed the volunteer crew for Lieutenant Ian McRoberts on the Qantas shuttle tender CA2.

◆ ◆ ◆

Major General David Blake was commander of the 7th Military District, which included Darwin. He was also the most senior military officer in Darwin. During the raid he had been sheltering in his 'sanger', a slit trench surrounded by a low mound, at Larrakeyah Barracks. As soon as the all-clear sounded he hot-footed it into town. 'My first job was to see how my batteries had fared,' he recalled. 'I went to Emery [a shore battery on Emery Point near Larrakeyah], and from there to town and the Administration, which had been heavily bombed, and then proceeded to the other battery at East Point to see how they had fared.' This was an eccentric choice of inspection sites. The Emery Point and East Point batteries were heavy guns pointing out to sea, designed to repel a naval attack. So far as I am aware, they didn't fire a single shot on 19 February 1942. Why the general chose to inspect them instead of chatting to the AA gunners, who might have done with a word or two of encouragement, is obscure.

On his tour, Major General Blake saw no evidence of panic. 'Those I saw were mostly Air Raid Precautions workers, and they were doing their job in getting the dead and wounded and that sort of thing.'

◆ ◆ ◆

Mick Ryan, secretary of the North Australia Workers' Union, which spoke for the wharfies among others, had been sheltering in a gully near the school during the raid. The school backed onto Woods Street, just outside the town centre. He recalled:

> Before the all-clear siren sounded, as it appeared to me to be clear enough to come out, I came out and I called to the men around me to come with me to the wharf in case we could be of some assistance there. I then got into the utility truck, which was standing outside our [Union] office. Then, along with several other men, we drove round through the streets proceeding toward the jetty. We called out to quite a number of men along the street, and the truck very quickly became overcrowded with men.

Then, as they got close to the wharf, they heard shouting: 'Here they are. They are coming again.' Ryan had been too quick in deciding it was safe to move out. Fuchida's planes were returning for another sweep. Ryan's group headed back to the gully near Woods Street and waited for the all-clear.

As soon as it sounded, Ryan and the crowded utility once more headed for the wharf. 'We got down near the bond store,' he recalled, 'and we were turned back by a military guard, who said that nobody would be permitted to go down to the jetty because of the danger that might arise from the likelihood of the munition boat exploding, that was on fire.' The motley group of would-be Samaritans climbed back into the utility and headed for possible rescue work at the Navy Victualling Yard, where, they were quickly told, there had been no damage. Undaunted, they pointed the utility back towards the school and the town.

Here, at last, was useful work. 'We found several men who had been on the wharf during the bombing,' Ryan remembered. 'One man was in a very bad state, and some of the men got a stretcher out of the school, laid him on it, put him in the truck and drove him to the hospital. Whilst this man was being taken to hospital, I assisted in carrying others in, who were arriving in military ambulances.'

Given that there were, officially, no air-raid wardens, the ARP operation in Darwin performed creditably. Edgar Harrison, the Permanent Officer, takes up the story again. After he raced to his headquarters in Mitchell Street to sound the alarm, 'Within half a minute Warden Foster reported to me and I got him to take his post outside the office and stop any people running along the road and to check them and get them to lie down in the grass. It was absolutely impossible to look for shelters because there were no shelters. In the paddock alongside my headquarters in Mitchell Street, at one stage we had anything from 80 to 90 people lying in the grass and did not have a casualty.'

The wardens also had responsibility for sounding the all-clear. Harrison again: 'We received instruction from Larrakeyah [Army headquarters] to sound the "All Clear". I sounded my siren, and then wardens who had been held up during the raid began to report. I gathered up 100 strangers, got the wardens going and sent them up to the spots I knew had been bombed heavily, and rescue work started.'

Harrison then set out to check how much of Darwin's administration had survived the raid. He was not much comforted by what he found. 'The whole Administration broke down entirely,' he said later.

Administration offices were badly cracked. Mr Giles [the Government Secretary] received a wound in the arm. The accountant, sub-accountant and others were badly upset by the blast, and the whole place became disorganised. I proceeded immediately after the 'All Clear' on a tour of inspection, and endeavoured to see what damage had been caused and how many casualties there had been. I went to the Administrator's office. He was obviously in a very dazed condition. He had received a very bad shaking—Mrs Abbott also, but she recovered her self-possession very quickly, and I must pay tribute to her bravery. She just looked at me and said: 'I am awfully sorry I am so dirty, Mr Harrison. Is there anything I can do for you?' I said: 'Yes, I would like to see you and the few remaining women out of town as soon as possible.' She said: 'Very well, I will pack my bags.' Later I saw the Administrator and he had pulled himself together, but he had received a very bad shaking.

When the all-clear sounded, Constable Bob Darken climbed out from under the car that had sheltered him. He had a fair idea of where help might be needed most. 'I went straight to the Post Office,' he recalled.

I noticed Mr Bald—I have always known him as that—was almost in a sitting position on top, partly covered by dirt. He was in a terribly battered condition. Most of the bones—his arms and legs—seemed to be broken.

I also recognised his daughter. She had part of her head blown away. I also recognised Mrs Young. The top of Mrs Young's head was blown off. I also saw another man whom Constables Hook and Withnall found lying over the fork of a tree. I saw him when he was being carried in on a stretcher.

Constable Darken and Constable McNab were clear about their first priority. They set about removing the bodies, planning to take them to the hospital morgue.

Brough Newell, the resigned Director of First Aid from the ARP, joined the two policemen at the Post Office. He began identifying the bodies, though their condition made this difficult. 'In one case I made a mistake about identification,' Newell recalled. 'I saw the man some minutes later—the worst shock I had that day, I think.'

The all-clear sounded at about 10.40 but Administrator Abbott, by his own account, stayed in his shelter until 11.15. He then came out to survey the damage. He wrote in his report: 'Although a bomb had fallen between two Government cars which were in Government House grounds at the time, one in a garage and one near the office, making a crater at least 15 feet deep, the two cars escaped with superficial damage, and were got out on the road.' His Honour's two surviving cars, and the use to which he put them, were to lead to some searching questions at the Royal Commission a few weeks later.

◆ ◆ ◆

For the AA gunners at the Oval, the sudden quiet was eerie after the bedlam of the preceding 42 minutes. Jack Mulholland had 'an uncanny feeling that it was all unreal'. He recalled: 'We came out of the gun pits somewhat "Zombie-like", with dry mouths, glad to be alive. Our main concerns were to see what damage had occurred and to check the safety of the other crews. To our great relief we did not suffer one casualty at the Oval.'

The gunners had used just about every anti-aircraft shell available to them, so their first job was to restock the ammunition recesses from the main storeroom under the Oval's grandstand. Mulholland remembers there was little talk as the gunners struggled with the heavy boxes. Mostly they were anxious to save their breath for the lifting work. But there would have been little point in talking anyway—the gunners were all deaf from the noise of firing. The guns would need cleaning, too. There was plenty to do.

◆ ◆ ◆

Stan Kennon gives an interesting perspective on the state of Darwin immediately after the raid. He was a carpenter on a building site in Smith Street in the centre of the town. He had been boiling a billy for smoko when the planes came.

> I stepped back and looked up and there was this magnificent formation coming straight towards us. I thought hello, the Yanks are here. The next thing I saw two white explosions in the sky [the first salvo from the AA battery]. That woke me up that they weren't Yanks.
>
> We had started an air raid shelter at the company's house, over a six foot chain wire fence. Somehow that six foot high wire fence disappeared—I found myself on the other side of it. I crawled into this ruddy air raid shelter that was about two feet high, concrete blocks just laid around, with sheets of flat iron and bits of timber on top for a roof. It was quite a stupid place to be if bullets came or anything—it was no shelter at all. So I backed out and stood by a tree.

Kennon spent the next 40 minutes shuffling around the tree, keeping it between him and any attacking aircraft.

When the all-clear sounded, he jumped on his bike and went for a tour around the town. His first impression was that damage was 'hardly noticeable'. He rode his bicycle home and grabbed an old movie camera. When he returned to the town he was able to capture moving pictures of the turmoil in the harbour, including shots of the *Manunda*. Then, as is the way of all temperamental machines at vital moments, the camera jammed. Kennon had to open the case and pull out yards of film, which was instantly spoiled. Some film survived, and for years afterwards Kennon showed it to his friends. Then the film was lost, and did not reappear until late 2007. It is now with the Australian War Memorial in Canberra, where experts are trying to salvage it.

◆ ◆ ◆

When the last Japanese plane left, Lieutenant Robert Oestreicher gratefully set his Kittyhawk down at the RAAF base. He landed with a flat tyre and some bullet holes in his wings, but was otherwise in fair shape. Oestreicher, ever the savvy veteran, parked his aircraft in a dispersal area well away from the main hangars.

◆ ◆ ◆

Judge Wells was standing in the back yard of his house on The Esplanade when he heard the first bombs fall. He heard no sirens. Following his own advice, he had built an air-raid shelter under his house, and he now set out to test his theories. They worked well. He remained unscathed, staying out of sight until the anti-aircraft batteries stopped firing. He recalled:

Immediately after that I left my house and walked down The Esplanade to see what damage had been done. I was anxious about my own staff.

I walked past the anti-aircraft battery and stopped and spoke to some of the men. I wanted to see how they were taking it. They were full of beans. They took it exceedingly well. They did a wonderfully good job. They were ragged at first but they put up a wonderfully good show. I spoke to them probably for a minute or so and walked along toward the Post Office and met the junior officer at the Post Office. He was in a very shaken state and said to me: 'Everybody in the Post Office is killed and I cannot find anybody in authority and I don't know what to do.' I said: 'You had better pull yourself together and see what you can do yourself.' I spoke to him for a couple of minutes and then he said: 'I will, I will go back.'

I then went on past the Post Office and passed the Administrator's residence. Mr and Mrs Abbott were out on the drive and the official car was apparently getting ready to leave. General Blake was also there, I think.

I then turned down to the left past the Administrator's

residence and met a man named McDonald who was formerly secretary of the North Australia Workers' Union. He had recently been working and supervising on the wharf. He told me there had been a number of people killed on the wharf and quite a lot thrown into the water.

I then went round to the Court House and found that none of my staff had been injured although they were badly shaken up. My staff had been in the slit trench and that probably saved them from injury. I then went to the Police Station and saw certain disorganisation there. I spoke to them for a minute or two and then went back to the Court House.

◆ ◆ ◆

Judge Wells leaves out of this account one of his more imaginative actions immediately after the first raid. Fannie Bay gaol sat on the edge of the civil airfield, which had been heavily strafed and hit with daisy-cutter anti-personnel bombs. One of the strafing Japanese pilots attacking the airfield switched his attention to the gaol, raking it with cannon fire.

Prisons Superintendent Jock Reid ordered all the prisoners released from their cells, and all internal gates and doors opened so the prisoners could take cover inside. When the all-clear sounded, Judge Wells went further. He authorised the release of all prisoners. Twenty Aboriginal prisoners and ten whites streaked through the prison gates and away.

One of the prisoners, Ivan Sinclair, did not simply head into the bush. He was serving a hefty sentence after a shooting incident, but he had previously led a blameless life. A trained ambulance man, he went straight to the hospital and offered his services, but was told they were closing down that night. He then went to the ARP office and was instantly accepted. He is credited with treating 113 victims of the raid, with remarkable dedication and skill. In recognition of this, the Governor-General granted him a full pardon. It was the first free pardon granted by any governor-general since the inception of the Commonwealth of Australia.

◆ ◆ ◆

Judge Wells's tour of inspection of the town establishes an important point. So far Darwin had acquitted itself well. The civilian population might have been shaken but they had not panicked. In general they found the best shelter they could and sat out the raid. The Army anti-aircraft gunners, despite their inexperience, fought doggedly and well, even scoring the odd victory. Ships on the harbour returned fire and managed to disrupt the attack even if they did not succeed in holding it off. The machine-gunners at the RAAF base could make a similar claim. A lone Kittyhawk had shot down two attackers. Volunteer rescuers on the harbour performed heroically in the face of strafing, bombing, exploding ships and burning oil. So far, so good. However, in both Edgar Harrison's and Judge Wells's accounts are the seeds of the problem that was about to engulf Darwin. In the first eerie calm of the all-clear, nobody took charge.

Then the Japanese came back.

Chapter 11

The second raid: Chinese whispers

The Vals and Kates that attacked Darwin in the first raid were one thing. The heavy bombers that now struck were an entirely different proposition. In all, 54 aircraft took part in the second attack: 27 G4M Betty bombers from Kendari, in the Celebes Islands, and 27 G3M Nells from the newly captured base on Ambon.[1] These were big, twin-engined bombers and each carried a payload of 1000 kg of bombs, more than three times the capacity of a Val and 250 kg more than a Kate. They carried heavier machine guns and cannons, and had a longer range than the carrier-based bombers.

This time the warning system worked a little better. The depot ship HMAS *Platypus* sounded her siren as the two bomber groups loomed into view. Army Headquarters informed RAAF Operations that a formation of enemy planes had passed over Larrakeyah and appeared to be headed for the RAAF base. Operations turned on the air-raid sirens and fired a red Very signal, both at 11.58 a.m. The base braced itself. Amidst all the anxiety, there was a degree of curiosity over what might tumble from the bellies of the planes. Paratroops? Or more bombs?

Once again, the Japanese tactics were worthy of an air show. A formation of 27 bombers attacked the airfield from the south-west, another formation of 27 from the north-east. They flew straight at each other at 18,000 feet in an immaculate V, more or less crossing over the RAAF airfield. As they crossed they released their first salvo of bombs. This massive load of explosives from 54 aircraft struck the entire area of the airfield simultaneously and with terrifying force.

For 20 minutes the disciplined waves of bombers wheeled and turned, rearranged themselves in tidy formations, and swept back over the RAAF base for another simultaneous release of up to 13,000 kg of high explosive. Airmen in trenches and shelters could feel the searing heat, deafening roar and violent pressure wave as each pattern of bombs threatened to engulf them. Concrete, metal and wooden debris showered all around them from smashed buildings, ruined workshops, wrecked aircraft and devastated parking aprons. A direct hit was fatal. A near miss could leave a man half buried in his slit trench.

◆ ◆ ◆

For the weary gunners at the Oval, a second air raid within two hours seemed like cruel and unusual punishment. As the gunners scrambled to their positions, Jack Mulholland found a rude rhyme going round and round in his head:

> Bugger me, said the Queen of Spain,
> Three minutes' pleasure and nine months' pain,
> Three months' rest and I'm at it again.

At the Oval section, the sergeant who called the firing orders had lost his voice during the first raid. Mulholland now found himself bellowing through a megaphone against the overwhelming din of the guns. This time the pain was brief: the second raid lasted only 20 minutes. The Japanese were so confident they would meet no resistance that they brought no escort of Zero fighters, so there was no strafing and no dive-bombing.

The second raid confined itself to the RAAF aerodrome. The people of the town, the ships on the harbour and anybody not immediately involved could watch the spectacle in comparative safety. As each pattern of bombs struck, with a gigantic flash of yellow flame followed by dense clouds of black smoke and thunderous rumbling, the eye-witnesses had only one thought for the men at the RAAF base: surely nobody can live through that.

To the bitter disappointment of the anti-aircraft batteries, the morning's problems with the fuse timers persisted. The shells continued to burst below and behind the bombers. At 18,000 feet the bombers were well beyond the range of the machine guns, so there was nothing to be gained from firing them. So far as is known, no Japanese plane received so much as a scratch in the second raid. The attackers had the skies to themselves.

◆ ◆ ◆

Although the air over Darwin was clear by 12.20, Mitsuo Fuchida's carrier-borne dive-bombers had not finished with the local shipping. Two freighters, *Florence D* and *Don Isidro*, were under way off the coast of Bathurst and Melville Islands. Both freighters had set off to run the Japanese blockade of the Philippines, bringing desperately needed ammunition to General Douglas MacArthur's besieged forces there. The entire Japanese wave would have passed over the two ships on their return journey to the carriers and noted their position. Early in the afternoon, a small task force of Vals took off with orders to mop up the two stragglers. *Don Isidro*, 40 kilometres north of Melville Island, was first to come under attack. She radioed for help, but it was too late. The Vals made short work of her. She rapidly caught fire and drifted helplessly until she beached on Melville Island. Eleven men were dead, 73 rescued.

The Vals now switched the attack to *Florence D*, off Bathurst Island. As we have seen, the *Florence D* had paused to gather up Thomas Moorer and the Catalina crew shot down earlier by the inbound Zeroes. The unfortunate Moorer and his men now found themselves under attack again, by the same force and with the same result. *Florence D* sank with four dead, including J.C. Schuler from the Catalina crew. Moorer and his surviving crew, together with survivors from the crew of *Florence D*, piled into two lifeboats. The wind blew them onto the coast of Bathurst Island, where they remained for two days without food or water before a passing RAAF plane spotted them and organised a supply drop and subsequent rescue. The Vals returned untroubled to the carriers. The carrier-borne assault on Darwin and its shipping was now over. Afterwards Fuchida wrote dismissively of the Darwin raid: 'As at Rabaul, the job to be done seemed hardly worthy of the Nagumo Force.'

◆ ◆ ◆

The Japanese did not escape entirely unscathed. There is still some uncertainty over Japanese losses. The Deputy Director of Japanese Naval History, Hitoshi Tsunoda, told Douglas Lockwood only two Japanese aircraft were lost. This is transparently false. Air Commodore Wilson told the Lowe Commission that Tokyo radio had announced the loss of 23 planes. I can find no record of that particular broadcast. In any case, Wilson's figure seems wildly high. Fuchida told Lockwood that the true figure was seven, and this seems likely to be correct.

We know of the two Vals shot down by Robert Oestreicher's Kittyhawk. Jack Mulholland's 3.7-inch gun at the Oval accounted for one Val, 'Darky' Hudson's machine gun accounted for one Zero, and Max Grant's Hotchkiss accounted for a second. A third Zero fell victim to its lack of armour. It was almost certainly brought down by a single .303 bullet, fired either from a single-shot Lee-Enfield rifle or from a Vickers or Lewis machine gun. There is no way of knowing who fired the fatal shot, but the bullet holed the Zero's oil tank and it drained, causing the engine to seize. The pilot, Petty Officer Hajime Toyoshima, glided his doomed plane into a lightly wooded valley on Melville Island and survived the subsequent crash. He was taken prisoner by a single Tiwi Islander, who told him: 'You come longa me, all same Hopalong Cassidy.'[2] Toyoshima was sent to the main Japanese prisoner-of-war camp, at Cowra in south-western New South Wales. He was one of the leaders of the Cowra uprising in August 1944 and died by his own hand on that terrible night. Toyoshima's wrecked aircraft is on display today in Darwin's excellent Australian Aviation Heritage Centre.

What of the other plane acknowledged by Fuchida as lost? The probability is that it met a fate similar to Toyoshima's Zero. All Japanese aircraft were notoriously under-protected by armour and self-sealing tanks, and would succumb to very light damage. The G4M Betty bomber came to be known derisively among Allied fighter pilots as the 'flying Zippo' or the 'one-shot lighter' when they discovered that a single bullet strike to the fuel tank was enough to produce a very satisfying fireball. The Vals in particular must have taken some battle damage from the likes of *Peary*, *William B. Preston*, *Platypus*, *Swan* and *Katoomba*. It would not come as a surprise if one or two of them failed to make it back to the carriers as a result.

◆　◆　◆

The second air raid by the heavy bombers produced nothing like the spread of devastation of Fuchida's mixed assault. Nevertheless it marked a turning point in Darwin's fortunes. So far there had been no panic and no disarray. Morale stood up well, both civilian and military. But the pitilessly brief break between the two raids, the brutal power of the second bombing, the absence of any Allied fighter aircraft mounting a counter-attack, and the inability of the AA guns to destroy or even seriously inconvenience the raiders led to a change of mood in the town.

Among the civilians there was a powerful feeling that there was now only one sensible course of action: get out. There should be no surprise at this. It is the common reaction of civilians of all countries and all centuries when wars take over their streets. Anyone who doubts it might like to take a look at news film shot in New York in the immediate aftermath of the attack on the World Trade Centre. The Big Apple's broad avenues were crammed with wild-eyed civilians screaming and running away. And why not? The civilians of Darwin did not scream, and none of them has been accused of breaking into a jog, let alone a run. But they were very clear what they wanted: out.

On the military side in Darwin, the worst affected were those at the RAAF airfield. They had just gone through one of the most terrifying

The remains of Darwin Post Office after the raid. The bomb scored a direct hit on a shelter, killing all ten occupants, including six women. (Photograph courtesy Australian War Memorial. Ref. P02759.004)

Several wrecked civil buildings after the raid. In the foreground, Jolly's store is completely destroyed. Behind it, the Bank of New South Wales (now Westpac) has been gutted. In the background at left the department store C.J. Cashman & Co. stands relatively unscathed. Burning lights in Cashman & Co. windows led to a violent response during earlier air-raid drills. (Photograph courtesy Australian War Memorial. Ref. P02759.009)

RAAF headquarters after the raid. The government's official statement, issued the day after the attack, included the phrase: 'No vital service installations were destroyed.' (Photograph courtesy Australian War Memorial. Ref. P01791.010)

An aerial picture of Darwin harbour after the raid. The hull of *Neptuna* lies overturned on the right. A large section of the wharf has been blown away entirely by the first stick of bombs, and the outer arm is severely damaged. The air-raid sirens, which might have warned the waterside workers, did not sound until the first bombs struck. (Photograph courtesy Australian War Memorial. Ref. 027350)

The wreckage of Toyoshima's crashed Zero on Melville Island. The plane's engine seized after a single bullet holed and drained the oil system. (Photograph courtesy Australian War Memorial. Ref. P00022.002)

The most terrible explosion of the day. The death of *Neptuna* produces a mushroom cloud over Darwin harbour, as tonnes of depth charges and other explosives detonate. In front of the explosion, the tiny naval auxiliary vessel HMAS *Vigilant* is carrying out rescue work. In the centre is the floating dock with the corvette HMAS *Katoomba* trapped inside. On the right, *Zealandia* has already begun to list before sinking. (Photograph courtesy Australian War Memorial. Ref. 134955)

This lone P40 Kittyhawk, on Darwin's RAAF airfield, is thought to be Robert
Oestreicher's. His was the only Allied fighter to survive the raid, and he is credited
with shooting down two Japanese Val dive-bombers, the first Allied aerial victories
under Australian skies. (Photograph courtesy Australian War Memorial. Ref.
P05303.003)

The final moment of the destroyer USS *Peary*, sinking under a plume of black smoke
in the entrance to Port Darwin. The hospital ship MV *Manunda* is on the left, not
far from *Peary*, and clearly in the danger zone. (Photograph courtesy Australian War
Memorial. Ref. 012970)

Aubrey Abbott, Administrator of the Northern Territory at the time of the time of the Japanese air raid. (Photograph courtesy National Library of Australia)

A 1941 photograph from Administrator Abbott's personal photograph collection. Left to right: His Honour C.L.A. Abbott, Brigadier E.F. Lind, Major-General David Blake (the most senior Army officer in Darwin), and Captain Penry Thomas, Naval Officer in Charge, Darwin. (Photograph courtesy National Library of Australia)

Captain Mitsuo Fuchida, who led the Japanese air attacks on Pearl Harbor and Darwin.

Sergeant Hajime Toyoshima, under escort, after his capture on Melville Island. (Photograph courtesy Australian War Memorial. Ref. P00022.001)

A bomber pilot's view of Darwin. This aerial photograph was taken by Robert Holland sometime in 1941. (Photograph courtesy Susan Holland)

An iconic photograph of Darwin AA gunners in action. Widely reproduced, this photograph has even been sold as a postcard. It is of particular interest in this narrative because the lanky figure exiting left is Jack Mulholland. He is anxious to make clear that he was not running away, but sprinting off to fetch more ammunition. (Photograph courtesy Jack Mulholland)

Left: 3.7-inch AA gun crew. Note the three gunners with their backs to the line of fire. These men aimed the gun using information fed to them electrically from the central command post. They could not see their targets, nor see the effect of their fire. (Photograph courtesy Jack Mulholland)

Below: Lewis AA gunners in action in Darwin. The guns had no proper mounts, so the gunners used improvised wooden stakes to swivel the gun as they tracked their target. (Photograph courtesy Jack Mulholland)

experiences any human being could be asked to endure. The Zeroes, Kates and Vals of the first raid left a trail of damage. The Bettys and Nells of the second raid simply wrecked the rest of the base. Almost nothing was left standing. In the understated words of the *Official History*: 'The station had lost its two hangars which, with the central store, had been burned out, and the transport section and the recreation hut had been wrecked beyond repair. Four blocks of airmen's quarters and the hospital had been severely damaged, and the officers' quarters and mess had been hit.' Six Hudson bombers were a total write-off, as were two Kittyhawks and a B24 Liberator bomber belonging to the Americans. A Wirraway and a Hudson were badly damaged. The first raid had led to only one death: that of Wing Commander Tindal. The second raid killed at least six, four felled by a single bomb that scored a direct hit on a trench. One of the dead was never identified. His body was found in the bush near the airfield. 'A bomb hit him and cut him to ribbons,' Group Captain Scherger said afterwards. 'He was wrapped around a tree. There was no article of clothing and he could not be identified. Nothing could be found. He was assumed to be an Air Force man because he had blue equipment on.'

Miraculously, Robert Oestreicher's Kittyhawk and the three Hudsons, all dispersed well away from the devastated hangars, survived the second raid too.

◆ ◆ ◆

At this point it is worth standing back a little and asking what exactly Darwin did need at 12.20 p.m. on 19 February 1942. All around were confusion and destruction. Nevertheless, the priorities were obvious enough. The military needed to assess the damage and get whatever weapons had survived the raid ready to fight again—the Japanese might come back at any time. With three serviceable Hudsons in hand, and a reserve of nine Wirraways not far away at Batchelor, some sort of counter-attack was still possible.

Meanwhile, people trapped in wreckage, both soldiers and civilians, needed to be located and freed. The wounded had to be given medical attention at either a first-aid post or a hospital. The dead needed to be removed to mortuaries or otherwise cleared from the streets, wrecked buildings and ships. Fires had to be put out, whether on land or in the harbour. Sailors who had abandoned sunk and beached ships needed to be picked up from the water or the mangroves. Above all, the first requirement after any disaster is for someone to get the tightest possible grip on the situation. Orders and advice need to be broadcast clearly and quickly, before rumours take hold. People need to be prevented from endangering themselves by entering risky areas. Human nature being what it is, those who seek to profit from the disaster by looting need to be stopped. The immediate aftermath requires public announcements that reach everybody. Areas must be sealed, and people stationed to guard them. Men and women are remarkably willing to brave dangers to help others, often displaying selfless and exemplary courage in the process. But they need to see clearly what to do, and they often need to be told to do it, and where to do it first. Like the dazed Post Office worker, the unionists in the utility truck and the policemen at the station, more than anything else Darwin needed someone to step forward and take charge.

◆ ◆ ◆

All the town's police had been told to assemble at the Police Station in the event of an air raid. After helping to deal with the carnage at the Post Office, Constable Bob Darken set out to walk back to the station. His route took him past Administrator Abbott's Residency, where he saw His Honour and Sergeant Bill Littlejohn bringing liquor out of Government House and loading it on to a truck. Darken continued on to the station, where he worked for some time collecting bodies and taking them to the hospital.

Darken's version of what happened next is perhaps the most furiously contested story of the entire Darwin saga. In particular, Administrator Abbott saw himself as the victim of perjury when it was put to him under cross-examination at the Royal Commission. When he heard the accusations, he asked Commissioner Lowe if he could be represented by counsel. Lowe refused, leading most writers to sympathise with Abbott.

But no other witness at the Royal Commission was represented by counsel, so Lowe was merely keeping Abbott on the same footing as everybody else. Lowe's principal objective was to save time. The key accusation came from Darken, and the reader will have to decide whom to believe, him or Abbott.

Darken said he arrived at the Residency after the all-clear sounded. There Littlejohn instructed him to remove the crested government crockery and load it onto Littlejohn's truck—presumably the same truck that had been used to remove the liquor. Two policemen were detailed to this work, Darken and Constable Hook. Abbott joined in, bringing out some of the crockery himself. It was bad enough that three desperately needed policemen plus the man who above all others should have been tightening a grip on the town instead busied themselves loading crockery. Worse was to follow.

DARKEN: People at the Residence at the time knew that the half-caste girl was still crying out for someone to take her out of the wreckage, and that carried on for half an hour or twenty minutes.

COMMISSIONER LOWE: Do you mean to tell me that the bystanders saw you leaving that woman there?

DARKEN: Yes. That is the position.

LOWE: That is the position? You understand the seriousness of the position, that you might have given help to this woman and saved a life but you were diverted from that to remove the china and crockery?

DARKEN: Yes.

LOWE: You appreciate the seriousness of that?

DARKEN: Yes.

LOWE: You have no doubt it was true?

DARKEN: It is true.

Administrator Abbott angrily denied this story in his own evidence. He said the whimpering had come from the Aboriginal boy, not Daisy

Martin. Of Martin, Abbott said: 'I was certain she was dead. There were two tons of masonry over her.' Why was he certain? 'The appearance of her limbs, and she had that pallor attributable to death, and she had not moved from the time she had been uncovered, and only her lower limbs were showing.'

John V. Barry, counsel assisting the Commissioner, was not satisfied. Darken had given evidence that when he helped to remove Daisy Martin's body next day, it was unmarked except for 'a little scratch on the lip'.

BARRY: Under those circumstances, there being two tons of masonry over her, you would be astounded to learn that her body was unmarked?

ABBOTT: The information I received was that she was badly crushed from the chest upwards. That was the information given to me before she was taken out.

BARRY: Who informed you of that?

ABBOTT: A Chinese, See Kee, who was my typist.

BARRY: Do you know when that was?

ABBOTT: Next day, I fancy. I had to ask the Superintendent of Police to get a demolition squad to endeavour to remove the masonry so she could be got out.

Bob Darken said extracting the body was comparatively simple and took half an hour using crowbars.

His Honour was unabashed about having ordered the removal of the crockery to safe keeping. He devotes a bit over a page of his five-and-a-half-page written report *Japanese Air Raid, Darwin, 19th February 1942— Movements and Actions of the Administrator Upon That and Following Days* to his solicitude towards the cups and saucers. He wrote:

I told General Blake that I thought I ought to save as much valuable Government property as possible and he agreed. I then saw Superintendent Stretton and Sergeant Littlejohn about getting material away. It was decided that we would endeavour to get two trucks away to the Adelaide River and then onto the railway and afterwards use these trucks between Larrimah, the railhead and Alice Springs. We knew that the Army transport would be far too busy to assist us and that we would have to do this ourselves.

I then mentioned what a terrible pity it was about all the glass and china in Government House which was of a high quality and quite valuable. Sergeant Littlejohn, a most resourceful Police Officer, then asked why I did not get it away. I said it would be impossible to pack it so that it would survive the road journey. He then said that he had transported china and glass many miles during his transfers and that the best way was not to pack them but to lay them separately upon a mattress and pack them with clothing. He said he was sure he could do this. I then agreed and told him to take what he could, but only to take the valuable china and glass which was marked with a crest. Sergeant Littlejohn did this early on Saturday morning, the 21st and I did not see the packing until it was practically completed.

His Honour is claiming that the packing took place two days after the raid and not on the same afternoon, as Darken alleged. For the record, Darwin's most senior policeman, Superintendent Alfred Stretton, confirms that the crockery packing began on the day of the raid and was completed next day. He told Commissioner Lowe that Abbott contacted him about 3 p.m. on 19 February, asking him to send over Sergeant Littlejohn and two Constables 'for the purpose of removing valuable government property from Government House'. Abbott himself said as much in one of his later reports when he wrote that on the first afternoon he had ordered the policemen to collect 'silver tea and coffee pots belonging to the Government and some pyjamas and clothes for myself'.

On the other hand Stretton, who had been at the Residency very soon after the raid, strongly refuted the Daisy Martin story. I believe the Daisy Martin story is untrue. Darken's evidence is hearsay, and he recanted it in an interview in 1999 with the historians Peter and Sheila Forrest. I have included it only because the story spread around Darwin immediately after the raid and added to the general public disillusionment with Abbott.

However, the balance of probabilities favours Darken's and Stretton's (and Abbott's) evidence that the movement of the crockery began on the afternoon of the raid. Littlejohn stated in writing on 6 April 1942 that he had packed only liquor on the 19th. He packed the disputed 'glass and chinaware, silverware, code books, confidential papers (official) and the flag' on the 21st. It is likely that Littlejohn wrote this memorandum under persuasion. His wording leaves open the possibility that Darken and Hook had packed the silverware and china on the 19th, and that Littlejohn finished the job on the 21st.

Eventually he delivered the following articles belonging to the Government to the Residency at Alice Springs:

Glass, including tumblers, wine glasses of all kind,— 415 pieces
China, including plates and dishes,— 351 pieces
Silver, including forks, spoons, fruit knives, etc,— 122 pieces
Cutlery, knives etc,— 33 pieces

Whether the infamous glass, china and cutlery moved on the afternoon of the raid or two days later, Abbott remains indicted on his own evidence of wasting a fair bit of police time as well as his own on a trivial matter. At the time Darwin had only 15 policemen. In general, a day shift consisted of only four men, so to pull three away from front-line policing was a serious decision. Superintendent Stretton told the Royal Commission that the three policemen involved in moving the crockery were not on duty but merely spare policemen who happened to be around at the time. Nevertheless, it beggars belief that three of them should, on the Administrator's orders, be whipped away from the emergency policing of the town and assigned instead to packing the Residency's cups and saucers. It is indeed hard to like Charles Lydiard Aubrey Abbott.

◆　　◆　　◆

Nobody has accepted credit for starting the Adelaide River Stakes, as the mass exodus from Darwin came to be known. The dunny truck is, however, a serious claimant for line honours. In 1942 Darwin had no sewerage, and very few houses had septic tanks. Instead sanitary carts toured the town twice a week and emptied the back-yard lavatories. Each dunny cart began its run with a load of empty lavatory pans, and worked its way around the houses removing the full pan and replacing it with an empty. It was not exactly a glamour job.

One cart had arrived in Smith Street, in the heart of town, when the first bombs fell. The driver, Ludo Dalby, sensibly dumped the pan he was carrying and dived into a trench in a back yard. When the first raid ended, both Dalby and the truck had moved on. History does not record the exact progress of the stately vehicle, but a few facts are known. By the time it left Darwin, it was under the command of a junior government official and had acquired a passenger load of eight prominent Darwin citizens, seated on the roof. It then set off down 'the Track' south towards Adelaide River township, about 120 kilometres away. According to legend, on its way it failed to negotiate a particularly tricky bend and shed its entire load of full and empty lavatory pans. This may be true, or it may just be part of a good story. Nevertheless, the sanitary cart is generally credited with being the first vehicle to arrive that afternoon in Adelaide River from Darwin. It was far from the last.[3] The Adelaide River Stakes had begun.

It gathered momentum with remarkable speed. The all-clear sounded at 12.20 p.m., lunch-time. Relieved citizens scrambled out of their shelters and headed for the refrigerator. In the absence of any clear direction from above, the rumour machine took over. The dominant rumour was stark and simple: civilians had been ordered to leave the town. In houses and pubs and hotels and cafés all over Darwin, people hastily decided to forgo lunch and flee, leaving behind half-eaten plates of food, even half-drunk glasses of precious beer.

The Administrator's wife Hilda was among the first to leave. In his written report, His Honour records that after the first raid he discussed the position with General Blake 'and received reports from the

Government Secretary, Mr Giles, the Superintendent of Police, and the Permanent Air Raids Precautions Officer, Mr Harrison'.

Understandably, Abbott wanted to get his badly shaken wife out of harm's way. His report continues:

> I then decided to send my wife and her household staff off in the two cars, and they left about 12 noon. As Kamper, my messenger, had only just learned to drive a car, Superintendent Stretton detailed a Police Officer, Constable Bowie, to drive one car and Mrs Abbott drove the other. She took the injured half-caste girl and the aboriginal in the car with her. This party took whatever they could hastily get hold of in the way of clothes and some blankets. No other personal effects were taken except a small portable typewriter which belonged to me and which had escaped damage.

Four of Darwin's 15 policemen were now engaged on domestic work for the Abbotts. Littlejohn, Darken and Hall worked on the liquor and the cups and saucers. Bowie drove the household staff. On Darken's evidence, His Honour did not simply leave them to get on with it. He selflessly and democratically abandoned his other work and gave a hand.

◆ ◆ ◆

From the beginning, the Army had been responsible for the evacuation of Darwin's civilians. Having organised his wife's safe exit in a convoy of two government cars, Abbott now went to Army Headquarters at Larrakeyah Barracks 'to see what could be done about getting the few remaining females out of the town'. The Army already had a plan. It hoped to get an evacuation train away about 2.30 that afternoon. Abbott returned to the town. Since his own offices had been wrecked, he set up headquarters in the Police Station. He asked the police to round up the surviving women and children and get them to the railway station at Parap by 2.30.

All of this no doubt laudable activity fell well short of getting a real grip on the crisis. In the absence of clarity, rumours spread. There was a well-justified fear that the air raid was a 'softening-up' operation, the usual preliminary to an invasion. Anybody who stayed could expect to be slaughtered next day when the bestial Japanese hit the beaches. The rumour mill ran hot. Every civilian was to evacuate at once. The police, who seem never to have been properly briefed either by the Administrator or by Superintendent Stretton, added to the confusion by giving contradictory advice and instructions. So did the air-raid wardens. So did the Army.

The result was inevitable. The road south filled with every kind of vehicle—cars, trucks, utilities, a road grader, horses, bicycles (including an ice-cream seller's bike, complete with cool box but no ice-cream), people on foot. Anything that could move did. The road jammed as drivers groped their way blindly in the choking red dust of the Track. Some cars and trucks carried food and personal effects. Other just drove, anything to get away from the bombers and the slaughter that would inevitably follow the arrival of the Japs.

◆ ◆ ◆

Mick Ryan, secretary of the North Australian Workers' Union, sat out the second raid in a culvert behind the union office. When the all-clear sounded, he took a walk around the town, looking for other members of his union executive to discuss what to do. During his wanderings he bumped into Brough Newell, erstwhile Director of First Aid in the ARP unit. Newell was a former Army officer and had, only two days earlier, been appointed Captain of the Volunteer Defence Corps. Ryan was a member of the VDC and he asked Newell what he should do. The VDC had been told they would automatically be taken into the Army in the event of enemy action. 'The Captain was unable to give me any information whatsoever,' Ryan recalled.

At this point Ryan set off again in the utility towards the Darwin Hotel, where some of his union executive were billeted. He went on:

I was in the vicinity of the Darwin Hotel together with some other men, and a police car passed by, and the police constable called out: 'All civil cars to proceed to the PWD [Public Works Department] depot to fill up with petrol. They have been commandeered for evacuation purposes.' We proceeded then to the PWD depot and lined up with the other cars. About an hour later the Administrator, Mr Abbott, came on the scene and gave instructions that no civil vehicles were to be given petrol unless they were on some special duty.

We then pulled out of the line of cars and went back down the town, to our union office and the office of the *Northern Standard*. We picked up some records and things, and decided we would go out of town a little way and then wait to find out what the position would be.

In his report to his superiors in the Department of the Interior in Canberra, and again in his evidence to the Royal Commission, Abbott set out to blame Ryan for triggering the Adelaide River Stakes. He wrote: 'Immediately after the raid the morale of the civilians was good, but it rapidly deteriorated, mainly, in my opinion, through the Secretary of the N.A.W.U. and other prominent union officials leaving the town by car as quickly as they could.' Given that Mrs Abbott was well up with the front runners when the civilian exodus began, departing some four hours ahead of what proved to be the temporary exit of Mick Ryan, this seems unfair, to put it mildly. And, Ryan pointed out in his evidence to the Royal Commission, they left in a utility truck, not a car.

◆ ◆ ◆

At 3.30 p.m. the military police stepped in to try to stem the Adelaide River tide. Lieutenant David Watson, the most senior Provost, gathered up four NCOs in a car and headed down the road. He placed two of them outside the Parap Police Station, close to the railway station, with orders to stop any civilians passing that point. Watson then continued 60 kilometres down the road, turning back any civilians he encountered. It was too late. The horse had well and truly bolted.

◆ ◆ ◆

While Group Captain Scherger fumed and raged over his inability to use the surviving fighting aircraft to launch a counter-strike, Wing Commander Sturt Griffith, the station commander at the RAAF base, was having trouble deciding what to do first. Incredibly, he chose not to organise any sort of salvage operation, leaving vital equipment and material to fend for itself in the damaged hangars, workshops and store-rooms. Instead he chose as his first priority getting the water going after a water main had burst. Water and electricity supplies had survived the first air raid. The second raid cut off both. Without power the warning sirens would not work, exposing everyone still on the base to danger if the Japanese came back. There was an emergency generator, but this needed water to function, so until water could be restored there could be no electricity. There was also an emergency water supply, but the tank was secured by a Yale lock and nobody could find the key. Griffith ordered maintenance teams to get to work on the burst water main as the best way of getting the base going again.

There is nothing quite like 20–20 hindsight for clarity of vision, and it is a matter of judgement whether Griffith had his priorities right. What can be said with certainty is that while restoring power was undoubtedly important, there were plenty of other jobs that could be done at the same time. In particular, there was a desperate need to salvage anything serviceable to give surviving aircraft a fighting chance if the Japanese came back. With luck, the salvage teams might even get some sort of ground-to-air radio working. Without it, the three undamaged Hudsons could not be used. The Hudsons were the key to any counter-attack, but they needed to be launched quickly to give them a chance to find the Japanese aircraft carriers. In the course of the afternoon Scherger pleaded six times for someone to get the ground-to-air working, to no avail. Other jobs came first.

With no salvage operation, there was very little else for the rest of the men to do. There were as many as 2000 men linked to the base, of whom only a handful could work on the water and electricity supply. The rest were left hanging about, exposed to danger if the Japanese returned.

Confronted with a large body of men under threat and with nothing to do, Griffith issued the order that led to the biggest fiasco of the entire sorry saga. Most people are familiar with the old game of Chinese Whispers, in which a dozen or so volunteers sit in a line. The maestro whispers something in the ear of the first volunteer, who is told to whisper it to the next person, and so on. The idea is to see how much the message has been distorted by the time it reaches the other end of the line. The most famous military example, supposedly from the First World War, tells of a commander who asked for the message 'Going to advance, send reinforcements' to be relayed verbally to headquarters by a series of runners. By the time it reached HQ, the vital message had become: 'Going to a dance. Send three and fourpence.'

The road to hell is said to be paved with good intentions. The farce that followed resulted from a well-intentioned plan to move those lads with nothing to do to a safer place and fix them up with a spot of lunch. Griffith recounted:

Group Captain Scherger and I discussed the matter and he agreed that it would be safer to remove the personnel from the aerodrome pending the rehabilitation of the water system. I suggested all the personnel including not only the station personnel but the Area Headquarters personnel should assemble at a point half a mile down the Batchelor Road and half a mile in the timber. The instruction was to Squadron Leader Swan [the station adjutant] that all ranks were to be assembled at this point. He was to move the men to the position indicated, feed them, and I would come over and address them.

There were two problems with this otherwise admirable proposal. Some of the men had already set off down the road, so it was too late to give them the correct order anyway. And those still at the base were scattered in sections over a huge area. Instead of calling them all together and marching them down the road in a body, which might have avoided confusion but would have exposed them to more danger, Swan allowed each section to pass the order to the next. Having received their orders and passed them on, the sections then moved off independently. Griffith spelled out what the reader has probably guessed.

> There seem to have been varying orders transmitted. Some men appear to have been told—though by whom I cannot track down—that they were to go to Batchelor [90 kilometres away]; some men that they had to go five miles down the road; some men that they had to go half a mile down the road; some that they had to go to the 22 mile. The men were prepared to listen to rumour, and if they saw a body of men moving down the road—for instance to the half-mile position—the rumour might have been: 'We are evacuating the aerodrome' or 'We are getting out into the bush,' which may have spread from section to section. Men started off without orders and to seek transport down the road, because there was any amount of civilian and Army transport, and I think the men merely took it into their heads, rightly or wrongly, that they were getting out of the aerodrome.

The result was a shambles on a gigantic scale, compounded by the fact that Swan and a colleague stopped trucks on the road and asked the drivers to give the men a lift. The airmen now had wheels, and they headed south with renewed enthusiasm and much-improved mobility. The mess officer set up a kitchen at the 13-mile point, and a few of the men actually made it there. The rest simply evaporated. One man, showing exemplary zeal and ingenuity, turned up in Melbourne 13 days later. Others reached Batchelor, Adelaide River, Katherine, Daly Waters, wherever they could hitch a ride.

♦ ♦ ♦

Those in authority hotly denied afterwards that there was panic in Darwin that day—the P word was never to be admitted in polite society. The dictionary defines panic as a sudden, overwhelming feeling of terror or anxiety, especially one affecting a group of people. Any distinction between what happened in Darwin and overwhelming anxiety affecting a group of people seems more semantic than real. The ex-ambulance man Ivan Sinclair, who had been freed from Fannie Bay prison under Judge Wells's orders, in evidence to the Royal Commission at first rejected the notion that Darwin had panicked. However, he offered the common-sense view that if someone had given a firm lead, the whole sorry business could have been avoided. It is hard to disagree with his simple summing up: 'My honest opinion is that if a man had been at the 2½-mile road where people were going out in such a panic, and had impressed on the general public that there was no necessity to leave Darwin as there was no immediate danger, I do not think one per cent of the population would have left. I think they would all have stopped here.'

Whatever word anyone chooses to describe what was happening in Darwin that day, worse was to follow. As the civilians abandoned their homes and workplaces and joined the swelling Adelaide River exodus, Darwin's houses, hotels, shops and offices were left empty, wide open and temptingly unprotected.

Chapter 12

Things go badly wrong

It is not possible to determine the exact time on the afternoon of 19 February 1942 when Darwin tipped from mild confusion and chaos into serious ugliness, but a single event probably marked the watershed. Sergeant MacArthur-Onslow of the Provost Corps, well drunk as usual, marched into the Police Station some time in the early afternoon, after the second raid.[1] Brandishing a revolver, he announced that Darwin was now under martial law. Constable Bob Darken, who was at the station at the time, remembers him bellowing: 'We are tops and you will take orders from us.' The tragedy is that the lower-ranking police officers believed him. Darwin was not then, or indeed ever, under martial law. But the police took MacArthur-Onslow's word that the town was now under military control, and they listened faithfully to the deluge of ill-informed, groundless and contradictory instructions arriving from all sides and purporting to emanate from the Army. Only one common thread ran through it all—civilians were under orders to get out of Darwin.

Just as there is no exact time for MacArthur-Onslow's outburst, so is there none for when the looting began. Administrator Abbott suspected that it started almost immediately. Constable Leo Law recalled:

After the second raid the Administrator sent for me. I went along and met him outside his residence near a bomb crater. He said to me: 'There has been some looting going on in my house already I suspect. I want you to go over for a while. I will be there presently.' I went over to his house. He followed me. He said to me: 'I want you to go down into my cellar and tell me what you can see there.' He supplied me with a torch. I went down into the cellar. All I could see there was a large quantity of liquor. I came up and informed him of the approximate numbers of bottles of liquor there. He said to me: 'All right, get a police car and we will take these to the Commandant.' I returned to the Superintendent of Police, and he said there was no car available.

Against His Honour's belief that the looting started with persons unknown at Government House, Gunner Jack Mulholland is willing to declare that he started it himself. His motives were of the highest. 'I don't think we had time to clean the guns properly after the first raid,' he recalled.

After the second raid, we started. The Army had given us a certain amount of rags to clean them. Well, the rags weren't enough. After all the firing, the guns were chopping the rags to smithereens. That's when we had the bright idea that the Darwin Hotel had plenty of serviettes, sheets and God knows what. That's what started the looting.

We were first into the Darwin Hotel. It was eerie. There were half cups of tea with a cigarette beside them. All the humans had disappeared. There was nothing—the hotel was empty. We could walk into the Qantas office, and there were parcels there. We didn't touch them. I don't know why not, but we didn't. We had a look in the fridges and found there was some good food there, which we ate.

The raiding party retreated, well fed and armed with enough white linen to give the guns the clean-up of a lifetime.

By the middle of the afternoon, the looting was in full swing. As Administrator Abbott wrote deferentially in his report to the Department of the Interior:

I regret very much to inform the Minister that looting became very prevalent in the town. I am afraid that I must state definitely that the main pillaging must be attributed to men of the three services in Darwin and officers must be included in it. I also do not except officers and men from the United States Army from this charge. The thefts include a great deal of valuable government property, including electric fans, kelvinators [refrigerators], and articles which could only be taken when transport and parties of men were available.

What Abbott is saying, in a nutshell, is that the looting was carried out by the military, and they took the stuff away in truckloads. This was confirmed by Police Sergeant Bill McKinnon: 'My idea is it was military. I know some was done by civilians. I do believe that some of the military police, although they were supposed to be in charge of the town, some members actually took part in the looting.' Note that McKinnon accepts that the military police were in charge of the town.

Constable Bob Darken agreed:

From what I have heard, the military police would go on to the shops and business premises with their own trucks and loaded materials and goods—they were taken away from the houses by the military police themselves. Sergeant McKinnon and I saw the back door open at the shop of Lorna Lim. We went round the back and an MP [Military Policeman] by the name of Stevens was inside the shop. I said to Stevens: 'Who is responsible for all this destruction?' At the time there was a great deal of goods trodden into the floor. I said jokingly: 'I suppose you Military Police have got most of the stuff?' He said: 'Oh, yes. When we were here someone was looting the place. We heard of it. We came down and everyone just took what they wanted.' Meaning, of course, every member of the military police.

Jack Mulholland concurs. 'As far as I can understand, they [the military police] split the town up among themselves, and you daren't go near any of their property.'

Edgar Harrison, the Permanent ARP Officer, confirmed Abbott's view that Americans were as much to blame as Australians: 'On the Sunday after the raid I went down to the Administrator's house in the course of inspection of the town, and there were a number of Americans coming out of the property with all sorts of articles, clothing etc.'

Some stories betray an almost breathtaking *chutzpah*. In his evidence to the Lowe Commission, Edgar Harrison gave this account of his personal involvement:

Last Sunday morning [1 March, ten days after the raid] I went to my own house to see what I could pick up. It was the first time I had any time to attend to my own personal matters. I found two military officers in the house. [Not junior officers, either. Harrison named them as Major Willshire and Captain Meiklejohn.] I asked them what they were doing in the house. Willshire said he was having a look round to see if there was anything that might be of value to him, and Meiklejohn said he was looking for a kerosene refrigerator. I then acquainted them with the fact that I was the tenant of the house, showed them the state of my personal possessions, and they expressed regret and went out. They did not take anything with them. I immediately gave a written report to His Honour, the Administrator. One of our junior officers who was with me counter-signed it as a witness.

Both Willshire and Meiklejohn appeared before the Lowe Commission, specifically to explain themselves. Both largely conceded that what Harrison had said about them was true. However, they offered an explanation. Willshire said he was looking for anything of military value, not of value to him. Meiklejohn, a medical supply officer, said he had indeed been looking for a kerosene refrigerator—several had been stolen from the Cullen Bay hospital and he had been told they had been seen disappearing on a lorry. The refrigerators were needed to preserve serums and other medical supplies. He had gone into Harrison's house, which appeared to be damaged, remarking to Major Willshire as he walked in: 'I wonder whether I might locate kerosene refrigerators here?'

To be fair, Meiklejohn had made a serious point, one to match Jack Mulholland's. One person's looting can often be another person's resourcefulness. In the immediate aftermath of the raid, Darwin faced a desperate situation. There was a real threat of shortages of food and other resources. In the circumstances, if people chose to leave their homes and flee, why not move in and make good use of whatever they left behind? Among other things, with the electricity supply disrupted, food would quickly rot in refrigerators. That argument is sound. But few could doubt that the 'borrowing' in Darwin went beyond resourcefulness and crossed the line that separates commendable initiative from outright theft. Removing and consuming perishable food from hotels and houses, especially when food might be hard to find elsewhere, is one thing. Stripping houses of tables and chairs, stoves and refrigerators, pianos and radios, bedding and blankets, china and glasses, is looting however you look at it.

Over the next few days, Darwin was picked bare. Officers' messes, which had been hot, bleak and uncomfortable the day before the raid, suddenly and mysteriously acquired electric fans, refrigerators, radios, carpets, cups and glasses, pleasant cane furniture, cushions, curtains and all the comforts of home. Somebody else's home.

The civilian police, who might have put a stop to it, were hampered from the beginning by the belief that the town was under military control, and that military authority trumped their civil jurisdiction. Constable Bob Darken told the Lowe Commission: 'It appeared to me that *if we had been in charge* [emphasis added] immediately after the raid, most of the looting could have been stopped.' The tragedy is that for four days after the raid they *were* in charge but didn't know it.

Captain Bernard Colman, who controlled the Provost Corps in Darwin, told the Lowe Commission he had been powerless to prevent this sorry state of affairs. 'The looting, I am told, started during the second raid, some in Wharf Street and Cavenagh Street, some near the Commonwealth Bank, and some near the Darwin Hotel. I had a limited number of men in town and they could not stop looting. They could stop it when they saw it.' The plain fact is that if Colman's men could stop looting when they saw it, they did not have far to look. They were doing it themselves.

◆ ◆ ◆

The legitimate evacuation of Darwin's remaining women and older men was scheduled to begin at 2.30 from the main railway station at Parap. It would be an uncomfortable journey. The Army had laid on a train, but the best it could find was a collection of cattle trucks and flat-top goods cars. That would have to do. The air-raid wardens scoured the town, telling women and old men to head for the station. There were even one or two children who'd been kept hidden at home after the earlier mass evacuation. Those heading for the station were mostly people who had actively resisted the earlier order to leave. Now they needed no urging. They were told they would travel by rail to Larrimah, then by road to Alice Springs. The 1500-kilometre journey would take five days.

There were scenes at Parap station to outdo even the unseemly scramble down the Adelaide River road. The train had been laid on for women and old men. Young men turned up and became abusive when they were told they could not go aboard. Arthur Miller, the chief air-raid warden, commanded the operation. As more people pressed into Parap, he sensed he was in danger of losing control. At his request, Army Headquarters at Larrakeyah sent two soldiers with sub-machine guns to back him up. According to Douglas Lockwood, Miller told them: 'A live burst at the feet of any young man who tries to get on this train. But don't kill anyone.' Miller had no trouble after that.

Every passenger's name was noted, and by 4 p.m. the train was ready to roll. In *Australia Under Attack*, Lockwood recounts an extraordinary last-minute drama. Just as the train was about to leave, Miller was told an unexploded bomb had been found buried in the middle of the railway line just near the RAAF airfield. Even if it was a dud, it might still be unstable. Worse, it might have a delayed-action fuse. Miller had to weigh the risk of sending his train to pass directly over the unexploded bomb with the very real possibility of setting it off. Otherwise, he could wait until the bomb was defused and removed, delaying the train by several hours. In the end he decided to chance it. 'Go now,' he said, 'but tell the driver to take it quietly past the aerodrome.' The train and its 71 passengers passed uneventfully over the bomb.

◆ ◆ ◆

Administrator Abbott's priorities are a never-ending source of wonder. After falsely blaming Mick Ryan for starting the stampede down the Adelaide River road, His Honour now discovered a new problem requiring his immediate and personal attention. 'The Chinese community joined in the rush and this resulted in cafés and restaurants being without cooks,' he wrote. 'The main objective [after organising the evacuation train] was to get kitchens going so that men who had stayed could be fed and I concentrated on this. Volunteer cooks were obtained and continuous meals (stew, bread and tea) were served from the Eastern Café.' With the town being looted, with civilians fleeing in droves, and with chaos all around him, the highest authority in the Northern Territory saw as his first priority rounding up cooks for the Eastern Café.

Abbott and Ryan could agree on one point: the Administrator went in person to the Public Works Depot some time in the afternoon to see if he could stem the tide of civilians pouring out of the town. 'I found a considerable amount of confusion,' he wrote afterwards. 'There were a line [sic] of civilian cars drawn up, all demanding petrol so that they could get away. I placed Sergeant Littlejohn in charge of the pump and told him that nobody could get petrol without an order from myself or the Superintendent of Police. I also instructed him to tell everyone that there was no order to leave the town and that I wanted everyone to carry on until they received definite instructions.' This last request fell on predictably deaf ears.

Abbott now turned his attention to the looting of his wine cellar. Constable Vic Hall had been at the police barracks when a bomb demolished it. He had been slightly injured. Abbott asked Superintendent Stretton if he could spare a policeman to guard the wine. Stretton nominated Hall. Abbott wrote: 'I asked Constable Hall, if he felt up to it to go down the cellar and bring all the wine up. He did this and later on Sergeant Littlejohn brought a car over and a large quantity of port, sherry and other wines were put in the car. I had this sent out to the Commandant's House where I was going to sleep and later on I asked Major General Blake if he would arrange to have this wine distributed among the various military messes.' Interestingly, considering he was to deny doing anything about the other 'valuable government property' that afternoon, Abbott goes on: 'I also sent out silver tea and coffee pots belonging to the Government and some pyjamas and clothes for myself.' You can't fault Abbott's priorities.

His Honour next went on a tour of the town. 'I had previously arranged to keep the Eastern Café open,' he wrote. 'With the assistance of one of the townsmen, Captain Gregory, volunteer cooks had been obtained and continuous meals were being served. I visited this Café and spoke to all the men there and told them to cheer up and settle down. I also visited the Darwin Civil Hospital and spoke to the patients and nurses.'

Last but not least, there was some serious business to attend to. In the event of an enemy attack, by longstanding plan the bank managers would collect money, securities and ledgers and head down the road to the safety of Alice Springs. At 7.30 p.m., Abbott sent out a summons to the four bank managers. When they dutifully turned up, Abbott was nowhere to be found. Police Superintendent Stretton told them to come back at 9.30 p.m. This time Abbott was there. He told them to be ready for evacuation in two hours, with cash and essential records. The bankers eventually left at 1 a.m. and arrived at Adelaide River seven hours later. They did not travel alone. There were other key citizens to move to safety. In Abbott's words: 'The Deputy Commissioner of Taxation accompanied them.'

♦ ♦ ♦

As night fell, the Provosts turned violent. They were by now largely drunk and well out of control. A second train had been organised to take remaining civilians south. Judge Wells recalled:

> About 8.30 p.m. I was told by Mr Abbott that there was some trouble at the 2½-mile, that the Provost Corps had stopped people and there was trouble. I went out there and saw the trouble. MacArthur-Onslow was there. He was even drunker than usual. He was pretty bad, and most of the Provost Corps, as far as I could see, were all in a pretty bad state.
>
> There was a train leaving shortly afterwards and at the time the army decided that no men should leave Darwin, so Jackson and I drafted them out. There were the old men and some who had been slightly wounded and some were sick. We picked out a number of men and told the others they would not be allowed to go. During this time the Provost Corps were firing over the heads of the crowd. The crowd were not giving any trouble at all. The Provost Corps said that if a man stepped forward, they would shoot him. They fired over the heads of the people. Then, if cars came along with lights on, they would stop the car and shoot at the light. It was a disgraceful matter.

Lieutenant David Watson, Deputy Assistant Provost Marshal and therefore the most senior MP in Darwin at the time, was not immune to trouble from his own men. On 20 February he wrote a frank and personal account of the events of the night before:

> At 2110 hours I returned to the camp by van which was showing regulation lights. On arrival at the camp Lieutenant Pye [second-in-command of the Provost Company] stepped on the road and

instructed the driver to extinguish the lights. The Lieutenant had then just arrived from supervising the loading of the train, which had departed at 2100 hours.

I asked Lieutenant Pye the reason for his instruction to the driver, and he replied that all lights in the town of Darwin were blacked out and that lights on m/vehicles were forbidden. He was unable to tell me who had issued this instruction, and had taken it for granted in view of the air raids during the day. I then asked Captain Colman if he had issued any instruction to that effect and he had not. Lieutenant Pye then stated that he and Sergeant MacArthur-Onslow had shot the lights out on several vehicles belonging to the American Armed Forces.

Administrator Abbott now summoned Watson to the police station in the town to explain all the shooting. Watson continues:

The Administrator was then out and I waited at the Station until 2200 hours. Mr Abbott then complimented the Provost Co^y for excellent work in the town during the Air Raids during the day and in the subsequent control of civilians and prevention of looting, but added that it had been reported to him that members of the Company in the vicinity of Parap had fired several shots and appeared to be excitable. He asked that these men be cautioned. Mr Abbott then drove off in his car without using his lights.

Watson returned to the camp and witnessed the arrest of Pye and MacArthur-Onslow by the Deputy Assistant Adjutant General. That calmed things down a little.

◆ ◆ ◆

The remaining population of Darwin took to their beds on the night of 19 February 1942 in a state of considerable disarray. They also faced something of an information vacuum. Civilians and airmen were camped out along the Adelaide River road, out of touch with civil and military authorities. Others made it to Adelaide River, where there was nothing like enough food or accommodation for them, and nobody to tell them what to do or where to go. Merchant seamen from the sunken ships set up a temporary camp in Doctor's Gully, at the site of the old Darwin Hospital, awaiting word on how they were to be evacuated. Until evacuation came, they could choose between joining the Adelaide River Stakes or indulging in a little light looting for food, blankets and shelter for the night.

Essential services had broken down. Electricity and water came back on in the afternoon, but the sanitary services had decamped south. Surviving ships desperately needed unloading, yet the wharfies had by evening joined the general exodus. The banks had gone. Shops were shut and deserted. So were hotels. Looting was rife. The civil police felt sidelined. The military police were out of control. The Administrator's port, sherry and other fine wines were in safe hands. Otherwise, Darwin was a mess.

Chapter 13

The military takes over

At the end of the first day the authorities in Darwin, military and civil, were all agreed on one thing: they had not seen the last of the Japanese. The Japs would surely be back within 48 hours, and the next attack would be far more destructive than the first. Indeed, it might very well be followed by an invasion. On the military side there was work to be done preparing positions. On the civil side, the town was incapable of functioning. All the bankers and at least half of the shopkeepers, businessmen, hotel keepers, café proprietors, cooks and garbage collectors had fled south with the wharfies and some merchant seamen. Ships in the harbour were stuck with no crews to move them, and often with their full cargoes still trapped in holds.

Having spent what little was left of the night of the raid at the home of Major General Blake, Administrator Abbott began the new day by calling in his Works Director, E.W. Stoddart, to his temporary headquarters at the Lands Office. Stoddart had already done sterling work on the afternoon of the raid restoring the town's water and electricity, and had begun the dispiriting job of clearing the wrecked civilian areas of the town. In Abbott's words:

It seemed to us at that time that steps would be taken to repair the damage at the wharf and that essential defence works would be continued. I visited the Eastern Café again and made sure that food was available and that the cooks were all on the job. Everything there was satisfactory. I then went to the remains of my Office and destroyed all the confidential papers by fire. My reason for doing this was that there had been practically a direct hit upon my confidential cabinet and files, very mutilated, were scattered everywhere. I was able to save the confidential code and cipher book with the exception of one cipher book which was badly damaged. This was also personally destroyed by me.

That took care of the morning. Abbott then met General Blake for lunch. Blake had taken a decision: it would be madness to try to defend Darwin from the Army's present position strung out along the shoreline. He would move his troops well back from the town and await the worst, meeting any Japanese attack with some kind of defence in depth. This was all very well and undoubtedly sensible, though overdue. However, it meant that Darwin became, in Abbott's phrase, 'a kind of no man's land'. The rampaging Japanese could have the town and its few remaining civilians to themselves, and the Army would not strike back until the invaders had rolled over the civilian population and moved inland.

The anti-aircraft gunners, who had performed so well the day before, were particularly miffed. They were not included in the withdrawal, and nobody told them it was happening. The first they knew of it was the sudden discovery that they had no food. The main body of the Army had taken all the stores. Help arrived in the form of tins of ham and rice, floating in boxes on the harbour and washed ashore by the tide. For days the gunners lived on nothing but the washed-up tins, three meals a day of ham and rice. Meanwhile, they faced the disquieting prospect of a Japanese invasion with no Army alongside them to resist it. If the Japanese came, as everybody expected they would, the gunners' reward for their courageous services on 19 February would be to be massacred in the first ten minutes.

Jack Mulholland recalls: 'We were just left up there—mainly search-lights, anti-aircraft and coastal artillery. We were ordered to put all our gear except one pair of boots and a couple of pairs of pants in kit bags with our names on them. They were going to take them down south and put them in a big dump where they would either burn them or give them back to us. We were practising spiking the guns and preparing to burn out. We had 44-gallon drums of petrol and oil.' If the Japs came, scorched earth would be the order of the day, with Mulholland and his gunners as the scorchers.

◆　◆　◆

At their lunch meeting, General Blake and Administrator Abbott discussed control of the town. Blake offered to appoint a Town Major to assist His Honour, and the Administrator agreed. Although the civil authorities remained in charge, Darwin moved one step closer to military control.

The General and the Administrator now turned their attention to the mounting chaos at the Adelaide River. 'We both agreed,' Abbott wrote, 'that I should go down there and with the assistance of Army Officers endeavour to clean it up.' Abbott left some time on Saturday, 21 February, in Police Sergeant Littlejohn's truck, together with the famous cups and saucers. They camped out overnight by the roadside and arrived at Adelaide River next morning, three days after the raid. His Honour wrote later:

> With the ready assistance of the Army Officers at the Adelaide River Camp, organisation was set in motion, the evacuees there were collected and rationed and the Area Officer compiled a list of eligibles for the Army. These were medically examined, and older men were sent back to Darwin or in the case of the old and infirm, evacuated down the line to Alice Springs and Adelaide.
>
> This took practically the whole day. I spent the night at Mount Bundy near the Adelaide [River] and returned to Darwin the following day.

On 23 February, the government in Canberra gave notice under National Security (Emergency Control) Regulations that the area of the Northern Territory north of Larrimah was under Army control. This amounted to about one-third of the Northern Territory and included Darwin. On his way back to town, Abbott met Blake, who had by now taken up his new battle positions well outside the town, and told him what had been achieved at Adelaide River: some 250 able-bodied men had been drafted into the Army and would shortly return to Darwin. The rest had been packed off south. Abbott presented a picture of Adelaide River and Darwin quickly being restored to order under his firm guidance. Others' experiences do not quite match this version of events.

◆　◆　◆

The word 'muster' is often used in military circles to describe calling the troops together for a parade or roll-call. The activities at the RAAF station in the days after the raid had more in common with a cattle muster. Officers headed off into the bush to round up stragglers. Just about everybody from the base had disappeared immediately after the second raid in the mistaken belief that they were under orders to get away. Some returned to the base on the evening of the raid. The rest had to be tracked down and brought back by truck or car from as far afield as Daly Waters.

Squadron Leader Swan, the station adjutant, kept a personal diary of the round-up. He wasn't counting on 19 or 20 February, when he was busiest, but he started to record numbers from the 21st. On that day he found 15 men on the road near the 20-mile point. Another 12 turned up on a truck at the 25-mile point, and 12 more on a similar truck at the 28-mile point, giving Swan a personal tally of 39 for the day. He had less to show for his efforts next day: a mere three men. At the end of the second raid on 19 February the RAAF station's strength stood at 1104 men. On the 23rd, four days after the raid, 826 men had returned to the station, leaving 278 still missing. From that point onwards, they were classed as deserters.

At the base itself, the atmosphere remained jittery for days. Wing Commander Scherger recalled:

Two days after the raid an alarm was sounded. All the staff in Area Combined Headquarters immediately ran at top speed to the nearest shelter trench. By the time the remaining officer and myself had ascertained the reason for the alarm being sounded and waited sufficiently long to ensure that it was a false alarm, we were unable to find any of the staff who had left the building. We looked in all the adjacent shelter trenches, and it was not until approximately 10 minutes after the all clear had been sounded that the staff returned.

It transpired they had taken shelter in the nearest sheltered trench and, as no attack eventuated immediately, they decided the trench was unsafe because it was near the building, so they retired to a sheltered trench further away where they thought they were practically safe. They got into the bush on the far side of the railway line.

◆ ◆ ◆

While the seamen's union in Australia in 1942 could not fully match the wharfies for 24/7 militancy and bloody-mindedness, they were not far behind. The merchant seamen brought ashore from wrecked ships had set up camp in Doctor's Gully, on the harbour foreshore. There was still plenty of work to be done on the surviving ships, with unloading the most immediate and urgent task. Some of the ships were capable of moving, and they needed crews to move them. The seamen would have none of it.

Lieutenant Commander James McManus, the senior Naval Intelligence Officer in Darwin, recalled: 'We wanted men to unload the ships. Our men were working day and night. We were being assisted by Army personnel and we wanted these merchant seamen to assist us.'

McManus went down to the camp and addressed the men. He was met with a blank refusal. 'They wanted to know how they stood,' he told the Lowe Commission. 'They were shipwrecked seamen and they were entitled to pay and return to their own port. One of their Articles is that they must not accept other work, otherwise they would lose all the benefits under the award.'

McManus was not the only speaker to plead with the men. Their own officers spoke to them, as did Navy Lieutenant Commander L.E. Tozer. In the end a few relented, but the rest simply sat. More than two weeks after the raid, 300 merchant seamen were still camping at Doctor's Gully. They turned ugly. Judge Wells told the Lowe Commission on 8 March:

> This morning we had a lot of trouble. The officer who has been more or less in charge of them—I think second or third mate or something—came and said he did not think he could keep them in control much longer. The cook refused duty this morning.
>
> Captain Thomas will probably tell you he offered to take them south on the *Tulagi*, and they refused to go on board. There is also a proposal which Captain Thomas made to take them by another ship. I do not know the name of the ship. I know that these seamen have said they will absolutely refuse to go on that boat. General Blake expressed the view to me that if they did not go on board he would make them. However that is going to be carried out I do not know. They are very definitely determined that they won't go by that boat, and they demand to be evacuated by road.

The recalcitrant sailors had their way. A few were persuaded to go south by sea. The Army eventually shouldered the burden and evacuated the rest by road and rail.

◆ ◆ ◆

The question of who controlled Darwin, civil administration or military, continued to cause confusion. When Administrator Abbott returned from Adelaide River, he complained: 'This [confusion] was greatly accentuated by various wireless broadcasting statements that Darwin was under martial law.' Why Abbott did not grab the microphone and make his own broadcast setting out the facts is hard to understand. I have been unable to trace any of the offending broadcasts, but this is not to doubt that they happened. The probability is that they emanated from the Australian Broadcasting Commission's mobile recording unit in Darwin. Those manning the unit were very likely as confused and misled as everybody else. Abbott clearly did not see it as part of his job to put them straight. As a result, the broadcasts were believed. After all, if the ABC said Darwin was under martial law, who would dare say otherwise?

As soon as Abbott returned to Darwin, he and General Blake agreed on a five-point plan for the future of civilians in Darwin. Abbott set it out in his 27 February report to the Department of the Interior.

1. Men for essential services such as sanitary, electric light and water services would be retained in Darwin and would carry on. If it became necessary these men would be organised into a military unit under Army control.

2. Non-essential civilians, aged persons, merchant seamen, hospital patients etc would be evacuated by the Army authorities as opportunity and transport offered, in order of priority. This priority would be determined by the Army.

3. The Commonwealth Bank staff, with their records, would be sent to Alice Springs as soon as possible so that the Commonwealth Bank could function with the least possible delay.

4. Essential Government property would be salvaged and sent south as transport becomes available.

5. All eligible men to be taken into the Army forthwith and men with technical and other training would be recruited into an Army organisation for work in Darwin or elsewhere.

Abbott wrote:

I estimate that the number of civilians in Darwin, exclusive of seamen who will be returned south as soon as possible, to be slightly under 500. This number is liable to increase as there are about 800 men between the Adelaide River and Katharine [sic] and some of them, realising that they cannot get further south, are drifting back to Darwin. These men, as they return, are rationed by the Administration which receives rations in bulk from the Army. In addition, the Administration is feeding all destitute sailors and has arranged supplies of clothing and food and boots.

So far as the future of Darwin is concerned, it would appear to be wise to base the Northern Territory Administration upon Alice Springs and maintain a small staff in Darwin to look after the town. As soon as the situation in Darwin is more or less static I shall go down to Alice Springs and get the Administration functioning smoothly there.

♦ ♦ ♦

Administrator Abbott was not the only Darwin resident to set his sights on Alice Springs. His and Blake's plan allowed for the departure of non-essential civilians. The Army would be responsible for their evacuation and would decide on priorities. Stan Kennon, who hid behind a tree during the first air raid, had been a member of the Volunteer Defence Corps. Like Mick Ryan, he expected to be taken straight into the Army if ever an emergency arose. 'A rumour started that we would be sent around the coastline as observers, but nothing happened,' Kennon recalled. After four days of cooling his heels, Kennon decided he would be more use elsewhere. Some time around 23 February, he chucked his bike in the back of the company ute and headed south with some mates. The mates aimed for Alice Springs. Kennon had more ambitious plans: he would ride his bike to Queensland.

The group made it as far as Adelaide River, and Kennon set up a fire beside the railway line to boil a billy of tea. A train stopped alongside and the driver leaned out and asked: 'What are you doing here?' Kennon knew the driver—they had been having dinner together every night for a year. Though places for able-bodied men on trains south were hard to come by, 'You'd better get on,' the driver told him. Kennon threw his bike on a flat-top truck and rode the train to Birdum, 350 kilometres south and the end of the line.

There was now nothing for it but to jump on the bike and start pedalling for Queensland. Kennon knew it could be done: a few years earlier he had driven from Brisbane to Darwin, leaving the roads behind at Camooweal and picking his way to Tennant Creek along rough tracks between cattle stations. If it could be done by car, it could also be done by bike. Kennon set Tennant Creek, about 450 kilometres south, as his next stopping point. His luck held. A truck took pity on him and gave him a lift all the way to the Creek, turning what might have been a five-day journey into a bumpy eight-hour ride. That still left the problem of getting to Queensland.

In Tennant Creek, Kennon had a word with the man from the mail delivery truck. 'If I start off on my pushbike across from Tennant to Mount Isa, will you give me a lift if you come along, when you've used up a bit of fuel?' he asked. Yes, the man said. 'So I headed off. That night I lay down by the road and got a bit of sleep. I was still there when they came along in the ute. They stopped the ute and threw me and the bike in the back.' A long day later Kennon was in Mount Isa.

He sold the bike and, with a bit of money cabled by his wife Audrey[*] to top up the proceeds, caught a train to Brisbane, to be reunited with her. His journey was more adventurous than most, but it was not untypical.

◆ ◆ ◆

The government in Canberra now extended the Army's area of control. At midnight on 27–28 February the whole of the Northern Territory was placed under Army rule. The proclamation set out three specific areas of Army responsibility: '(a) persons evacuated from Darwin as regards their destination; (b) enforcement of their return to Darwin, or to such other places as may be necessary; (c) power to enforce evacuation from Alice Springs of any civilians whom it is considered not essential.'

---

[*]Audrey Kennon appeared in Chapter 7 as the hard-pressed shipping clerk deciding who should stay and who should go in the evacuation ships.

Administrator Abbott was clearly deemed essential. He left Darwin for Alice Springs on Monday, 2 March, 12 days after the raid. Abbott faced his fair share of criticism over his handling of the Darwin air raid, including the repeated allegation that he had fled town on the afternoon of the raid with the rest of the Adelaide River refugees. This particular calumny is in print today in a semi-official diary of the raid, part of a display in Darwin's Air Raid Arcade. The note says: '20th February. Administrator and Superintendent of Police left Darwin and the Military Barracks empty.' It is simply untrue. Abbott has a fair bit to answer for over his failure to impose order on Darwin after the raid, but the charge that he deserted will not stick.

Chapter 14

Telling the world

Lou Curnock, surely one of the quiet heroes of the Darwin saga, stayed on duty at VID aeradio station throughout the two raids. The station was a little outside the centre of the town and therefore not on the main line of attack. Nevertheless, he was close enough to hear the bombs exploding and could even feel the earth shake when they hit. As he tended to his microphones, Morse keys and meticulous signal logs, Curnock was certainly at serious risk if the bombers broadened their target area and VID took a direct hit.

In his methodical way, he set about telling his superiors in Melbourne that all was not well in Darwin. In the gap between the two raids, Curnock transmitted a brief message in Morse to his bosses at the Department of Civil Aviation: 'Devastating air raid. Staff and station intact.' Darwin was not then connected by telephone to the rest of Australia. Not that it mattered. With the telephone exchange and cable station in ruins, VID at this point may have been the only working line of communication between Darwin and the outside world. So far as I can trace, Curnock's terse seven-word message, delivered to the Department of Civil Aviation in Melbourne, gave the first inkling outside Darwin of the seriousness of the raid.

Within minutes of Curnock's message, Darwin opened up a second line to the outside world. The engineers at the cable station had already prepared for the kind of emergency Darwin now faced, setting up a branch cable that terminated at the Lands Office in Cavenagh Street. Two engineers from the cable office, Harry Hawke and William Duke, rescued an undamaged Morse key and associated equipment from the wreckage of the Post Office and carried it all to the Cavenagh Street emergency base. At 11.25 a.m., 45 minutes after the first raid ended, they had hooked up their Morse keys and were ready to transmit. Understandably, their long report concentrated on the effect of the raid on postal and cable links. But they began by telling their Adelaide office: 'We have just had bombing raid which appeared centred on and near postal buildings causing much damage. Several officers lives lost many injured.'

This new line of communication did not last. The second raid on the RAAF base cut the cable. Hawke, the senior engineer, sized up the situation. Their new office was in a frail wooden building that would not withstand another attack. It was also too small to accommodate the cable station crew. Hawke realised he would have to shift base again. He chose a makeshift camp site near an abandoned railway hut 16 kilometres from the town. Some 50 engineers and technicians grabbed what equipment they could, plus some essential belongings, crammed themselves and their kit into some severely battered engineers' vans, and moved. By 3 p.m. they had the line working again. Messages travelled by a tortuous route, first to Batavia, then to Cocos Island, then to a relay station in the Perth suburb of Cottesloe before being sent on to Melbourne.

Meanwhile, Lou Curnock found himself under pressure. At the civil aerodrome, some radio transmitters and receivers had survived the raid. However, the main electricity supply from Darwin had been cut, so the airfield's two-way radio remained useless. It was vitally important to warn civil aircraft to stay away from Darwin. By a great stroke of luck, the direct telephone link between the airfield and VID survived the raid. One of the airfield staff, Ted Betts, established that VID was still on the air. He borrowed a truck and raced across to the VID station. He and

Curnock managed to get a message through to the Department of Civil Aviation in Melbourne telling them to keep all civil aircraft away from Darwin. Curnock and Betts also gave some rudimentary information about the raid.

Curnock stayed on duty continuously for two days following the raid. For the next five days all communication with civilian flights passed through VID. The station was also the sole contact with merchant navy ships at sea and with the civilian coastwatchers. VID also had to cope with armies of Darwin citizens wanting to send reassuring messages to friends and relatives in the south.

Although VID was very likely the first to send details of the raid, it was not the only long-range radio transmitter functioning in Darwin. The Royal Australian Navy maintained a shore-based signal station, HMAS *Coonawarra*, to relay messages to and from ships at sea and Naval Headquarters in Melbourne. Although *Coonawarra* took some minor damage, it functioned perfectly well after the raid. It seems to have been slow to get going on the day of the raid, but by the evening it was busily sending damage reports to the Naval Board.

Finally, the Australian Broadcasting Commission had set up a mobile recording unit in Darwin in December 1941 to transmit news for re-broadcast by the main radio stations in the capital cities. (The ABC had earlier set up a similar unit in Gaza, Egypt, and subsequently established a mobile field unit in Papua New Guinea.) The Brisbane *Courier-Mail* reported that the first the outside world knew of the Darwin attack came from the ABC mobile unit. The Deputy Postal Director in Darwin, a Mr Fanning, had radioed at 10.05 a.m., when the first raid was a mere seven minutes old, to say that the town was being raided and the broadcasting station was closing down.

◆ ◆ ◆

The Australian government directed the war from two councils: the War Cabinet, which was an inner circle of the full Cabinet and therefore drew its membership from the government alone; and the War Advisory Council, which included Opposition representatives and other senior political figures as well as the government members of the War Cabinet. The War Advisory Council's next meeting happened to be in Sydney on the morning of 19 February, with the Chiefs of Staff of the three services in attendance. The Prime Minister, John Curtin, had been in St Vincent's Hospital, Sydney, since 17 February, suffering from exhaustion. He did not attend this meeting or the subsequent meeting of the War Cabinet. Both were chaired in his absence by the Deputy Prime Minister, Frank Forde.

On Darwin's big day Curtin was in the middle of a furious cable row with Churchill and Roosevelt. Curtin wanted to pull two divisions of Australian troops from the Middle East to defend Australia. The War Advisory Council spent most of the meeting discussing this very matter, concentrating on the return of the Australian 9th Division. Government members were firmly committed to bringing the boys home. Opposition members argued for diverting them to Burma, as Churchill had requested. One wonders if they would have continued to pursue this line had they known what was happening on their own soil at that very moment. The Council even found time to discuss the advisability of stocking up on rubber shoes, which the soldiers of the 8th Division had found useful in the jungles of Malaya. Darwin did not get a mention. Nobody knew about it. The full War Cabinet met later the same morning, again in Sydney. Still no mention.

One of the enduring controversies of the Darwin air raid is the extent to which the government lied about it. In general, historians have castigated Curtin and his ministers for wildly understating the extent of the damage, the numbers of dead and injured, and the level of anarchy that was already engulfing Darwin. It has to be said, in the government's defence, that on the afternoon and evening of 19 February 1942 it did not set out to lie. It simply didn't know.

Before dealing with the government's version of events, it is necessary to sketch in a little background. On 4 January 1942, almost seven weeks before the real Darwin raid, the Sydney *Sunday Telegraph* and the Brisbane *Truth* had published false stories of a bombing attack on Darwin. They got their information from enemy propaganda broadcasts. The government was understandably horrified: the evacuation of Darwin was then well under way, and the last thing the government needed was untrue scare stories about air raids devastating those left behind.

The Chief Publicity Censor moved quickly, issuing an instruction on 5 January 'forbidding publication of sensational reports from enemy sources'. Later that day he amplified this with the following instruction: 'Reports from enemy sources claiming successes in any Australian territory, including mandated territories, whether such reports are received in Australia by cable from Empire points or by other means except through the BBC, must not be published without official comment by the Defence Ministry or Service Chief concerned. If no such comment be forthcoming, the item may not be used. BBC statements if used must be quoted accurately without embellishment or comment.' The Newspaper Proprietors' Association discussed the Censor's ruling informally and happily agreed to go along with it.

A week later, at the War Advisory Council meeting on 12 January, former Prime Minister Billy Hughes took the ruling a stage further. He asked that 'reports of this nature are not to be published or referred to on Press posters unless they are sanctioned by a responsible authority of the Commonwealth Government'. On 20 January the War Advisory Council noted 'the instruction by the Chief Publicity Censor, Department of Information, forbidding publication of sensational reports of enemy operations, unless officially confirmed'. Thus in the space of two weeks the Censor's instructions to the media moved from a fairly respectable clampdown on repeating bad news from enemy sources, and became a block on 'sensational reports of enemy operations, unless officially confirmed'. I can find no trace of any specific censorship ruling dealing with the 19 February attack on Darwin, but from 12 January onwards both sides—media and government—accepted that the government or the service chiefs were to be the only source of information on the war, particularly when the story affected Australia. War correspondents had their stories cleared by the Censor's office. As for the rest, the government's version of events would be the first, final and only word.

✦ ✦ ✦

The first public announcement of the raid came from Prime Minister Curtin. Some time early in the afternoon of 19 February he issued a brief statement from his hospital bed. In part it said:

> I have been advised by the Department of the Air that a number of bombs were dropped on Darwin this morning. Australia has now experienced physical contact of war within Australia. The extent of the raid and the results of the attack are not yet known. As the head of the Australian Government I know there is no need to say anything other than these words—total mobilisation is the Government's policy for Australia. Until the time elapses when all necessary machinery can be put into effect, all Australians must voluntarily answer the Government's call for complete giving of everything to the nation.

So the first announcement was very short on detail, and came from the Air Ministry, suggesting that Lou Curnock was the original source. Curtin concluded with a warning: 'I make it clear that the statement that has been made is official and authoritive. Nothing has been hidden. There is no ground for rumour. If rumours circulate, take no notice of them, and deal sharply with any person who circulates them. The Government has told you the truth. Face it as Australians.'

Arthur Drakeford, Minister for Air, went into more detail. He issued a statement shortly afterwards saying: 'Japanese bombers raided Darwin this morning. Preliminary reports from Darwin indicate that the attack was concentrated on the township. Shipping in the harbour was also bombed. There were some casualties and some damage was done to service installations, details of which are not yet known. The raid lasted about one hour.' This was followed by an announcement from Deputy Prime Minister Forde that there were communication difficulties with Darwin and no information regarding details of the raid or damage could be obtained. Later the Postmaster General and Information Minister, Senator William Ashley, announced that cable communication had been reestablished. From the fact that the most detailed information came from the Minister for Air, we can deduce that Curnock's messages rather than Harry Hawke's gave the government what little information it had.

Up to this point, the government played it pretty straight. However, it is notable that no newspaper carried reports direct from Darwin. There were three correspondents in Darwin on the day of the raid, including Douglas Lockwood, one of Australia's finest journalists. Each took his story to the makeshift cable office just outside Darwin, where he was told that military traffic had priority and the cable office was unable to file his news stories. Nevertheless, and despite the sketchiness of the information they had, all Australian newspapers understandably reached for their blackest headline type to report the first external attack on Australian soil since the arrival of Europeans in 1788. 'DARWIN BOMBED HEAVILY IN TWO DAY RAIDS: 93 Enemy Planes In First Swoop: 4 Brought Down,' said *The Courier-Mail*. 'DARWIN BOMBED BY JAPANESE PLANES: "Face It!"—Curtin Tells Australians,' said the less restrained Sydney *Daily Mirror*.

◆ ◆ ◆

On the morning of 20 February, the day after the raid, Arthur Drakeford issued a detailed communique giving the casualties in Darwin: 15 killed, 24 hurt. His announcement read:

> There were two separate raids. The first, about 10 a.m., was made by a force of 72 twin-engined aircraft, with a fighter escort of Zero type aircraft. This force split into two parts, one of which concentrated on the town, wharves and shipping, while the other flew inland. Several ships were hit and damage was done to wharves and buildings. No vital service installations were destroyed. During the attack on the town, civilian buildings were hit, and some Commonwealth employees were killed. So far as is known, the total killed in the town numbered nine women and two men. About noon a second raid was made and directed

mainly at RAAF installations by a force of 21 bombers unaccompanied by fighters. Service buildings and aerodromes were bombed and machine-gunned and some damage was caused. There were four confirmed casualties to service personnel. Damage to the aerodrome was not serious.

During the raid several hospitals, both service and civilian, were bombed and machine-gunned. Some patients were wounded and one is known to have been killed. Of other casualties not mentioned above, there are known to have been three killed and 20 injured. Some of our aircraft were damaged on the ground. At least six enemy aircraft were shot down, but it is not clear whether by our fighters or anti-aircraft guns. Some of the enemy aircraft involved are presumed to have come from an aircraft carrier standing off the North Australian coast.

Although this statement is riddled with errors, it is hardly a cover-up. The 72 twin-engined bombers in the first raid were, in fact, 152 single-engined bombers. The 21 bombers in the second raid were, in fact, 54. However, this reflected inaccurate information coming out of Darwin rather than an attempt to hide the facts. Some of the misinformation was probably deliberate: 'No vital service installations were destroyed'; 'Damage to the aerodrome was not serious.' All governments do this in war. But in general the statement told the truth as best the government knew it at the time while not giving the enemy valuable information about the extent of the damage.

Next day the government raised the death toll to 19. The Melbourne *Herald* on 21 February carried this report, datelined Canberra: 'It was stated officially today that 19 people were killed during the Japanese air raids on Darwin on Thursday. The original official announcement said that 15 were killed—11 civilians and four defence personnel. Later last night it was disclosed that eight service personnel were killed, making the death toll 19.' The same day, the *Herald* carried a first-person report from Douglas Lockwood, cabled from Katherine, giving an account of the raid but revealing no details of casualties or damage. No doubt the censors saw to that. It appeared under the nicely ambiguous headline: 'AA Gunners Gave Jap Raiders All They Had'.

Again, the 21 February statement was far from a cover-up. Consider this cable, sent on the 19th, on the evening of the raids, from the Naval section of Area Combined Headquarters in Darwin. The cable is timed at 1321 Greenwich Mean Time—10.51 p.m. Darwin time—and addressed to ABDACOM, the American, British, Dutch and Australian joint command, which included Darwin.

1. PRINCIPAL DAMAGE AND CASUALTIES TO FOLLOWING SHIPS AND ESTABLISHMENTS. SWAN MINOR DAMAGE. A/S [anti-submarine] GEAR OUT OF ACTION. 3 KILLED 14 SERIOUSLY INJURED. PLATYPUS GUNBAR COONGOOLA MINOR DAMAGE. B.W.V'S [boom-working vessels] 6 INJURED. U.S. DESTROYER PEARY SUNK. MAVIE SUNK. MERCHANT SHIPS ZEALANDIA BRITISH MOTORIST MOANA LOA [sic] NEPTUNA MEIGS SUNK. PORT MAR AND BAROSSA EXTENSIVELY DAMAGED. MANUNDA MINOR DAMAGE. COONAWARRA W/T [wireless telegraph] STATION MINOR DAMAGE EFFICIENCY UNIMPAIRED. OIL FUEL INSTALLATION NO 5 TANK CONTAINING ONLY SMALL QUANTITY FUEL SERIOUSLY DAMAGED. NO 6 TANK HOLED ABOUT 6 FEET FROM THE TOP.

2. STOCK OF FRESH AND DRY PROVISIONS VICTUALLING YARD SUFFICIENT ONLY FOR 7 DAYS NORMAL RATIONS.

3. DAMAGE TO MAIN JETTY PRECLUDES USE BY SHIPS AND FUELLING AND WATERING CAN BE CARRIED OUT BY LIGHTER ONLY.

The cable lists only three dead, from HMAS *Swan*. In fact the numbers killed on the named ships were: HMAS *Swan* 3; *Gunbar* 1; boom-working vessels *Kara Kara* 2, *Kangaroo* 1; USS *Peary* 91; *Zealandia* 3; *British Motorist* 2; *Mauna Loa* 5; *Neptuna* 45; *Meigs* 2; and *Port Mar* 1. The number dead was not three. It was 156. The point is that when the government first announced low casualties on the morning after the raid, it was acting on the best information it had at the time.

It continued to receive misinformation for at least four more days. The Chief of Air Staff, Sir Charles Burnett, flew in to Darwin on 22 February to investigate on the spot. Next day he submitted a report to the War Advisory Council and War Cabinet that fell woefully short of any realistic numbers. Marked Most Secret, the report is 'based on information received up to 1200 hours 23rd February'. It concludes by setting out the casualties to service personnel 'reported to date'. These were:

6 injured on the naval boom working vessel

3 Australian RAAF personnel including W/C Tindal
    at RAAF Station

1 American at RAAF Station

1 killed Berrima Hospital

1 injured Berrima Hospital

3 killed on HMAS Swan

14 injured on HMAS Swan

4 pilots missing believed killed

Burnett's report acknowledged 12 service personnel dead, including the four missing pilots, and 21 injured. It made no reference to civilian casualties, and no reference to chaos, looting or the civilian exodus. More dishonestly, it made no reference to the RAAF's evaporation in the wake of the second raid. So the government, still defending the announcement of 19 dead and 24 injured, could hardly be accused of deliberately lying. This was the very best information it could get, from a senior officer sent specifically to find out the facts. However, government ministers must have begun to get a whiff of the real story, and the need to keep it to themselves: at the same War Cabinet meeting that received Burnett's report, 'it was approved that credentials should not be given by Ministers to newspaper representatives proceeding to Northern Australia'.

The government's version, not many dead and not much damage, was reinforced by a series of mendacious cables from Administrator Abbott to the Ministry for the Interior in Canberra. On 24 February, five days after the raid, Abbott cabled, in full: 'DARWIN NOW NORMAL AND ESSENTIAL SERVICES IN HAND STOP SHOPS CAN REOPEN STOP PLEASE ARRANGE URGENTLY FOR COMMON-WEALTH BANK TO FUNCTION UPON TEMPORARY BASIS IN DARWIN SO THAT PAYS CAN BE MADE WORKMEN AND OTHERS.' Next day, 25 February, in full: 'DARWIN QUITE NORMAL STOP SHOPS OPEN STOP GLAD TO RECEIVE ADVICE REGARDING COMMONWEALTH BANK FUNC-TIONING AGAIN.' In part, on 26 February: 'EVERYTHING NORMAL STOP CONSIDER DISTRESSED MERCANTILE MARINE SHOULD BE RETURNED AT ONCE BY SPECIAL CONVOY.'

This picture of Darwin back to normal was nonsense, and well Abbott knew it. The only possible explanation for these cables is his wish to conceal from Canberra the extent to which he had allowed the town to fall into chaos.

Now consider a cable sent from Darwin on 1 March, ten days after the raid. This went to the Australian Navy Board in Melbourne from Captain Penry Thomas, the Naval Officer in Charge, Darwin. Thomas told the Navy Board:

> Merchant seaman casualties not yet complete. Known casualties to date, killed 15 Europeans, 10 Asiatics. Missing believed killed 6 Europeans, 25 Asiatics. Missing believed en route Katherine 4 Europeans 16 Asiatics. Injured 12 Europeans 24 Asiatics. A.R.P. estimate of civil casualties is killed 40 mostly Europeans. Injured 250. Estimate of injured considered high. U.S. destroyer Peary casualties estimated 82 killed, 10 injured. Injured from Peary believed evacuated by Manunda. Greatest difficulty experienced in obtaining names.

This second cable gives a total of 178 dead,[1] still well short of the final official figure of 243 (of which more later). The point here is that ten days after the raid the figures were rising sharply, though they were still incorrect and still too low. The bigger point is that, for better or worse, the authorities decided to keep the higher numbers to themselves, at least for the time being. They now knew for certain that casualty numbers went way beyond the original 19 killed and 24 hurt. If they said nothing, then the Censor's ruling blocking publication of 'sensational reports of enemy operations' unless confirmed by the Commonwealth government or service sources would carry on the job. Nothing could be published unless the government offered it, so silence was golden. At the risk of introducing an inappropriate note of levity into what is unquestionably a tragic story, the Australian government chose to follow a trail blazed by sub-editors of *The Times* of London. On quiet news days the subs regularly ran a competition among themselves to invent the world's most boring headline. One of the winners was SMALL EARTHQUAKE IN CHILE: Not Many Dead. The parallel message AIR RAID IN DARWIN: Not Many Dead, together with an assurance that everything had quickly settled back to normal, would keep the story off the front pages for the time being. The censors could do the rest.

◆ ◆ ◆

The government's final announcement of the numbers killed was issued on 30 March 1942, immediately after Curtin received the secret report of the Lowe Commission. Although this statement gave dramatically larger numbers, it was played down by the newspapers, clearly under guidance from the censors. Newspapers printed the story in two or three paragraphs on inside pages. The Melbourne *Herald*'s report appeared on page three under the headline: '240 killed in First Raid on Darwin—Shipping Losses Given in Report'. It would have taken a keen-eyed reader to spot the three-paragraph story. Curtin's statement began: 'The number killed on land, sea and in the air during the first Japanese attack on Darwin on February 19 did not exceed 240.' Curtin then suggested that even this number might be reduced when missing wharfies communicated with the Railways Commissioner or the shipping agents. He concluded apologetically: 'The interests of security prevented me from stating previously the number who were killed or drowned at the harbour and on the wharves. That information, together with the shipping losses, constituted information which the enemy would have valued had it been made public immediately.' This was the last word on the subject from the government until October 1945.

Curtin and his government have been pilloried from that day to this for covering up the facts of the Darwin raid. Professor Alan Powell, in his excellent book *The Shadow's Edge*, wrote that one reason the raid had so little impact on the Australian people at the time was that 'their government would not trust them with the truth'. However, the government did set out to tell the truth in the first 24 hours, and for several days afterwards. Its crime—and major error—was to allow the military authorities to bully it into withholding the full story.

There is good evidence that Curtin himself saw the folly of holding back information. On 4 March 1942, the day after Japanese bombers struck at Broome and Wyndham in the north of Western Australia, Mr McLaughlin of the Department of Defence Co-Ordination sent a teleprinter message to Mr Farrands of the same department: 'In view of the stories being circulated by evacuees from Darwin, which suggest very large death toll, the Prime Minister desires to release an official and authoritative statement showing numbers killed and injured, both services and civilian.' Would Mr Farrands please ask the service Chiefs of Staff if they had any objection, asked Mr McLaughlin, making it plain that the PM was in a tearing hurry. The teleprinter message is timed at 3.57 p.m. The Prime Minister wanted an answer on his desk by 5.30 p.m. that day. Mr Farrands missed the deadline by ten minutes but obliged with the following message: 'The Chiefs of Staff consider that it would not be in the national interest to make any statement giving the details of casualties at any particular place, as to do so would give the enemy valuable information. They also consider that to make a statement in relation to the raids at Darwin, Broome and Wyndham would establish a precedent which would require a similar statement to be made in the case of all future raids.' However reluctantly, Curtin accepted their advice. There would be no statement. And without a statement, there would be no newspaper stories. It is hard to avoid the suspicion that the 'national interest'—does that phrase not have a familiar ring today?—that the Chiefs of Staff were so assiduously defending was in fact their own interest. The full story might have raised some uncomfortable questions about inadequate defences and lack of preparation.

From the *Herald*'s tiny '240 killed' story on 30 March until the end of the war, Darwin's story simply disappeared from public gaze. It was left to the rumour mill to keep Australians informed. The only breach in this wall of silence came, oddly enough, from the Army itself. Throughout the war the Australian War Memorial in Canberra, in conjunction with the Army, published a series of annuals containing articles, poems, cartoons and stories about Australians at war. Authorship was attributed to 'Some of the Boys'. The War Memorial distributed the annuals among the troops and subsequently made them available to the general public, all in an effort to boost morale. Each edition had a different title: *Jungle Warfare*, *Khaki and Green*, and so on. The 1942 volume was called *Soldiering On*. It contained a long article about the bombing of Darwin, signed by 'XV115', under the headline 'WAR CAME TO AUST-RALIA'. XV115 was a *nom de plume* for the Darwin representative of Defence's public relations director. The anonymous public servant wrote a graphic and dramatic account of the raid, painting a much more lurid picture of its scale and intensity than the bland statements issued by the government. A description of the Kittyhawks' tragic challenge to the bombers ended with the statement: 'Four of the American pilots lost their lives in a vain attempt to get into the air and fight.' Then: 'The first bomb to fall on Australia—a 1000-pounder—scored a direct hit on the wharf, killing 20 labourers.' Then: 'Burning oil from an oil tanker spread over the water of the harbour, adding to the holocaust. Men drowned because they could not swim in the heavy oil. Men burnt because they could not escape the flames.' And: 'The *Peary* sank with two-thirds of her complement.' However, XV115 carefully avoided any mention of chaos, looting or the civilian exodus. Those facts were still not for public consumption.

Nevertheless, the *Soldiering On* story was the first insight into what had really happened in Darwin. On 9 December, newspapers around Australia picked it up. The *Sydney Morning Herald* summarised it under the bland headline 'Darwin Air Raid Story—Disclosures in Army Book'. The Melbourne *Herald* was less restrained. 'FIRST OFFICIAL STORY OF RAIN OF DEATH ON DARWIN—BRAVERY OF GUNNERS', it shouted. The *Herald*'s story began: 'A thrilling story of the first raid on Darwin by the Japanese last February, giving many remarkable details not previously released, is contained in "Soldiering On," a new Christmas book for the Australian Army.' Again the government was asked to make a clear statement. On 28 January 1943 Senator Collett tabled a parliamentary question: 'To ask the minister representing the Minister for Defence—As the story of the enemy attack on Broome has been given to the press, will the Government now make available to the public a full account of the bombardment by the Japanese of the Port of Darwin?' The reply to the senator repeated the words of the Chiefs of Staff. It would not be in the national interest to make a statement, so best say nothing.

The military line was seriously counterproductive, as censorship usually is. Curtin had realised that those who left Darwin after the raids were under no obligation to conceal from their friends what they had seen—or heard. As survivors fled south, the rest of Australia rapidly filled with wild rumours about the fate of Darwin. Thousands had died. Looters had been shot. So had deserters. Darwin had been wiped out. Everyone had panicked. The government was covering it up. The Japs would be here soon. After Darwin, Sydney would be next. Or Perth. Or Brisbane. A sharp dose of the truth might have done more to settle nerves than provocative silence in the face of spreading rumours.

To be fair, those left behind in Darwin generally supported the government's silence. Lou Curnock told the Lowe Commission he preferred not to worry friends and relatives outside Darwin. However, the government line created a problem for those left behind. Fed with bland information, people down south simply didn't appreciate the massive problems these stalwarts faced. Lou Curnock told Commissioner Lowe: 'They probably thought it was a picnic—a few planes came across and, after dropping a few bombs, went away.'

Surely the clinching argument for telling the truth is the American experience in the wake of Pearl Harbor. Roosevelt had spared his public nothing when telling the story of the raid, including a clear account of the numbers killed and the extent of the damage. American public indignation over the 'day of infamy' did more than anything else to spur a reluctant and isolationist country into enthusiastically supporting total war. There is no reason to suppose the Australian public would have reacted differently. The most likely consequence of a truthful account of the Darwin raid would have been a surge of national fury, followed by an angry determination to fight back. The Australian government railed endlessly against public indifference to the war effort. The full horror of the attack on Darwin was its best chance to jolt Australians out of their apathy. Unwisely, it chose not to take it.

Chapter 15

Not many dead

The question of how many died in Darwin as a result of the two raids is still controversial. Jack Burton, a former mayor who was in the town on 19 February 1942, estimated the number killed at 'about 900'. Some have put the number as high as 1100—echoing a rumoured early estimate by Army Intelligence. An anonymous contributor to the compilation *Darwin's Battle for Australia*, published by Darwin Defenders 1942–45 Inc., submitted this graphic account: 'I have spoken to four soldiers who were among those detailed to deal with the problem. One said that they were told to collect the bodies and take them down to Mindil Beach. He said: "We stacked them two deep on the back of the trucks." Another said they dug down to the water level and stacked them in. Another said he counted over 300 into one mass grave, he didn't look in the other one. Padre Richards said: "243? I buried more than that myself." These men had no reason to lie, and I believe the Army Intelligence number [1100] to be substantially correct.' So the Darwin Defenders supported the idea that the true toll was anything up to four or five times the official one.

We can make a clean start by demolishing the figure of 243, which is still the 'official' count established by the Lowe Commission. This number is simply wrong. It is made up as follows:

Neptuna	45
Zealandia	3
British Motorist	2
Manunda	12
Swan	4
Karakara	5
Gunbower (presumably Gunbar)	1
Peary	80
Meigs	2
Port Mar	1
Mauna Loa	5
Don Isidro	11
Florence D	4
The Army	2
The Air Force	6
US Army and Air Force	7
Civilians in the town	14
Civilians on the wharf	39

The list leaves out the 15 dead from the USS *William B. Preston* and puts *Peary*'s number too low, at 80. The correct figure of 91 for *Peary* was known by 6 March 1942, the date of an action report filed by Lieutenant William Catlatt, a *Peary* officer. Catlatt's report gives not just the number of dead but includes the names of those who died, and can be taken as accurate. The Lowe Commission began sitting in Darwin on 5 March, so the correct figure was both known and available at the time it was collecting evidence. The figure for the Air Force should be at least seven, not six. (It might be eight—the evidence is confusing.) On the other side of the ledger, the figure for *Swan* should be three, not four.

◆ ◆ ◆

The task of collecting and burying the dead could be carried out only by police or soldiers. It was a gruesome and dispiriting business, made no easier by the fact that tropical heat could play havoc with a body. Speed was important. So was the need to identify the bodies. The dead were congregated in four main areas: in the harbour; around the wharf; in the town, particularly the area around the Post Office; and at the RAAF station. Because the tide was ebbing at the time of the raid, bodies from sunken or damaged ships were first dragged out to sea. When the tide turned, bodies washed up on the beaches or drifted into the mangroves, where they were hard to find and even harder to extract.

Surely Edgar Harrison, the Permanent ARP Officer, was right when he said: 'I am afraid the actual figures will never be known. We do not know whether there are five, 50 or 500 in the swamp. With the sharks and other vermin, I think quite a number of bodies have gone.'

Police Sergeant William McKinnon told the Lowe Commission: 'As far as I know, when the bodies were found they were either buried where they lay or conveyed to suitable places for burial without any documentary authorisation.' The police dug the graves themselves. If the ground was too hard to dig deep, the bodies were moved elsewhere. The police tried to keep a record of the numbers they buried, but the urgency of the work and the general confusion meant the records were far from perfect.

On the beach, police laid out in rows the oil-covered and burnt bodies of seamen and asked surviving crew members to identify them where possible. It was a hopeless task. The bodies were simply unrecognisable. Civilian dead generally went to the hospital morgue, where friends and workmates did their best to say who they were. After the first day, the heat made this task impossible. From the second day onwards, decomposed and unrecognisable bodies were buried on the spot. The police did their best to identify them, but the need to bury them quickly overrode all other considerations.

There was no time for ceremony. Henry Hunter, the mess manager at the East Point shore battery, had been at the hospital as an out-patient on the day of the raid. He said later: 'To my way of thinking it was quite disgusting. There was no service. Whether it was read afterwards, or before they went down, I do not know. Women and men were placed in a common grave.'

Much later, bodies were exhumed and moved to graves in the Adelaide River War Cemetery, the largest group of war graves on Australian soil. Row upon row of crosses mark their final resting place. Some graves carry the name of the victim. Others mark the final rest of unidentified seamen 'known unto God'. To one side of the cemetery lies a group of graves for civilians. A special section, with its own group headstone, guards the bodies of the ten postal workers.

◆ ◆ ◆

So how many died? I can only agree with Edgar Harrison that the final total will never be known. While the official figure of 243 can be proved to be low, numbers such as 1100 are fancifully high. If so many died, who were they? Any claim that large numbers of people died but were not counted rests on the fact that bodies may have drifted out to sea, got lost in the mangroves, or been taken by sharks or crocodiles. If so, the victims must have come from the ships or the wharf. Survivors from ships in the harbour, particularly military ships, had a pretty fair idea of how many were aboard when the raid took place. They would be unlikely to underestimate the death toll by hundreds. And if 900 or 1100 died, why were the numbers of injured so low? The count of the injured is more accurate, because they were treated in hospital or shipped out aboard the *Manunda*. The hospitals and *Manunda* noted names and numbers of those they treated. The Lowe Commission put the number of injured 'between 300 and 400', and there is no reason to doubt that figure. It is implausible that the number killed would be three or four times greater than the number injured. Some wharfies remained unaccounted for, but they are more likely to have disappeared down the Adelaide River road than died on the wharf and drifted away on the harbour.

And what of the mass graves on Mindil Beach, and bodies piled two deep on trucks and tipped into mass graves? Nobody has ever come forward and said they drove the truck or dug the grave. Darwin could stake a fair claim to being the rumour capital of the world in the aftermath of the raid, and these stories are no more than second- or third-hand hearsay.

The most accurate 'official' figure to date appears on a plaque unveiled in 2001 on The Esplanade, near Government House. Placed by the Northern Territory's Administration to mark the centenary of Federation, it amends the *Peary*'s death toll to the correct 91 and lists *William B. Preston*'s fatalities as 10, rather than the correct 15. The plaque increases the RAAF number to seven, the Australian Army number to three, and the *Don Isidro* figure to 14. It then adds 19 who died of wounds on the *Manunda*, and 22 further fatalities among 'various seamen and civilians—circumstances unclear'. Its final total is 292 dead:

Killed on Darwin Wharf	22
Killed in the town area	17
MV *Neptuna*	45
USS *Peary*	91
SS *Zealandia*	3
SS *British Motorist*	2
SS *Mauna Loa*	5
USAT *Meigs*	1
AHS *Manunda*	12
HMAS *Swan*	3
HMAS *Kangaroo*	1
HMAS *Kara Kara*	2
HMAS *Gunbar*	1
SS *Port Mar*	1
USS *William B. Preston*	10
MV *Don Isidro*	14
MV *Florence D*	3
PATWING 10 Catalina	1
Royal Australian Air Force personnel	7
Australian Army personnel	3
US Army personnel	3
US Army Air Force personnel	4
Died of wounds aboard *Manunda*	19
Various civilians and seamen	22
TOTAL	292

With the *William B. Preston* toll corrected to 15, a figure of 297 known dead is the best count anyone is likely to achieve.* If we then accept Edgar Harrison's view that an unknown number of bodies drifted out to sea or were caught up in the mangroves or taken by sharks or crocodiles, and temper that view by saying the number unaccounted for is bound to be low, the full death toll is likely to be a little over 300, perhaps as many as 310 or 320.

Does this make the Darwin raid Australia's worst disaster? The only challenge comes from Cyclone Mahina, which struck Bathurst Bay, near Cape Melville on the far north-east coast of Queensland, on 22 March 1899. Mahina wrecked a pearling fleet. The death toll is unverifiable, and most authorities settle for a figure of 'over 300', with some putting the number dead as high as 400. A minimum figure of 297 for the Darwin raid is provable from records. Mahina's death count is simply an estimate, based on a rough count of the number of ships sunk. In the absence of accurate figures from Bathurst Bay, Darwin's claim is strong.

Prime Minister Curtin said later: 'The results of the raid were not such as to give any satisfaction to the enemy.' Tom Minto, the First Officer of the *Manunda*, responded: 'Well, the enemy must have been very hard to please.'

---

* My certainty on the higher figure for that ship is based on the action reports filed by Les Wood and Jimmy Grant, the ship's First Officer and Captain respectively, which name 15 dead.

Chapter 16

Post mortem

To understand the Australian government's reaction to the events in Darwin, it is necessary to look at them in historical context. Quite simply, 1942 was the worst year of the Second World War for Australia. And in that terrible year, the week beginning 15 February 1942 was the worst week.

The Curtin government was comparatively new. On 28 August 1941, the long-serving conservative Prime Minister, Robert Menzies, bowed to pressure from within his party to resign. He handed over to his deputy, Arthur Fadden, whose government fell five weeks later, when two independent members voted down Fadden's Budget. Curtin's Labor Party took over from Fadden on 3 October 1941. So Curtin became Prime Minister not because the Australian public had voted for him at an election but because the conservatives had lost the confidence of the House of Representatives. The Governor-General, Lord Gowrie, simply sent for the Labor leader and asked him to take over.

On 27 December, with his government a mere 12 weeks old, Curtin stood Australian foreign policy on its head by declaring that the country now 'looked to America' for protection from the Japanese. Until this ringing pronouncement, Australia, in truth, barely had a foreign policy.

As a British Dominion and part of the Empire, its foreign policy amounted to little more than adding a squeaky 'me, too' to whatever Britain decided.

Australians had always been uneasy about threats from the north, whether from China, Japan or Russia. Against this threat stood the mighty British bastion of Singapore. Let no enemy contemplate a southward thrust towards Australia: the invincible Royal Navy and its impregnable Singapore base would rapidly put a stop to that.

As Japanese forces swept unstoppably through Indo-China, Burma, Malaya, Singapore and the Dutch East Indies, the Curtin government could see Australia falling while most of its Army was fighting at Britain's side in the Middle East.

On 15 February 1942, two events of shattering importance dominated the councils of the Australian government. Singapore fell. And Curtin cabled Churchill asking for the return of two Australian divisions from the Middle East. For the next five days, furious cables flew between Curtin, Churchill and Roosevelt. Churchill was willing to see the Australians pull out of the Middle East, but he wanted them to go to Rangoon to defend Burma and therefore India. Curtin wanted them back in Java to block the Japanese advance or, better still, back in Australia to defend the homeland. The strain of these two events—Australia's worst military disaster in Singapore, and a bitter row with Australia's two most important allies—was enough to put an exhausted Curtin in hospital on 17 February.

Then, two days later, came news of the Darwin raid. Invasion appeared imminent. No Australian government or prime minister has ever faced such a quick succession of terrible events. So if, with the benefit of 20–20 hindsight, we can see that not every decision taken over Darwin was wise or sure-footed, it is surely right to point out that Curtin and his ministers had a lot to think about at the time.

♦ ♦ ♦

Nothing in the minutes of the War Cabinet or War Advisory Council in February or March 1942 gives a clue as to when the government began to grasp the appalling implications of the Darwin raid. The minutes barely refer to the attack. The full horror began to dawn after receipt of a report from Administrator Abbott to the Department of the Interior, dated 27 February. Of all the documents His Honour produced in the aftermath of the raid, this is his best. It is honest, clear-headed and direct. It pulls no punches in describing the looting and the anarchy that swept through Darwin. He wrote:

> The psychological effect of a bombing raid upon civilians is one which should be deeply considered by the government. The confusion which followed the raid was very bad and was greatly accentuated by unauthorised actions by various service sections, including the Provost Corps. Discipline there was very bad, men were drunk, and salutary action including the arrest of an Officer and a Non-Commissioned Officer had to be taken. The worst feature was that soldiers, entirely without orders, kept advising civilians to leave the town. This resulted in a stream of cars, cyclists and pedestrians making down the road as far and even past the Adelaide River. Had it been necessary to fight an action the confusion might have been most disastrous. No official instruction was ever issued by me for male civilians to evacuate.
>
> *A similar type of raid in a large town might have very serious panic results.* [emphasis added]
>
> In regard to casualties and particularly fatalities, I have been endeavouring to get a complete list but this is exceedingly difficult on account of the confusion which extended after the raid. A reasonable estimate is about 300 killed, which includes the personnel of ships attacked and sunk.

This was the first clear indication the government had of just how serious were the results of the raid. Only four days earlier the Chief of Air Staff, Sir Charles Burnett, had come up with a figure of 12 servicemen dead. Now the Administrator was talking about 300. It was also the first full account the government had of the flight of civilian refugees. The Adelaide River Stakes spooked the government as no other aspect of the Darwin raid had done. Did it reveal some previously hidden character flaw in Australians? Might the same sort of thing happen if the Japanese attacked the much larger cities in the south? The thought of hundreds of thousands of people from Sydney or Melbourne taking to the roads in flight was too terrible to contemplate.

The government made two decisions. First, it agreed to accept the advice of the Defence Chiefs of Staff and reveal nothing to the wider public of the extent of the calamity. Possibly it reasoned that the fall of Singapore and the consequent loss of an entire Australian division was enough bad news for the public to digest in a single week. Second, it resolved to find out independently and impartially exactly what had happened. On 3 March 1942, 12 days after the raid, the government appointed Charles Lowe, a Supreme Court judge in the state of Victoria, to head a Royal Commission. His brief was to inquire into and report on all the circumstances connected with the attack, including the preparedness of 'naval, military, air and civil authorities'; the damage and casualties sustained; the degree of cooperation existing between the various services; the steps taken to meet the attack or minimise its effects; whether the Commanders or other officers of the naval, military and air forces or any civil authority failed to discharge the responsibilities entrusted to them; and to recommend what changes in defence measures might be considered necessary to meet a second attack.

There was no delay. After accepting the appointment, Lowe flew out of Melbourne at 1.30 a.m. on 4 March, accompanied by two assistants, John V. Barry, King's Counsel, and Basil Murphy, who fell ill on the plane and was replaced by an Adelaide lawyer, H.G. Alderman. The inquiry began hearing evidence at the Darwin Hotel at 10 a.m. on 5 March. A few days later, it moved to the Parap Hotel, where facilities were better and it was less exposed to constant interruption from air-raid warnings. All evidence was heard in camera. Witnesses were encouraged to be frank, knowing that anything they said would remain secret.

◆ ◆ ◆

The Lowe Commission deserves a place in the legal history books as an example of what can be done in a short time without serious compromise to good legal practice. Lowe submitted his first report on 6 March—a cable to the Prime Minister stressing the urgent need to station fighter aircraft in Darwin: 'In its existing condition Darwin could not be successfully defended against a major enemy attack. Immediately necessary to have the air defences of four fighter squadrons and recce aircraft, and two additional radar installations.' Lowe was off to a good start.

Between 5 and 10 March, he heard some 70 witnesses. The hearings continued late into the night, stopping only for meals and sleep. Teams of stenographers laboured into the early hours transcribing evidence. On the 12th Lowe and his team returned to Melbourne, where stenographers continued the overwhelming task of typing up the witnesses' words. Lowe resumed the hearings in Melbourne on the 19th, and continued to take evidence until the 25th, examining another 30 witnesses. Incredibly, he submitted his first report, of more than 10,000 words, on 27 March. He then reviewed the entire transcript of evidence (which runs to some 917 pages) and the hefty folders of exhibits, including log books, reports and cables. In the light of this additional reading, Lowe submitted a much briefer, 2600-word supplementary report on 9 April. The whole process, from Lowe's appointment to his final report, was completed in 38 days.

Key passages of Lowe's two reports are reproduced in Appendix II. In essence, his criticisms were simple and unchallengeable. Darwin suffered from a lack of leadership, military and civil. And its defences were inadequate, particularly in the area of fighter aircraft and radar to direct them.

Lowe singled out two clearly identifiable individuals as culpable: Administrator Abbott and the RAAF station commander, Sturt Griffith. In particular Lowe focused on Abbott's failure to get a grip on the town, thereby opening the gate to civilian disorder. 'Had there been effective leadership [immediately following the raids],' he wrote, 'I think that normal conditions might very rapidly have been attained, but leadership was conspicuously lacking.' The row between Abbott and the air-raid wardens was a further blight on civilian order. 'I am clear that this difference prevented the police being aided by officers of the A.R.P. in preserving law and order after the raid,' Lowe added.

He was particularly harsh on the failure of RAAF Operations to raise the alarm after receiving Father McGrath's warning. 'The failure by Royal Australian Air Force Operations to communicate with A.R.P. Headquarters is inexplicable,' he wrote, adding: 'The delay in giving a general warning was fraught with disaster. It is impossible to say with certainty what would have happened if the warning had been promptly given when received by the Royal Australian Air Force Operations at 9.37 a.m., but it is at least probable that a number of men who lost their lives while working on ships at the pier might have escaped to a place of safety.'

He singled out Griffith for blame over the disorderly exodus of RAAF personnel from the air base. 'I am convinced [that] with competent leadership the personnel would rapidly have resumed their duties,' Lowe wrote. 'An order, however, was given by the Station Commander, which I think was extremely unfortunate.' Lowe went on to describe the emptying of the base, and the 278 men still missing four days after the raid. 'As the casualties were small, the result can only be regarded as deplorable,' he concluded.

In the light of subsequent events, it is also worth quoting Lowe's verdict on Group Captain Scherger. 'He was present in Darwin on the day of the raid and acted, in my opinion, with great courage and energy,' Lowe wrote. 'I desire to record the view that, on all the evidence before me, his conduct in connection with the raid was deserving of the highest praise.'

The reader might wonder, at this point, whether heads rolled in the wake of the damning verdicts. The government certainly looked at the possibility of sacking Abbott but decided against it. Only one head rolled. There is a laconic account of what happened in the oral history files of the Northern Territory Archives service in Darwin. The voice is Scherger's: 'The Chiefs of Staff in Melbourne had decided that there must be scapegoats. Now the one man who could not have been criticised under any conditions was Captain Penry Thomas [Naval Officer in Charge, Darwin], who'd been a retired RN bloke called back to the colours. I could find nothing, nothing at all, to throw at him.' Moving to the Army, Scherger continued: 'Now no one ever landed or tried to land so nothing was wrong with Blake [Major General and Army Commandant].' That left the RAAF to take the fall. In April 1942, two months after the raid, Scherger was relieved of his command. It did his RAAF career no permanent harm. As Air Marshall Sir Frederick Scherger, he went on to become a worthy and much admired head of the RAAF.

◆ ◆ ◆

The Darwin raid was by no means Australia's national day of shame, as Paul Hasluck declared. Yet there is no getting away from the fact that Australia did not exactly cover itself in glory on 19 February 1942.

The talk of shame usually flows from accounts of the Adelaide River Stakes. The truth, of course, is that the citizens of Darwin behaved as civilians usually do when bombs start falling. What shocked Australians was the discovery that they were no more stoic or heroic than anybody else. They had seen newsreel films of pathetic lines of refugees fleeing the violence of war in Europe. They called these people 'reffos', a term of mild derision. Reffos who turned up in Australia were foreigners: poor, sad, defeated people in ragged clothes, accompanied by ragged children and clutching at ragged possessions. Australians would never act like that.

With the publication of the Lowe Commission report and the revelation of the Adelaide River Stakes, Australians were confronted with a picture of their fellow countrymen behaving just like reffos. Their self-image as a strong and independent people, cool under fire, brave and resourceful, was shattered. Could these be the sons and daughters of men who had fought in Gallipoli, in Flanders, in Palestine? Worse, since 1940 Australians had been fed endless newspaper and newsreel stories of plucky East Enders smiling stoically through the London Blitz. Surely the Poms were not braver in the face of bombing than the bronzed heroes of God's own country? (The truth, of course, is different. Anyone who has read transcripts of the excellent Mass Observation oral histories of the Blitz knows that the plucky East Enders whinged and complained like nobody's business, and would have cheerfully moved out if there was anywhere else to go.)

If the civilian exodus was not a source of shame, what about the looting? After allowing for the understandable grabbing of survival rations, the plain fact is that the looting became an organised rort using Army trucks and other vehicles to strip Darwin bare. Looting in the wake of military defeat—for the Battle of Darwin was nothing if not a military defeat for Australian and American forces—is a dishonourable tradition dating back to ancient history. However, there was a difference in Darwin: looting is usually carried out by the winners. In Darwin, the losers took all.

What of the lack of military preparation? Certainly there was a shortage of available resources. No doubt Darwin could have used four squadrons of fighter aircraft and some reconnaissance planes to scour the seaward approaches. The ships and the RAAF base could have used some pom-pom anti-aircraft guns to tackle the fighters and dive-bombers. The Army could have done with more 3.7-inch anti-aircraft guns. There were none to be had.

It has been argued that Pell's squadron should never have flown out and left Darwin with no fighter cover. But this is hindsight. Pell's Kittyhawks were always destined for Java. Pure luck brought them to Darwin to give temporary fighter protection to the ill-fated convoy. When there was no convoy to protect, they simply reverted to their original orders and continued their journey to the Dutch East Indies.

Should not the military authorities, particularly the RAAF, have glanced at a map and realised that Darwin was suddenly on the front line? And having seen that, should they have sent more fighter aircraft to protect it? Yes, but which fighter aircraft? There were few available. With the Pacific war only ten weeks old, a lot of the RAAF's fighter strength was still in the Middle East. Should it have reduced the threadbare fighter defences of Sydney, Melbourne and Brisbane still further to shore up Darwin? Maybe. But the political consequences would have been unbearable if the Japanese had chosen one of Australia's major cities as their first target, and the government had meanwhile sent the scarce southern fighters north to defend the tiny town of Darwin.

Specifically, should the nine Wirraways at Batchelor not have mounted an air combat patrol over Darwin that day to protect the port and the RAAF field? With hindsight, yes, of course. But mounting such a patrol would almost certainly have led to nine Wirraways shot down and nine Australian pilots dead, with very little impression made on the Japanese attacking force. The absence of a combat patrol probably counts more as a lucky escape than as evidence of incompetence on the part of the RAAF.

The real failures of Darwin are three. As we have seen, an air attack on the town was widely expected. So although Darwin anticipated an air attack, it did not prepare for it. The civilian air-raid precautions in particular were pitifully thin. Administrator Abbott's failure to give anything like proper backing to the ARP wardens meant that there was no coherent plan for dealing with the consequences of an attack. To be fair, the government endlessly complained that Australians in general were not taking the war seriously. So it may seem harsh to blame Abbott for failing to persuade Darwin residents to show more willingness than southerners. Nevertheless, failure to prepare became one of the town's deadliest killers.

The second failure might be forgiven. While both the military and civilians anticipated a Japanese attack, nobody expected an attack of the scale or ferocity of the one that came. It is notable that everybody in the town underestimated the number of aircraft taking part. The first headlines talked about 93. Lowe accepted estimates of 27 high-level bombers and a total of fewer than 50 dive-bombers and fighters in the first raid, and 27 heavy bombers in the second raid. The true numbers, unknown until after the war, were 81 high-level bombers, not 27, 94 dive-bombers and fighters, not 50, and 54 heavy bombers in the second raid, not 27. The true numbers would have seemed incredible to the stunned defenders. What had Darwin done to deserve an attack on this scale? The anti-aircraft gunners, backed by Pell's ten Kittyhawks, might have disrupted 30 or 40 attacking planes. They did not stand a chance against 242. So Darwin's second failure was in neglecting to anticipate and prepare for what was then one of the biggest air raids of the war.

The final failure was the deadliest: a massive failure of leadership. If readers feel I have been harsh in singling out Administrator Abbott, let me put a question in response. Who else was there who could have shown the leadership needed? Abbott was chairman of the Darwin Defence Committee, which brought together the heads of the Army, Navy and Air Force to coordinate the defence of the town. He was also Commissioner of Police. He was unquestionably the man in charge. It is perhaps unfair to compare the way Mayor Rudolph Giuliani took command in New York in the wake of 9/11 and the way Abbott failed to get a grip in Darwin. He was undoubtedly and understandably shaken by the bombing of his office and his narrow escape from death, but his focus on his wine cellar and his cups and saucers in the immediate aftermath of the raid, when there was a civilian population to be calmed and returned to order, widespread looting to be stopped, an evacuation to be organised, damage to be repaired, and the wounded and dying to be attended to and comforted, indicates a man who was not up to the job.

Wing Commander Griffith's failure to maintain discipline at the RAAF base was surely culpable, as was Major General Blake's failure to keep order among his troops, particularly the Provost Corps. Griffith's sense of priorities is open to challenge. There were more useful things to do at the base than mend the water pipe and move the men down the road. Lowe quoted evidence from 'a very senior officer'—in fact it was Scherger—that Griffith 'was rattled and did not know which were the first things and which were the second things'. His failure of leadership led to the fiasco of the desertion of the base. Restoring morale and confidence must have been a painful task.

Nevertheless, this was no day of shame. The doggedness of the Army and Navy gunners, the heroism of the Kittyhawk pilots, the selfless bravery of the harbour rescuers, the dutiful response of the disbanded

ARP wardens, the parallel response of the hard-pressed police, all add up to something Australians can look on with pride. But that must be put alongside a recognition of failures: of preparation, of leadership, and of discipline. Forget about the Adelaide River Stakes. That was normal civilian behaviour, made all the more forgivable by the fact that the fleeing citizens believed they were under orders from the military to leave town. Look instead at the looting, the leaderless chaos, the undisciplined shooting-out of car headlights, the unseemly scramble to shove women and children aside at Parap railway station, and the bloody-mindedness of the merchant seamen and wharfies when it was clearly time to forget about the rule book and pitch in. If Australians wish to hang their collective heads, it should be over those lapses.

◆ ◆ ◆

The raid on Darwin is often described as Australia's Pearl Harbor. The parallels are obvious. But there were differences. Pearl Harbor came as a complete surprise. The Darwin attack was widely anticipated. America's leaders used Pearl Harbor to galvanise a wary and isolationist nation into willing mobilisation. Australia's leaders chose to play down the bombing of Darwin for fear of its impact on national morale.

The numbers are striking. More bombs fell on Darwin than on Pearl Harbor. More aircraft attacked Darwin in the first wave than attacked Pearl Harbor in the first wave. In Darwin eight ships were sunk. In Pearl Harbor four went to the bottom, with two more capsized. The Japanese attacked civilian targets in the town of Darwin, killing 61 civilians. They left Honolulu alone—the 68 civilians who died there were killed by fallout from American guns. Of course, the tonnage of shipping sunk in Darwin was far less than in Pearl Harbor for the obvious reason that the Japanese were attacking bigger ships in Pearl Harbor. The death toll in Darwin was very much smaller than in Pearl Harbor, because the larger ships in Pearl Harbor had bigger crews. And the bombs used in Darwin were lighter anti-personnel bombs rather than the 800-kg torpedoes used against the battleships. So while more bombs fell on Darwin, the weight of bombs was greater at Pearl Harbor.

The Japanese assault on Darwin did not end with the two raids of 19 February. Over the next 21 months, the town faced no fewer than 64 attacks by Japanese bombers. The onslaught ended with a final raid on 12 November 1943. None of the subsequent raids matched the scale or ferocity of the first. The attacks were part of a largely forgotten air war in northern Australia that involved no fewer than 97 attacks on Darwin, Broome, Wyndham, Derby, Katherine, Horn Island, Townsville, Mossman, Port Hedland, Noonamah, Exmouth Gulf, Onslow, Drysdale River Mission and Coomalie Creek.

The attacks grew less frequent as time wore on. The Australian and American fighter pilots and anti-aircraft gunners gradually got the upper hand. Jack Mulholland remembers one raid of nine bombers arriving over Darwin. By then the gunners on the ground were hardened by experience, and problems with fuse setting had been overcome. The gun sections' routine first salvo of four rounds certainly worked this time. It sent four of the nine bombers to the ground in flames. The fighter pilots then radioed to ask the gunners to hold fire while they attacked. They quickly saw off the remaining five bombers. With such losses as this, the Japanese were paying too high a price for attacking Darwin, and they backed off.

The town's fighter defences, both Australian and American, steadily improved in strength and skill. Kittyhawks remained the backbone of the air defence. In January 1943, much-admired Spitfires joined the fray. Although they had proved highly effective in the Battle of Britain, they were less useful in tropical Darwin.

The tide of war began to turn in May 1942, when the Japanese invasion of Port Moresby was blocked by American, Australian and British forces in the Battle of the Coral Sea. Japan never again won a major strategic battle. The tide turned decisively in June 1942, at the Battle of Midway. Darwin's tormentors, the four aircraft carriers of Nagumo force, were all sunk. Japanese sea power never recovered. With control of the sea and sky gradually passing to Allied ships and aircraft, Japan's long retreat to defeat and humiliation had begun.

Darwin continued to play a major part, this time as a base for Allied offensives against Japanese positions in the Dutch East Indies. It was now the turn of the Japanese to dive into slit trenches as waves of Allied bombers from Darwin and other northern bases harried and hammered them.

◆ ◆ ◆

Within a month of the first Japanese air raid, Darwin became a de facto military camp. Most civilians moved out and did not return until well after the end of the war. Administrator Abbott moved his headquarters to Alice Springs, away from the sound of gunfire. He has been criticised for this. One highly respected Northern Territorian confided to me that this was the part of Abbott's performance that most stuck in his throat. 'The King and Queen of England stayed in London right through the bombing,' he said. 'I think Abbott should have set an example and done the same.' Well, maybe. Abbott certainly paid a price for his retreat south. Judge Wells stayed in Darwin throughout the war. Abbott did not. Wells is remembered to this day with affection. Abbott is not.

◆ ◆ ◆

When the Lowe Commission report was published, in October 1945, the public reacted with shock. The Melbourne *Herald* headlined its story: 'JUDGE ON DARWIN RAID PANIC—LEADERSHIP AND DELAYED WARNING BLAMED'. Subheads scattered through the story give the flavour: 'Alien stampede', 'Warning delayed', 'Rush from town', 'Lessons unlearnt', and 'Malicious lying'. It did not make for pretty reading. The reporting concentrated on the Adelaide River Stakes while making room for the inadequate preparations and the poor leadership. The bravery of the gunners and the heroism of the harbour rescuers somehow seemed less important than the disastrous picture of The Town That Ran Away. The legend of Australia's national 'day of shame' sprung from these reports. Darwin is still trying to live it down.

◆ ◆ ◆

I went to Darwin in February 2008 to attend the anniversary ceremony. It is held at the Cenotaph in Bicentennial Park, more or less on the site of the old Oval and Jack Mulholland's guns. In fact there are several ceremonies. The Australian American Association held a 'meet and greet' on the evening of 18 February at the Trailer Boat Club, attended by the American Consul General to Melbourne, Earl Irving. There was a cash bar and finger food provided by the Association. Dress was smart casual. It was a subdued affair. About 20 people turned up.

Next day was typical Darwin weather. The rain drizzled down lightly at first, barely damping the 50 or 60 who turned up for a wreath-laying ceremony at the USS *Peary* memorial on The Esplanade. Dress was Territory rig: men—long-sleeve shirt and tie, long trousers; women—day dress. There was a brief speech by Earl Irving.

We all then traipsed the 500 metres or so from the *Peary* memorial to the Cenotaph, in increasing rain. By the time we were seated in the large marquee, about 1000 of us, the rain was pelting down in drowning tropical bucketloads. Before the speeches, at exactly 9.58 a.m., the air-raid sirens sounded and the Army fired blank rounds with highly coloured smoke from some field guns on the harbour's edge. The noise was shocking, as it was meant to be. I particularly felt for the Army machine-gunners, in their camouflage, who had to lie prone on the waterlogged ground and fire a belt or two of machine-gun blanks. They could comfort themselves with the thought that their soaking in the mud and slush was less lethal than the hail of bombs and bullets their counterparts faced 66 years earlier.

The Navy had stationed some small ships in the harbour, and they fired their guns too. It was impossible to see them in the blinding rain, but they added to the cacophony. An old DC3 flew over us, followed by a couple of FA-18 fighters from Tindal Air Base. I didn't envy the pilots. I would guess that the cloud base was no more than 400 feet, and Darwin has its share of tall buildings. Flying low enough for us to see them took skill and courage. I couldn't help thinking how lucky the Japanese had been with the weather on 19 February 1942. If we are looking for failures, we might add a sour note of condemnation for the weather gods who failed to deliver a normal wet day on 19 February a lifetime ago. They might have saved the town.

There was a recurring theme in the speeches. The rest of Australia is still ignorant about what happened in Darwin, not just in the first two raids but in the 62 that followed. The defenders of northern Australia feel neglected and forgotten. The government decision to conceal the full horror of the raids reverberates to this day. I can only agree with the speakers. While researching this book, I was astonished by how little Australians know of the succession of bloody battles fought under their skies.

After the Cenotaph ceremony, there was a reception in the lobby of the Northern Territory Assembly building, and I chatted briefly to the engaging Chief Minister, Paul Henderson. He was a former Education Minister, and he thought Australian history books needed to be rewritten to give proper space to Australia's northern war. Again, I can only agree. The Australian War Memorial in Canberra gives it a cursory few metres of glass case while devoting huge floor space to single actions such as the sinking of the *Emden*. Darwin could contribute a bit of self-help of its own. The excellent Northern Territory Museum and Art Gallery, near Mindil Beach, devotes huge space and energy to recreating the devastating noise and damage from Cyclone Tracy. It might like to do the same for the bombing of Darwin.

One of the more notable aspects of the commemoration is that the numbers attending have been swelling over the years. The 1000 or so people who watched at the Cenotaph in 2008 formed one of the largest crowds ever. Two days later the *Northern Territory News* ran an editorial under the headline 'Military past an attraction'. The leader writer noted that tourism is a cut-throat business and operators must forever look for new ways to attract visitors. He continued: 'The Territory has one under-exploited attraction—its military history. It has been suggested that a military heritage trail be marked out for visitors. This is a good idea.'

At first I was irked by the editorial, which seemed to me to trivialise what is, after all, the worst disaster on Australian soil. But then I softened. Australians spend large sums to visit remote battlefields such as Gallipoli and to walk the Kokoda Trail. If more of them felt like a trip to Darwin, to walk around the gun sites, the oil tunnels, the makeshift airfields, and to visit the Aviation Heritage Centre, they might be as surprised as I was at what they find.

Epilogue

Whatever happened to . . .?

THE CITY

Darwin remained a military camp for the rest of the Second World War. The ships sunk during the first raid stayed as hazards in Port Darwin until long after the war. (See The Sunken Ships, below.) Many of the wrecked civil buildings went unrepaired until the return of the civilian population, which did not get under way until 1946. Tragedy struck on Christmas Eve, 1974, when Cyclone Tracy flattened the town once more, killing 71 people. Darwin was patiently rebuilt, this time on more storm-proof foundations.

Today Darwin is surely one of Australia's most attractive cities. The lush green tropical landscape, wide streets, busy shops and excellent restaurants make it entirely liveable. While it is now in every sense a modern city, Darwin retains an attractively louche character, a charming reminder of its frontier past. It thrives on tourism. Grey nomads stream through in their camper vans and four-wheel-drives, or fly in to catch the Ghan train south for the two-day journey via Alice Springs through the red heart of Australia to Adelaide. Young backpackers, mostly Australian and European, treat Darwin as a staging post on whatever epic journey has taken their fancy. It is the trading centre for the booming mining, agricultural, fisheries and forestry industries of the Northern Territory. Ironically, the military today is a major contributor to the

Northern Territory's GDP, with some 13,000 Army and Air Force personnel and their families based there. The lessons of 1942 and 1943 have been well learned: Australian governments now regard a strong northern line of defence as essential for Australia's protection.

THE MEN

Aubrey Abbott remained in his post of Administrator of the Northern Territory until 26 May 1946, when he left the Territory on sick leave. He was replaced the next day. In Sydney he wrote a much-admired book on the Northern Territory, *Australia's Frontier Province*, published in 1950. He retired to Bowral in New South Wales and continued with occasional writing. Whatever his failings, there can be no doubt that Abbott's affection for the Northern Territory was profound. He died in Sydney on 30 April 1975, and was accorded a state funeral at St Mark's Church, Darling Point.

Captain Mitsuo Fuchida survived the war. He was struck down by appendicitis on 27 May 1942, a week before the Battle of Midway, and took no part in that decisive action. (See Nagumo Force, below.) He was rescued from the sinking *Akagi* during the battle, and returned to Japan on the hospital ship *Hikawa Maru*. Back in Japan, he and others who knew the truth of Midway were kept isolated from their fellow countrymen while their government tried to conceal the immensity of the Midway disaster. He spent the rest of the war at a desk, or teaching at the Naval War College. His subsequent story is both unexpected and exotic. In 1950 General MacArthur, still governing Japan in the wake of that country's defeat, asked to meet the destroyer of Pearl Harbor. On his way to the meeting, Fuchida was handed a pamphlet in the street by an American Christian missionary. He underwent a profound conversion, and became a zealous promoter of Christianity in Japan, and later in the United States. He died in Japan on 30 May 1976. Before his death he earned a modest supplementary income from books and articles, and as an advisor to makers of Hollywood films featuring the Pearl Harbor attack. The quick-eyed will find his name buried in the small print of the credits on many of them.

Wing Commander Sturt Griffith survived the criticism of the Lowe Report. In civilian life he was an engineer and patent attorney, and in June 1942 he transferred to No. 5 Maintenance Group in Sydney. In December 1943 he was promoted to Group Captain and assumed command of No. 1 Aircraft Depot in Laverton, Victoria. After the war he took to testing and writing about cars as the *Sydney Morning Herald*'s motoring correspondent. He famously tested cars to their limits, hurling them around a course he had designed, near Leura, in the Blue Mountains west of Sydney, while junior *Herald* staff sat in terror in the front passenger seat. Car manufacturers were equally terrified: a Sturt Griffith report could make or break a new model. He died on 14 December 1979.

Commander Herb Kriloff survived the war, something he still looks on with awe and surprise. He transferred from USS *William B. Preston* to command a destroyer in the bitter submarine war in the North Atlantic. After the war he worked as a research engineer in the US. He then moved to the Portuguese island of Madeira, where he lived for 25 years. He now lives in Melbourne, Australia, with his remarkable English wife Dagmar, whom he met in Sydney in 1942 and married in Perth a year later. Readers who keep back issues of Australian *Vogue* might like to look at page 52 of the July 2007 issue, where the vivacious and stylish Dagmar models a few of her favourite outfits and dispenses some worldly and excellent fashion advice. She turned 100 in January 2009.

Charles Lowe, later Sir Charles Lowe, became one of the most respected Australian judges of the 20th century. He enjoyed an enviable reputation for having his decisions upheld on appeal, even when the appeal went as far as the Privy Council. He presided over two further Royal Commissions, including the high-profile Royal Commission into the allegation that the Menzies government had adopted a 'defeatist' plan to abandon the defence of northern and western Australia and retreat behind a 'Brisbane Line'. In addition to his legal career, Lowe became a much-admired chancellor of the University of Melbourne. He died in 1969.

Gunner Jack Mulholland survived the war. He returned to his old civilian job in banking, and continued as a banker until his retirement in 1981. Now a widower well into his eighties, he lives in Wyoming, a suburb of Gosford, north of Sydney, and stays in contact with survivors of the 1942 air raid. His book *Darwin Bombed: An A/A Gunner's Reflections* is a vivid and attractively modest account of the gunners' roles from 1940 to the end of the war. Jack is a very tall man, and his role firing the 3.7-inch gun required him to stand on a platform beside the gun with his whole body exposed well above the protecting revetment. During an air raid, the Japanese had the better part of two and a half metres of Jack and his platform as a target. Happily, they consistently missed both.

2nd Lieutenant Robert Oestreicher was awarded the Distinguished Service Cross for his part in the defence of Darwin. However the citation credited him with shooting down only one enemy aircraft, not two. On 27 February 1942 he was ordered to join the US Army Air Corp's 49th Pursuit Group based in Bankstown, Sydney. On his way south his Kittyhawk, the only fighter to survive the Darwin raid, crashed in Cloncurry, and was wrecked. Oestreicher emerged from the crash, in his own words, 'without a scratch'. He continued flying to the end of the war, including a posting in Darwin with the 49th. On 19 February 1982 he returned to the Northern Territory to accept a small plaque presented by the grateful people of the Cox Peninsula.

Group Captain Frederick Scherger was the only senior official, military or civilian, to face disciplinary action over the Darwin raid. He had been the highest-ranking Air Force officer at Area Command Headquarters on the day of the raid, and therefore the most senior officer of the most conspicuously unsuccessful service. He was relieved of his command two months later. Scherger understandably felt hard done by, and chose the high-risk strategy of appealing against the decision to Arthur Drakeford, the Minister for the Air, over the heads of the RAAF Chiefs of Staff. He was supported in his appeal by, among others, Commissioner Lowe. In service ethos, going to a politician rather than keeping the matter

214 AN AWKWARD TRUTH

inside the RAAF family would have cost him dearly had he lost the appeal. In the event, he won the day. His career was unchecked, and he went on to attain the rank of Air Chief Marshal and become head of the RAAF and later Chairman of the Chiefs of Staff Committee—in effect the head of all Australian defence forces. He died in 1984.

Judge Wells remained in Darwin throughout the war. At a time when Administrator Abbott had moved with most of the public service to Alice Springs, Wells became de facto administrator of Darwin, and the handful of remaining civilians looked to him for leadership and advice. Circumstances were often difficult: at one point he conducted court hearings outdoors, under a tree. Wells continued as Judge of the Supreme Court of the Northern Territory after the war. He had a stroke in February 1951 and retired in 1952. He died in Darwin on 13 September 1954. His most notorious judgment, the death sentence imposed on an Aboriginal man named Dhakiyarr in 1934, is remembered in Darwin today. Inside the Supreme Court building, a monument of traditional Aboriginal artefacts commemorates an act of reconciliation between Dhakiyarr's family and the family of the policeman he killed.

THE SHIPS
USS *Houston*, the heavy cruiser that almost single-handedly held off the Japanese air attack on the ill-fated convoy for Koepang, was one of three Allied cruisers and five destroyers sunk 12 days later at the Battle of the Java Sea, on 27 February 1942. The battle marked the beginning of the end for ABDA, the ill-considered joint command of American, British, Dutch and Australian forces. The Japanese lost no fighting ships, though four loaded troop transports were sunk and an unrecorded number of men killed. The Allies suffered 2300 dead. It was one of the worst Allied naval defeats of the Pacific War.

HMAS *Platypus*, the base ship that fought back so bravely during the first raid, survived the war. She remained in Darwin until 1 January 1943, then moved to Cairns and later to New Guinea, operating in the Madang, Hollandia and Morotai areas until November 1945. On

20 February 1958 she was sold for scrap to Mitsubishi Shoji Kaisha Ltd of Tokyo, and shipped in pieces to Japan aboard the salvage vessel *Tukoshima Maru*.

MV *Manunda* survived the war. She was returned to civilian service in 1947 and operated as a passenger and cruise ship between Melbourne and Cairns until 1956. She was then sold for scrap, to a Japanese ship breaker.

Nagumo Force, the formidable aircraft-carrier fleet that rewrote the rules of modern naval warfare with its attack on Pearl Harbor, had one more success after the Darwin raid. Mitsuo Fuchida again led a force of 36 Zero fighters, 54 Val dive-bombers and 90 Kate bombers in an attack on Colombo, Ceylon (now Sri Lanka). They were followed by a second force of 80 Vals. The British lost four ships sunk and 27 aircraft destroyed, with 424 dead. The Japanese lost five aircraft. Nagumo Force then returned to the Pacific as the spearhead of what was to prove the decisive naval battle of the Pacific War. It attacked the American base at Midway, intending to invade and hold it as a staging post to the Hawaiian Islands and Pearl Harbor. American code-breakers gave accurate advance warning, and Admiral Chester Nimitz was able to make good use of American aircraft, both land and carrier based. Luck also favoured the Americans. The result was a horrendous defeat for the Imperial Japanese Navy, with all four of their key aircraft carriers sent to the bottom along with a heavy cruiser, and severe damage to other ships in the force. While the Japanese hung on tenaciously for more than three years after the Battle of Midway, the tide of the war had turned. Nagumo Force had been a decisive element in the Imperial Japanese Navy's run of successes, and its destruction proved equally decisive in ending Japanese command of the Pacific seas and skies.

The Sunken Ships *British Motorist*, *Kelat*, *Mauna Loa*, *Mavie*, *Meigs*, *Neptuna*, *Peary* and *Zealandia* remained on the bottom of Port Darwin for the rest of the war and long after. Amid some controversy, the job of removing them was finally handed over to the Japanese salvage company Fujita. In conditions of tight security, the salvage work began in 1959.

The US government refused permission for the Japanese to remove any of the lost cargo, and the bottom of Port Darwin still plays host to a collection of trucks, jeeps, motorcycles, Bren-gun carriers, ammunition and some lengths of railway line scattered from the holds and decks of the ships. The Fujita salvage team cut up most of the wrecks for scrap but refloated *British Motorist* and used her for storage and as crew quarters. Three sunken Catalina seaplanes also remain on the bottom of Port Darwin, ignored by the Japanese salvage team. 'A good dive for small groups,' the Darwin Dive Centre advises on its website.

MV *Tulagi*, used as a troop transport and civilian evacuation ship and beached after damage in the first raid, was quickly refloated and continued to supply Australian and US forces in the Pacific area until 1944. On 27 March 1944, *Tulagi* was attacked by the German submarine U532 en route from Sydney to Colombo. She was hit by a single torpedo and sank within 20 seconds, killing 39 aboard. Then began one of the epic survival stories of the Second World War. The survivors drifted on two rafts tied together by a rope. After more than a month, the rope snapped. One raft with eight survivors was never seen again. The second raft, with seven on board, drifted to the island of Bijoutier in the Seychelles, where the survivors were found and moved first to the island of Alphonse, then on to Bombay and safety.

USS *William B. Preston* left Darwin immediately after the raid and headed down the west coast of Australia looking for a suitable dockyard to repair the very substantial damage she suffered. *Willy B* stopped at Broome and Fremantle but, unable to find a yard, continued to Sydney. There, she completed repairs at the Cockatoo Island naval dockyard on 31 May 1942. Maintaining her impressive record for being in the right place at dangerous moments, *Willy B* returned to anchor in Sydney Harbour a few hours ahead of the midget submarine attack that evening. She survived unmolested and continued to operate in Australian waters until 1944, before moving on to New Guinea and later the US. On 6 November 1946 she was sold to the Northern Metals Company of Philadelphia for scrap.

Appendix I

Evacuation notice

In a leaflet distributed to every Darwin household on 15 December 1941, the two most senior air-raid wardens, Arthur Miller and Edgar Harrison, set out the rules for the evacuation of the civilian population. The initial notice gave no clue as to when this might take place or who would be evacuated. It left the strong impression that the evacuation would apply to the whole civilian population, not just the women and children. This certainly made more credible the Chinese whispers on the day of the raid to the effect that all civilians were to leave by order of the military authorities.

The notice is amateurishly written and shows every sign of haste and wishful thinking. Its author also had a terrible Weakness for Capital Letters.

NATIONAL EMERGENCY SERVICES

Civil Defence—Darwin, N.T.

SPECIAL—Notice to all householders, and occupiers of dwelling houses or any other habitation.

In the event of Enemy Raid or other form of Attack upon or in the vicinity of Darwin, it may become necessary for the Authorities to Issue an Order for the Evacuation of the Civil Population to some other place or places of safety.

Such Order to Evacuate will not be issued until after the Proper Authority or Authorities has or have issued a Proclamation declaring a State of Emergency.

The Civil Population will, after such State of emergency has been declared, receive from the Senior Air-raid Warden a Notice to Prepare for Evacuation.

Such Notice will be issued by one or all of the following methods:

1. Written Notice issued to every Householder or Occupier of a Dwelling House or other habitation.
2. Verbal Notice issued to every householder or Occupier of a Dwelling House or other habitation.
3. A GENERAL ASSEMBLY of the Civil Population at their respective Zone Headquarters.
4. Special Notice in the Northern Standard Newspaper, and/or Notices posted in prominent places throughout the area.

Immediately such Notice of Intention to Evacuate has been issued, each and every person warned to Evacuate will make all necessary preparations to do so.

Each and every Evacuee will be entitled to take the following articles, as personal belongings:

(a) One small Calico Bag containing Hair and Tooth Brushes, Toilet Soap, Towel, etc. (personal only)
(b) One Suit Case or Bag containing Clothing, and such shall not exceed 35 lbs. gross weight.
(c) A Maximum of two Blankets per person.
(d) Eating and Drinking Utensils.

(e) One 2 gal. Water Bag filled for each family.

NOTE: Officers in charge of Evacuation have the power to examine luggage and determine what constitutes personal luggage.

The Senior Warden of the Group will communicate, through his Wardens, full instructions to every Evacuee as to method of Evacuation and time and place of Assembly.

Every Evacuee will be provided with IDENTIFICATION CARDS in duplicate, one of which will be handed to the Evacuation Officer on DEMAND, and the other KEPT ON THE PERSON.

EVACUEES WILL BE DIVIDED INTO SECTIONS OF FOURTEEN (14) PERSONS, ONE OF WHOM WILL BE DETAILED AS SECTION LEADER AND RESPONSIBLE FOR THE CONDUCT OF THE GROUP OR SECTION.

RATIONS WILL BE PROVIDED BY THE AUTHORITIES AND ISSUED TO THE SECTION LEADERS FOR DISTRIBUTION.

PERSONS OTHER THAN THOSE TO BE EVACUATED WILL REMAIN IN DARWIN, AND OBEY THE INSTRUCTIONS ISSUED BY THE CHIEF AIR RAID WARDEN.

No Evacuee shall take, or attempt to take, with him or her, any domestic pet, either animal or bird, and any such pets owned by the Evacuees should be destroyed prior to the Evacuation.

No facilities will exist for feeding of these pets after the Evacuation.

Domestic Poultry would be an Auxiliary Food Supply for those remaining in Darwin, and as such will not be destroyed under any circumstances.

No person or persons will be entitled or allowed to use any privately owned vehicle, or vehicle plying for Public Hire, for the purpose of Evacuation from Darwin, and no method other than that ordered by The Commandant 7th Military District, and affected by the A.R.P. Authorities under such jurisdiction will be permitted in any circumstance.

N.B.—Any Person or Persons acting contrary to these Instructions or additional instructions issued by the A.R.P. Authorities may cause serious upset to the Evacuation Scheme, thereby endangering the lives of themselves and others.

Any Breach of the said Instructions will therefore be dealt with under the National Security Act, and the Offender or Offenders severely punished.

A.R. MILLER, Chief Warden, A.R.P.

EDGAR T. HARRISON, Permanent Officer Civil Defence

DARWIN, N.T.

December, 1941

Appendix II

Report of the Lowe Commission

B y any standards, the Lowe Commission investigation into the 19 February 1942 air raids was a remarkable piece of work. As we have seen, Mr Justice Lowe accepted the commission on 3 March, flew to Darwin in the early hours of the next morning, and began hearing witnesses the day after that. He sent a first cabled report on 6 March urging the government to station fighter aircraft in Darwin. By 25 March he had heard 102 witnesses, at sittings in Darwin and Melbourne. On the 27th he handed over his first, 10,271-word report, highlights of which are reproduced below. He then read through all 917 pages of the transcript of evidence, together with two fat folders of exhibits, including diaries, log books, written reports, copies of cables, intelligence reports, action reports and diagrams, and on 9 April produced a 2608-word addendum. The report and its afterthought are models of clarity and commonsense.

What follows is an edited version of the full report, concentrating on its most important findings. Anyone wishing to read the report uncut can find it online at www.naa.gov.au, under reference A431 and titled *Bombing of Darwin—Report by Mr Justice Lowe*. The original is held by the Canberra office of the NAA, and is available for reading there.

Readers may raise an eyebrow over the sub-section on page 231 dealing with fifth-column activity and wonder why I did not mention it in the main narrative. The evidence Lowe refers to came from Wing Commander Gerald Packer, the RAAF's Director of Air Intelligence. While Packer had hard intelligence of local Japanese releasing meteorological balloons to assist in the high-level bombing of Port Moresby, the evidence of local Japanese support for the Darwin air raid is somewhere between thin and nonexistent. Packer gave no dates or physical evidence for the alleged discovery of the balloons, nor did he have any logs giving times, dates and contents of alleged intercepted radio transmissions. Packer himself did not assert the truth of the story, nor did it form part of his first evidence to the Commission. Quite correctly, when he heard the rumours a few days later, he asked to appear again before Commissioner Lowe and pass on what he had been told. Lowe seems not to have believed it, and nor do I.

COMMONWEALTH OF AUSTRALIA
COMMISSION OF INQUIRY
UNDER THE NATIONAL SECURITY (INQUIRIES)
REGULATIONS
IN THE MATTER OF AN INQUIRY CONCERNING
THE CIRCUMSTANCES CONNECTED WITH THE
ATTACK MADE BY ENEMY AIRCRAFT AT DARWIN ON
19TH FEBRUARY 1942
BEFORE HIS HONOUR MR JUSTICE LOWE,
COMMISSIONER
FIRST REPORT OF COMMISSIONER
To The Hon. The Minister of State for Defence
Co-ordination:

I have restricted my consideration to matters which throw light upon the raid itself, the damage arising from it, and the measures to be taken to prevent a like result following from a similar raid. But there are many indications in the evidence of this historical background affecting opinions expressed either in documents sent to the Services or the Government, or in evidence given before me, and exaggerated statements have been made which the evidence does not support. Specific illustrations appear in—

(a) The suggestion that shipping in the harbour at the time of the raid was unduly large because of labour troubles at Darwin. With the possible exception of the *Zealandia* and the *Port Mar* there is no foundation in any evidence given before me for this allegation. Delays undoubtedly occurred and the performance of labour was often unsatisfactory, but these results seem to have been mainly due to lack of facilities in the port equipment, defects of management, and the fact that climatic conditions affected the output of labour as compared with Southern ports.

(b) One official report refers to an exodus of workmen from the town preceded by the Secretary of the North Australia's Workers' Union, Mr. Mick Ryan, and another states, 'Every wharf labourer left the town immediately after the raids and most of them were understood to have mobbed the train which departed Thursday evening.' These statements are only true in the sense that Mr. Ryan and the wharf labourers acted as the mass of civilian population did in leaving the town, and I shall have to refer later to the lack of leadership which, in my opinion, was responsible for this conduct.

(c) A further statement refers to the probable refusal of train crews to perform their duties and to desert. There is no truth in this statement and it was afterwards withdrawn by the person making it.

The evidence also disclosed the existence in some sections of the population of a lack of confidence in and resentment towards the Administrator. It so happened that most of the witnesses who gave evidence before me on this matter were of this section, and I feel that it is at least dangerous to draw an inference on partial evidence against the Administrator when an examination of all the relevant evidence which may well cover a lengthy period might lead to a different conclusion.

An allegation was made that the Administrator on the day of the raids and after the second raid had removed liquor and crockery and clothing from Government House by the use of police officers when the condition of affairs in the town urgently required the attendance of those police officers for the duties of preserving order. That the Administrator did order the removal of liquor is, I think, plain and indeed not disputed, but I can find no reason for criticizing his action in that respect.

Had action been taken in regard to liquor stocks in hotels in the same way or by effectively picketing it some of the disorder which followed might have been avoided. The allegation against the Administrator in regard to moving crockery on the day of the raid was emphatically denied by him and the Police Superintendent, and has not I think, been established, although the next day or the day following that the crockery, which was Government property, was removed to Alice Springs. The only clothing which I think was removed on the 19th February was contained in certain suit-cases which were taken by Mrs. Abbott, on departing after the raid for Alice Springs.

THE RAIDS.

The first raid commenced just before 10 a.m. I have accepted the evidence of a witness who fixes the time as 9.58 a.m., as he particularly noted it and as he was the person to receive the first warning of the enemy approach. A number of high altitude bombers came in from the south-east of the town, flying in a 'V' formation and at a height which was variously estimated by witnesses but was probably not less than 15,000 feet. One formation consisted of 27 bombers. The bombing was that which is known as pattern bombing in which the individual machines drop their bombs at a signal from the Squadron Leader.

The first bombs fell over the harbour. Having completed their run this group of bombers after a circuit returned and dropped bombs again in pattern over the town. Much difference of opinion was expressed by witnesses as to the number of machines engaged in this attack. I am inclined to think that the view of Air Marshal Williams is correct and that the number of high altitude bombers did not much (if at all) exceed 27.

After the high altitude bombers there came a number of dive bombers escorted by fighters, and these attacked the shipping in the harbour. The number of dive bombers and fighters is uncertain, but I think it probable that Air Marshal Williams is correct in his view that the total number of high altitude dive bombers and fighters did not exceed 50. The cause of confusion lies I think in the impression conveyed to witnesses that the same squadron returning for another run was an added group of enemy planes. An attack was also made about the same time by enemy machines on the Royal Australian Air Force aerodrome and on the civil aerodrome, and by machine-gun fire on the hospital at Berrima [sic] some 9 miles from the town, and in each case a good deal of damage was done which I shall presently particularize. The "All-clear" was sounded about 10.40 a.m.

THE DAMAGE.

(a) *On Water.*—The attack upon the harbour caused great damage to installations and shipping. The seaward limb of the pier was struck, part of the decking was destroyed, and the metal attachments (rails, &c.) completely distorted. Alongside the inner limb of the pier when the raid started were berthed the *Neptuna* and the *Barossa*. The *Neptuna* had among her cargo a quantity of explosives. She was set on fire by enemy bombs, as was also the *Barossa* on the opposite side of the pier. After the enemy planes had departed the *Neptuna* blew up and caused the destruction of a large section of the inner limb of the pier, and it is probable, too, that the *Barossa* was injured by this explosion. The damage to the pier is thus seen to be very extensive. The outer limb cannot be used and repair to the inner limb will take some months to effect.

Other ships lost in addition to the *Neptuna* were the *Zealandia*, the *Meigs*, the *Maunaloa* [*sic*], the *British Motorist* and the U.S.S. destroyer *Peary*. Ships damaged were the *Barossa*, the *Port Mar* (U.S.) and the hospital ship *Manunda*. In addition, two Catalina flying boats were destroyed. All these losses were in the Darwin Harbour. I have not attempted to determine in what order the enemy inflicted the damage suffered by these ships.

In addition, the enemy planes on their way to or returning from Darwin destroyed another Catalina flying boat and two American vessels, the *Don Isidro* and the *Florence Dee* [*sic*].

(b) *Oil Tanks*.—The oil tanks suffered very little damage and relatively little oil was lost. The damage done to the tanks probably occurred from shrapnel or portions of shell casings or by fragments thrown up by the explosion of the *Neptuna*.

(c) *On Land*.—On land the Administrator's office was hit by an enemy bomb and is a total loss. The front part of Government House had been affected by bomb blast, but the rear portion appears not to have been injured. The Police Barracks are a total loss, together with the Police Station and the Government Offices attached. The Post Office, the Telegraph Office, the Cable Office and the Postmaster's residence all suffered either by a direct hit or blast and are a complete loss. The Civil Hospital was much damaged and it is estimated that the cost of repairs will be in the neighbourhood of £25,000. There was some damage done to two or three private residences, which are probably also to be counted a complete loss. Some huge craters are said to have been caused by bombs of 1,050 lb. weight.

A second raid occurred about 11.55 a.m. and lasted for about 20 to 25 minutes. This raid was by upwards of 27 heavy bombers which flew at a great height and indulged in pattern bombing, more than 200 bombs being dropped according to one observer. These bombers were unescorted by fighters. This raid caused much damage to the surface of the Royal Australian Air Force Station and to the Hospital thereon. No attempt was made in the second raid to bomb the town or the port.

(d) *The Aerodrome.*—I have not sought to discriminate between the damage done on the Royal Australian Air Force Station by these two raids. The hangars and repairs shops were destroyed, the hospital damaged, and damage was also done to the hutments. The losses in aircraft were as follows:—

Australian—

6 Hudsons destroyed on the ground.

1 Hudson in hangar badly damaged.

1 Wirraway badly damaged.

American—

8 P.40's destroyed in the air.

2 P.40's destroyed on the ground.

1 B.24 destroyed on the ground.

1 P.40 damaged in the air.

(e) *Railways.*—The railway line at a point 4 miles out of Darwin was damaged by the dropping of one 250-lb. G.P. [general purpose] bomb close to the permanent way. This was repaired in a few hours, when traffic resumed in a normal fashion. When the pier was bombed a railway engine was blown into the water and remains there. The railway lines on the pier were extensively damaged.

(f) *Other Utilities.*—No damage was done to the water supply of the town generally, though the destruction of portion of the pier destroyed with it the water and oil pipes which were attached, and water pipes on the Royal Australian Air Force aerodrome were also put out of use. The destruction of the Post Office staff put out of action the telephone system of the town, and the electric lighting system was also affected.

LOSS OF LIFE.

The extent of the casualties incurred in the raids has been investigated for me with great thoroughness by Mr Alderman, and I adopt the conclusions which he has arrived at in his inquiry. It is impossible to speak with certainty of the number of people who lost their lives but I am satisfied that the number is approximately 250, and I doubt whether any further investigation will result in ascertaining a more precise figure. [. . .]

INJURED.

Mr. Alderman satisfied himself that it was not possible to compile a complete list of those injured in the raid. The evidence before me also suggests that no accurate estimate of the injured can be obtained, but various suggestions were made, and I think that the number of 400 is probably in excess of those who sustained any substantial injury. An estimate of between 300 and 400 is probably as accurate as any that can be made.

WARNING OF THE RAID.

[. . .] The delay in giving the general warning was fraught with disaster. It is impossible to say with certainty what would have happened if the warning had been promptly given when received by Royal Australian Air Force Operations at 9.37 a.m., but it is at least probable that a number of men who lost their lives while working on ships at the pier might have escaped to a place of safety.

There is other evidence to indicate that this particular Service was conducted with some laxity. No log book was kept before 6th February, 1942, and the log book kept after that date discloses a gap in the entries between 16th and 20th February, 1942.

MEANS OF DEFENCE TO THE ENEMY RAID.

The only defence to the enemy raid over the harbour and over the town was by means of anti-aircraft guns and such defence as the ships in the harbour possessed. There was no defence by air. The evidence before me was all to the effect that the anti-aircraft batteries operated efficiently and that the personnel of the A.M.F. performed very creditably in their baptism of fire. Their earlier shooting seemed somewhat short of the planes at which they were firing, but later their range was better and the defence became effective. The ships in the harbour defended themselves vigorously but with little success in most cases. At the Royal Australian Air Force Station the American P.40's which were grounded attempted to take off and to attack the Japanese planes. They were, without exception, shot down. Thereafter the only defence offered was by means of anti-aircraft fire.

DAMAGE TO THE ENEMY.

There is no very clear evidence as to the damage sustained by the enemy. The best estimate I can make is that the enemy lost five planes certainly and probably five others. It was stated by Air Commodore Wilson that the Tokyo Radio Station had broadcast that the Japanese had lost 23 planes in the attack. Apart from this I do not know the origin of such a statement, and I am far from satisfied that the Japanese loss was so high.

CONDITIONS WHICH DEVELOPED AFTER THE RAIDS.

(a) The Town.—Immediately following the raids, the morale of the townspeople was not noticeably affected, and there is evidence to show that nothing in the nature of panic then developed. Had there been effective leadership at that stage I think that normal conditions might very rapidly have been attained. But leadership was conspicuously lacking. Houses were abandoned in haste. I myself observed in the Darwin Hotel tables upon which drinks remained half-consumed, letters started but not finished, papers strewn about, beds unmade in bedrooms, and other signs of a very hasty exit.

On the night of the 19th looting broke out in some of the business premises and sporadic looting occurred thereafter even to the time when the Commission was sitting in Darwin. This looting was indulged in both by civilians and members of the Military Forces. It is hard to believe that, if proper supervision had been exercised throughout, such looting could have gone on.

I am satisfied that the Administrator was not fully acquainted with the conditions which were developing and the telegrams which he sent to the Minister for the Interior failed to give any adequate idea of those conditions. In my opinion, this condition of affairs was largely due to the fact that there had been no adequate foresight of what might result after an enemy raid, and consequently no plans made for the rapid resumption of normal conditions when the raid ceased. There had been an unfortunate difference between the Administrator and the A.R.P. organization in January. I am clear that this difference prevented the police being aided by officers of the A.R.P in preserving law and order after the raid.

(b) *The Air Station.*—The effects of the raid at the Air Station were extremely serious. Much damage had been done, and the personnel, most of whom were experiencing enemy attack for the first time, were shaken by the attack. But at that stage (I am convinced) with competent leadership the personnel would rapidly have resumed their duties.

An order, however, was given by the Station Commander, which I think was extremely unfortunate. He directed that the men should gather in order to be fed at a point half a mile down the road from the aerodrome and half a mile into the bush. The order was completely distorted and by repetition ultimately reached the men in various forms. Some men stated that they were ordered to go 3 miles, others 7 miles, and others 11 miles. Many of the men simply took to the bush. Some were found as far afield as Batchelor, some at Adelaide River, one was found at Daly Waters, and another, by an extreme feat, reached Melbourne in thirteen days.

The Air Station itself was practically deserted. For several days afterwards men were straggling back to the Station, and at a parade on 23rd February, the muster showed 278 men missing. As the casualties were very small, the result can only be regarded as deplorable.

FIFTH COLUMN ACTIVITY.

One matter to which I was asked to direct my attention was whether there was reason to believe that the raids had in any way been assisted by enemy action within Australia itself. Up to almost the last day of the sittings, I should have had to answer this question with a plain negative, because all the witnesses to whom that question was put agreed that there was no foundation for such a suggestion. On the last day but one of the sittings in Melbourne, however, evidence was given which I think cannot be disregarded though it may still leave unchanged a negative answer as to these raids. I was told that meteorological balloons had been found in the vicinity of the aerodrome at Darwin. Similar balloons had been noted at Port Moresby concurrently with a raid upon that town. Their purpose is to indicate air currents in the upper air so as to guide the pilot of a bomber in the operation of his bomb release.

At Port Moresby the matter was immediately investigated, and the release was found to be almost certainly due to the presence of Japanese. The discovery of similar balloons at Darwin led to observation being made, the result of which was that messages in Japanese Morse were detected both outwardly and after a lapse of 40 minutes inwardly towards a point in the direction of Daly Waters. These facts, coupled with the disappearance from Darwin on the outbreak of war of Japanese then residing there, who have not since been traced, furnishes at least a suspicion that there is activity in the neighbourhood of Darwin which may be not unconnected with the raids which took place.

INSTALLATIONS AVOIDED BY THE JAPANESE.

It may not be inappropriate here to remark that there was a large body of opinion expressed before me that the Japanese had deliberately refrained from attacking the oil tanks, the floating dock and the water supply and that, had they wished to destroy any of these installations, they could in the absence of air opposition—which existed on that day—have easily effected their purpose. It is unnecessary to dilate upon the inference that is to be drawn from this abstention on the part of the Japanese. It will be appreciated no doubt that if the opinion of these witnesses is sound, such abstention holds a grave threat of later enemy action against Darwin.[1]

PREPAREDNESS OF THE SERVICES IN RELATION TO THE RAID.

(a) The Navy.—The Navy, in my opinion, had taken all proper steps in preparation for an attack. [. . .]

(b) The Military Forces.—The only part of the Military Forces required for action in the raid itself were the anti-aircraft equipment and personnel; as I have already indicated in an earlier part of this report, the conduct of the personnel is to be highly commended. [. . .]

(c) The Air Force.—Group Captain Scherger acted in command of the north-west area. He was present in Darwin on the day of the raid and acted, in my opinion, with great courage and energy. I desire to record the view that, on all the evidence before me, his conduct in connexion with the raid was deserving of the highest praise. Another officer whose conduct during and after the raid merits commendation is Squadron Leader Swan.

The officer in command of the Darwin Station was Wing-Commander Griffith. He also has had but a short period of service at Darwin, coming there about the beginning of February. [. . .]

It is probably unfair to attribute blame for this lack of organization and dispersal wholly to the Commander of the Station whose service there had been so short, but, in my opinion, the condition of the Station was a prime factor in the extent of the losses which followed.

(d) The Civil Authorities.—What I have already said indicates that I feel the Civil Authorities were lacking in foresight in not envisaging the possible conditions which would follow upon the raid. The result was that no plan had been formed to deal with conditions such as those which arose. If the Civil Authorities found themselves insufficiently equipped to meet the situation, I think the

Administrator should have, at an earlier stage than he did, sought the aid of the Military Authorities. [. . .]

(Sgd.) CHARLES J. LOWE
Commissioner.
27th March, 1942

FULL AND FINAL REPORT OF COMMISSIONER
TO THE RIGHT HON. THE MINISTER FOR DEFENCE
CO-ORDINATION:

Having now perused the transcript of the evidence taken at Darwin, I have the honour to make this supplementary and final report upon the attacks made by enemy aircraft at Darwin on the 19th February, 1942. [. . .]

FURTHER DETAILS OF MATTERS REPORTED UPON

(a) *Naval Installations and Equipment.*—H.M.A.S. *Platypus* is a repair ship. Acting-Commander Tonkin gave evidence that there was not sufficient equipment on the ship to enable the full complement of the vessel to get safely away if the ship were sunk. In addition he said that the ship required further guns to give it adequate protection. He suggested that six of the Oerlikon type and also Breda guns were required to attain that object. In his view, unless the ship were adequately armed there was grave danger that she would be destroyed and not be able to discharge her function of repair ship. No other repair ship is available at Darwin.

(b) *Pier.*—Much evidence was given that the pier before its destruction was quite insufficient for the handling of shipping under war-time conditions. The main report has indicated the damage which was done to this pier and an indication was given of the time requisite for the repair of the pier.

(c) *Oil Pipes.*—I drew attention in my Report to the destruction of the oil pipes which were attached to the pier. There was evidence before me that it would be better to adopt the practice which is in existence in many parts of the world of taking the oil pipe under the water to a buoy in the harbour and there supplying ships.

(d) *Minesweeping Equipment.*—The Naval Commandant at Darwin drew my attention to the danger of destruction to minesweeping equipment from the lack of aircraft at Darwin. I quote from his evidence as the most effective way of emphasizing the point he made. He said: On the 5th March—

. . . I received a report from the *Deloraine* to the effect that she was being bombed by enemy aircraft and required assistance. Application was made to A.C.H. (Area Combined Head-quarters) in the normal manner for this assistance within five minutes of the attack commencing. There were enemy fighter aircraft in the air. I was informed by A.C.H. that no fighter aircraft were available in Darwin to render assistance to the *Deloraine* and she got none. She was not damaged by a hit but there were some very near misses which were sufficiently close to put out of action the anti-submarine detection apparatus. It was purely accidental that the ship was not either sunk or severely damaged and put out of action until replacement parts were obtained from the south. This ship happened to be the only ship in northern or north-western Australian waters fitted with the necessary apparatus for sweeping the magnetic and acoustic mine.

(e) Royal Australian Air Force.—In my Report I drew attention to the disorganization which occurred on the Darwin Station after the raids. It is important, I think, also to call attention to some of the results which, as the evidence disclosed, followed from this disorganization. I have mentioned that certain Hudson machines were not damaged in the raid.

(f) Effects of Disorganization.—(1) *Inability to Use Aircraft.*—A senior officer gave evidence that six times during the afternoon he endeavoured to get these Hudsons into the air in order to search out the whereabouts of the enemy aircraft carrier and to attack it. Owing to the disorganization existing, he was completely unable to get a communication to the necessary quarter. This was largely due to the fact that the Station Commander was unable to organize a ground-to-air wireless link at a time when the organizing of such communication was vital.

The same officer expressed the opinion that at that time the Station Commander was rattled and did not know which were the first things and which were the second things.

(2) *Salvage Not Attempted.*—Moreover, no attempt was made

to salvage equipment and material from the hangars or to salvage stores although in the opinion of competent witnesses such salvage was possible.

(3) *Emergency Water Supply Not Used.*—The water main laid on to the station was damaged in the raid, but to meet such a contingency an emergency water service was in existence from an elevated tank with the necessary reticulation. When it was attempted to use this during the raid, it was found to be chained and locked with a Yale lock, and in the result it proved impossible in the time to make use of this emergency service. [. . .]

(q) *Slit Trenches.*—Much evidence was given before me of the effectiveness of slit trenches to protect those who took shelter in them. The only instances in which they did not prevent injury to those sheltering were the cases of the Post Office and of one trench on the Royal Australian Air Force Station. At the Post Office there was a direct hit upon the trench and the occupants were killed. At the Royal Australian Air Force Station one officer was shot through the throat and killed.

(r) *Commendation.*—I should like to draw attention to the work done by Constable McNabb. All those who spoke of his conduct agreed in the view that his actions on the day of the raid were worthy of the highest praise.

ADDITIONAL MATTERS REPORTED ON.

(cc) *Natives of Melville Island.*—Evidence was given before me that the natives of Melville Island were in all probability more favourably disposed towards the Japanese than towards ourselves. The matter was not fully investigated by me, and a contrary opinion in relation to the majority of natives was expressed by Brother McCarthy, of the Catholic Mission on Bathurst Island.

I draw the Government's attention to these opinions in order that the matter may be more fully investigated if it is thought necessary.

This Report completes my survey of the evidence and of the matters upon which I have been asked to report, and I return herewith my commission.

(Sgd.) CHARLES J. LOWE,
Commissioner.
9th April, 1942

Acknowledgements

So many people have freely given time and trouble to help with the
writing of this book that it is hard to know where to start. I owe a
particular debt to my cousin Penny Cook, former Director of the
National Trust of the Northern Territory, whose affection for Darwin
and subtle understanding of Territory social history saved me from many
an error of fact or judgement. Some of the buildings mentioned in this
narrative are still standing, most notably the mission church on Bathurst
Island, thanks in no small part to Penny's energy, charm and persistence.

My lively veterans Herb Kriloff and Jack Mulholland gave me
invaluable first-hand accounts of the Darwin raid and its aftermath. They
were endlessly patient with my barrage of email and telephone questions,
and finally in face-to-face interviews. Jack's book *Darwin Bombed* is a
wonderfully evocative account of an ordinary soldier's experience of the
war. Herb's book *Officer of the Deck* is an equally graphic account of
the extraordinary adventures of USS *William B. Preston*.

Jack Mulholland introduced me to Austin Asche, former
Administrator of the Northern Territory. His Honour generously
undertook to look after me when I visited Darwin in February 2008 to
complete my research. Austin and his wife Val shepherded me through a
series of commemorations and reunions where I had a chance to meet

and talk to survivors of the 19 February raids. Austin's own sympathetic knowledge of the Northern Territory and its history provided me with an invaluable bridge to that colourful past.

Gordon 'Gordy' Birkett's encyclopaedic knowledge of Kittyhawk history in Australia, including some remarkable detective work on serial numbers and individual aircraft, allowed me to present the pilots' stories in detail, often in their own words. His files include signals traffic and other contemporary records, and they brought a directness and authority to what might otherwise have been no more than the usual mishmash of myth and legend. His group Adf Serials works entirely voluntarily. Anyone interested in more information can go to its website, www.adf-serials.com.

Brian Manning, former secretary of the Waterside Workers Union in Darwin, was unsparingly helpful with descriptions of the workings of the wharf, and with insights into the complex political history of trade unions in the Territory. He is a wonderful raconteur, and his stories of his time in office in Darwin, when his house was known as The Kremlin, would fill a book. I would not expect him to agree with my judgements on the role of the unions in the Second World War, and I hope he will forgive me for them. The wharfies, who suffered horrifically in the first few minutes of the raid, showed more fortitude during and after it than most of their critics. They deserve a fair hearing.

Peter Forrest and his wife Sheila are the Northern Territory's premier historians. I went to school with Peter and, on that flimsy excuse, sought him out. He gave me the touching Arthur Wellington letter reproduced in Chapter 7, and a lot of sound advice. Peter had long thought of writing a book about the Darwin raid, and my arrival on the scene cannot have been good news for him. Nevertheless, he gave generously and freely of his time, for which I am deeply grateful. My equal thanks to Arthur Wellington's daughter Aldyth, who gave me permission to quote the letter in full.

Warrant Officer Gnaire Foster put me in contact with Ian Ward, of the Darwin Defenders' Association, and Ian led me to other local veterans who gave invaluable firsthand accounts of the raid.

A remarkable chain of luck led me to Susan Holland in the tiny French village of Mortagne-sur-Gironde (population 967) in June 2008, just as I was finishing the book. Her father Robert Holland lived in Darwin from 1936, before joining the Australian Army in 1941 (and finishing the war as a guest of the Japanese government in Thailand, after being captured in Timor). She kindly gave me permission to use some of her father's Darwin photographs, particularly the aerial picture of Darwin which vividly brought to life the layout of the town and harbour at the time of the raid. Her father is second from the left in the group picture on the front cover.

The Lowe Commission examined its last witness on 25 March 1942, less than five weeks after the raid. So while the witnesses may not all have told the truth, the whole truth and nothing but the truth, what they did tell was certainly fresh in their memory. I have often used the transcript of the Lowe Commission evidence to allow my cast to tell their story in their own words. The evidence was quietly made public in 1972 when it was deposited with the Federal Parliamentary Library in Canberra, but it was not until 1997 that it became available, again with no fanfare, in the National Archive. All 918 pages are now available at its website, www.naa.gov.au. Two fat manila folders of exhibits are available in the National Archive in Melbourne. Some of the subsidiary documents had not been made public when I began writing this book, and some were released at my request. While no one could accuse successive Australian governments of covering up this material, it is fair to say that none went out of their way to lead the public to it.

All authors owe a debt to those who have tackled their subject beforehand. Douglas Lockwood's book *Australia Under Attack: The Bombing of Darwin 1942* (first published in 1966 as *Australia's Pearl Harbour*) is a first-class account of the raid, as anyone would expect from that great journalist. Lockwood had the advantage over me of being in Darwin on the day of the raid. On the other hand, he was denied access to the transcript of evidence given to the Lowe Commission and was even refused a request for a list of witnesses. As a result, he was forced to rely on his own and other people's memories 25 years after the event.

Sometimes individual accounts altered between Lowe and Lockwood, and whether the tellers' memories improved or faded in the interim is a matter for conjecture. Throughout the book, unless indicated in the text, I have used the Lowe rather than the Lockwood version.

Alan Powell's *The Shadow's Edge: Australia's Northern War* combines those rarest of qualities in history writing: authority and good humour. Professor Powell chose to write little about the events of 19 February 1942, saying modestly that 'the tale of the raids on Darwin that day has been twice told at length, by [Douglas] Lockwood with acumen, by [Timothy] Hall with hyperbole, and needs no general retelling'. I have taken the liberty of going against his advice and embarking on a general retelling. Meanwhile, I happily acknowledge the importance of Powell's research in giving me an authoritative time frame and, particularly, a detailed account of military movements before the raid.

Mitsuo Fuchida's book *Midway: The Battle That Doomed Japan, The Japanese Navy's Story*, written with Masatake Okumiya and published in English in 1955 by the Naval Institute Press in Washington, is a remarkably unapologetic and revealing account of the Imperial Japanese Navy's thinking and day-to-day tactics in 1941–42. Fuchida helped to plan both the Pearl Harbor and Darwin raids, and he was privy to his Navy's strategic calculations from 1941 to the middle years of the war. His book, and my old boss Charles 'Hank' Bateson's *The War With Japan, A Concise History*, enabled me to piece together the Japanese side of the story.

Sir Max Hastings' spellbinding book *Nemesis: The Battle For Japan, 1944–45* tells the story of Japan's descent in the final years of the Pacific War from the cocksure triumphs of the preceding pages to the starving, cornered and ultimately overwhelmed military nation it became. By 1945 the Japanese were surviving on little more than blind tenacity and denial in the face of certain defeat. Max's book—I presume to call him by his first name on the basis of a brief working connection many years ago—was badly received by some in Australia because it deals, however sympathetically, with the sidelining of Australian land forces towards the end of the Pacific War. Australians would do well to grow up and accept the reality of their history, as I have tried to do in this book.

The staff of the Northern Territory Archives Service were endlessly helpful with both research and photocopying. My particular thanks to Cathy Flint and Françoise Barr. The staff of the National Archives of Australia in Darwin, Canberra and Melbourne were equally forthcoming, as were the staff of the Australian War Memorial in Canberra. The Northern Territory Library, housed in the Legislative Assembly building, provided excellent background material, including contemporary newspapers.

The Sea Power Centre in Canberra is a gold mine of information on ships' histories, much of it available online. It proved particularly helpful in providing accurate casualty figures. My particular thanks to John Perryman, the Senior Naval Historical Officer there.

The National Archives and Records Administration in Maryland, USA, were tirelessly helpful in producing action reports. These reports, written within a few days of 19 February 1942 by the officers of the US Navy ships in Darwin during the raid, are matchless in their immediacy and authority. My particular thanks to Jodi Foor, who went to great trouble to dig out original documents that proved, among other things, that the official body count for the raid is nonsense.

Penny Cook, Austin Asche, Jack Mulholland, Herb Kriloff and Helen Young all bowed to my bullying and read the manuscript, subsequently saving me from my many sins. As always, all errors are entirely mine. I am grateful to Penny, Austin, Jack, Herb and Hellie for steering me away from the worst of them.

Mary McCune volunteered to type the Lowe report (Appendix II), thereby sparing me hours of drudgery. Mary has developed something of an addiction to low flying, and accompanied me on the Kittyhawk trail in Foxtrot Juliet Foxtrot (see p. 246, Chapter 5, n. 2). She showed great promise as an air navigator. The Kittyhawk pilots of 1942 might have made a better fist of Outback flying if they had been lucky enough to have Mary in the cockpit and in charge of the map.

My publishers Allen & Unwin remain a powerhouse of flair and good humour, qualities not often in evidence in the accountant-driven book industry of the twenty-first century. My particular thanks to managing editor Rebecca Kaiser for untiring support, and for her patience while we agonised over book titles. (I'm still fond of Bloody Darwin, but that's just me.) My editor Angela Handley did her customary stylish job of converting my words into a book, while Liz Keenan's sharp eye for the most economical way to shape a sentence trimmed away any loose ends I'd carelessly left behind.

Finally, my heartfelt thanks to those who gave me a home while I was researching this book: in Sydney, Karma Abraham and Lenore Nicklin, Mary and Van McCune, and Paul and Debbie Dykzeul; in Melbourne, Robert Foster and Jack Bell.

Notes

Chapter 1: 'Big flight of planes . . . Very high'

1   McManus recalled afterwards: 'We worked it out a long while ago.
We based it on 140 knots and the distance from Bathurst Island to
Darwin: I think it is 43 miles or 47 miles by air. We allowed
four miles a minute to be on the safe side.' In fact the distance
between Nguiu on Bathurst Island and Darwin airfield is
42 nautical miles, which an aeroplane flying at 140 knots would
cover in 18 minutes. Despite McManus's dodgy arithmetic, his
figure of 12 minutes proved remarkably accurate.

Chapter 2: A very sinful people

1   It is only fair to point out that some of the creation stories of the
Northern Territory Aboriginal people involve places as far off as
Port Augusta in South Australia. Aboriginal trade routes linked
northern and southern Australia thousands of years before John
McDouall Stuart.

2   It is important to distinguish between Darwin, meaning the town
itself, Port Darwin, the large stretch of water enclosed by the East
Arm on one side and the town of Darwin on the other, and Darwin
Harbour, the tiny enclosed wharf area on the western side of the
port and next to the town centre.

3   When the wharf was rebuilt after the Japanese air raid, the new
     design followed a single curve from ship to shore, eliminating the
     need for turntables, donkey engines and manhandled railway cars.

Chapter 3: Horribly strained relations

1   The Allies gave Japanese bombers girls' names, and Japanese fighters
     boys' names. Under this system, the Zero was called a Zeke. How-
     ever, this proved less easy to remember than Zero, and the Japanese
     aircraft-type number stuck.

2   Given that the Japanese had no shortage of diplomats and spies in
     Honolulu at the time, this was an unusually faulty piece of
     intelligence. Only two carriers were then available to the American
     Pacific Fleet, USS *Lexington* and USS *Enterprise*. USS *Yorktown* was
     still operating in the Atlantic. On 7 December 1941 *Enterprise*
     was on its way from Pearl Harbor to Wake Island, ferrying aircraft,
     while *Lexington* was on a similar delivery run to Midway. The third
     Pacific Fleet carrier USS *Saratoga* (not the *Hornet,* which was never
     involved) was still in San Diego on the American west coast, after
     completing a refit.

3   As a bizarre footnote to history, all 68 civilians killed at Pearl
     Harbor died from 'friendly fire', mostly anti-aircraft shells dropping
     back into the city of Honolulu. The Japanese lost 55 killed to the
     same guns. Not a single civilian death could be laid at the feet of
     the attacking Japanese. At Pearl Harbor, defending US forces killed
     more of their own countrymen than they did their supposed target,
     the enemy attackers.

Chapter 4: One suitcase, one small calico bag

1   In 1942 Cullen Bay was more commonly known as Kahlin Bay,
     after the old Aboriginal 'compound' at Kahlin near Larrakeyah.
     Throughout the text I have preferred the current usage. The name
     Kahlin survives in the city's most important cricket field, Kahlin
     Oval, on Cullen Bay.

2   The RAAF airfield, much expanded and improved, is now Darwin
     International Airport. The civil airfield is no more: the runway has

become Ross Smith Avenue, Parap. Its only surviving artefact is the old Qantas hangar, now owned by the Museum and Art Gallery of the Northern Territory and used as a workshop and vintage car display area by the Motor Vehicle Enthusiasts' Club.

Chapter 5: No place and no time for argument

1 The Kittyhawk looked a bit like the Zero, leading to the famous 1942 training film *The Identification of the Japanese Zero*. In the film, a young Ronald Reagan almost shoots down his buddy's P40 before learning to tell the difference and go on (of course) to shoot down a real Zero.

2 I can sympathise with their problems. As part of the research for this book, in July 2007 I flew the route myself, starting from Camden, west of Sydney, and finishing at the smart new Darwin International Airport. I was piloting a single-engine Beech Debonair, call sign VH-FJF. Foxtrot Juliet Foxtrot and I had the benefit of a GPS and a lot of other 21st-century electronic wizardry. The Kittyhawk pilots had not much more than a rudimentary map, a compass and a stopwatch. I flew up via Walgett, Charleville, Winton, Mt Isa, and Borroloola to Darwin, and back to Camden via Tennant Creek, Birdsville and Bourke. (Someone must have been along with a dustpan and brush after the war, because I saw no sign of crashed planes along the way.)

Elements of the journey were pretty alarming. Pilots navigating 'visually' (as opposed to following radio beacons or other electronic aids) generally draw a line on a map and mark 'waypoints' every 30 or 40 kilometres—a river fork here, a town with a racecourse there, a railway bridge across a highway somewhere else—and fly from waypoint to waypoint. The Kittyhawk pilots were all navigating visually. In central Australia there are no waypoints. On my flight from Tennant Creek to Birdsville, there was a stretch of 173 nautical miles (320 kilometres) across the Simpson Desert without a single ground feature I could use. For more than an hour all I could do was point the aircraft in what I hoped was the right direction and pray that Birdsville would appear ahead of me.

Without the GPS I seriously doubt that I would ever have found it. The Kittyhawk pilots had no GPS and little or nothing else to help them. They navigated by following roads, railways and telegraph lines. For huge stretches of the journey there were none. Their planes regularly overheated and developed engine problems en route. Others got lost and ran out of fuel, crash-landing in the desert before they had a chance to engage the enemy.

3   The citizens of the Northern Territory have good reason to this day to thank 'coloured labour units' from America. Black American troops were the main labour force building what is now called the Barkly Highway road link between western Queensland and the Northern Territory.

4   Author's note: the correct number of children was 969. Harrison, in his evidence to the Royal Commission, said there was a discrepancy of about 500 between the police survey and the wardens' survey, with the error on the police side. V.G. Carrington, the Acting Government Secretary, confirmed to the Commission that there were discrepancies, but said the errors were on the wardens' side. Clearly, this was not a happy ship.

Chapter 7: Convoy to Koepang to return to Darwin

1   In the early days of the Pacific War, the US Army Air Corps used the word 'Pursuit' in squadron names in the way most other air forces used 'Fighter'. The 3rd Pursuit Squadron would now be called 3rd Fighter Squadron. The terms are interchangeable, but I have stuck to the original.

Chapter 8: 'Zeroes! Zeroes! Zeroes!'

1   Griffith told a different and even less credible story to the Lowe Commission. In Griffith's version: 'At a little after 10 a.m. on the 19th the station Operations Room phoned me that there was a report of enemy aircraft approaching. I went immediately to the Operations Room, which is directly above my own office, and was informed by the controller that a message had been telephoned through from Bathurst Island that a large force of unidentified

aircraft was approaching from the north. I remained on the verandah of the Operations Room and ordered the air raid alarm to be sounded. I saw some aircraft attacking the town of Darwin, and then, with the Operations staff that remained, took shelter in a trench.'

2   There is a bizarre footnote to Lieutenant Hughes's tragic story. Although McMahon was able to give a fair idea of the crash site, neither the wrecked plane nor Hughes's body was ever found. He is officially listed as 'MIA', Missing In Action, rather than 'KIA', Killed In Action.

Chapter 9: QQQ QQQ QQQ de VZDN

1   Tindal's name lives on today. The RAAF base near Katherine, 280 kilometres south-east of Darwin, and at the time of writing home to 75 Squadron's FA-18 fighters, was named RAAF Tindal in his memory.

Chapter 10: Between the raids: Can anyone drive?

1   To be fair, it would have taken a shark or crocodile of more than usual coolness under fire to loiter in Port Darwin that day. There is no record of any crocodile or shark attack during the rescue operations. Even the ubiquitous box jellyfish seem to have thought better of it.

2   I can find no trace of the A24s Scherger refers to. There were none in Darwin that day. They were not at Batchelor, nor at Daly Waters further south. The only other aircraft within reach were eight Hudsons at Daly Waters, but they had no crews.

Chapter 11: The second raid: Chinese whispers

1   There is some doubt over their airfields of origin. The official Australian Navy history says Kendari only. The official Army history says Ambon only. The official RAAF history says nothing. Douglas Lockwood says both Kendari and Ambon. The official Japanese history supports Lockwood.

2   A popular star of B-movie Westerns of the day.

3   For the record, Darwin's entire contingent of sanitary carts disappeared in similar fashion down 'the Track'. A Mr Monks was

eventually dispatched to Adelaide River to retrieve the errant vehicles, and returned them to service three days later. Darwin had no sanitary collection for five days after the raid. Some houses waited ten days for their next collection.

Chapter 12: Things go badly wrong

1 James Arthur MacArthur-Onslow's service record was sealed until 2012, and parts of it are still inaccessible. It's a weird story. He was the son of Major General James MacArthur-Onslow, of the great Australian grazier dynasty. He joined the Australian Army on 13 May 1940 under an assumed name—James Vernon. On 30 January 1942, three weeks before the Darwin raid, he was promoted to sergeant (under his real name) but on 19 April 1942 he was demoted to corporal and then to private. Two months later he was discharged. The Wikipedia entry for his father notes that the major general had three children. Of James Arthur it says: 'disinherited and bankrupted by his father'. He died on 17 June 1959.

Chapter 14: Telling the world

1 In files held at the Australian National Archive in Darwin is an undated handwritten note from Flight Lieutenant Colin Bell addressed to Group Captain Scherger setting out the numbers killed and injured. Bell's memorandum comes up with the same figure of 178 dead. His calculation uses almost identical figures to those given in the Navy cable of 1 March, suggesting that the two writers had conferred, and that the two documents were prepared at about the same time. Thomas's figures may even have been based on Bell's. Both documents illustrate the fact that the true numbers were still unclear more than a week after the raid.

Appendix II: Report of the Lowe Commission

1 Lowe is referring elliptically to the widespread belief in Darwin that the Japanese left the oil tanks alone because they wanted the oil for their own use after an invasion. We now know that this was false: they did not set out to preserve the oil tanks, they simply failed to hit them.

Bibliography

Alford, Bob, *Darwin's Air War 1942–1945: An Illustrated History*, Aviation Historical Society of the Northern Territory, Darwin, 1991

Bateson, Charles, *The War With Japan: A Concise History*, Ure Smith, Sydney; Barrie and Jenkins, London; Michigan State University Press, East Lansing, 1968

Calvocoressi, Peter, Guy Wint and John Pritchard, *Total War: The Causes and Courses of the Second World War*, Viking, London, 1972, revised 1989

Edmonds, Walter D., *They Fought With What They Had: The Story of the Army Air Forces in the South West Pacific, 1941–42*, Little, Brown and Company, Boston, 1951

Edwards, John, *Curtin's Gift*, Allen & Unwin, Sydney, 2005

Forrest, Peter and Sheila Forrest, *Federation Frontline: A People's History of World War II in the Northern Territory*, Centenary of Federation Northern Territory, Darwin, 2001

Fuchida, Mitsuo and Masatake Okumiya, *Midway: The Battle That Doomed Japan, The Japanese Navy Story*, Naval Institute Press, Annapolis, 1955

Hall, Timothy, *Darwin 1942: Australia's Darkest Hour*, Methuen Australia, 1980

Hastings, Max, *Nemesis: The Battle for Japan, 1944–45*, Harper Press, London, 2007

James, Barbara, *No Man's Land: Women of the Northern Territory*, Collins Australia, Sydney, 1989

Kriloff, Herbert, *Officer of the Deck: A Memoir of the Pacific War and the Sea*, Pacifica Press, Pacifica, 2000

—— *Proceed Orange: Assume Command*, Detseleg Enterprises, Calgary, 2002

Lockwood, Douglas, *Australia Under Attack: The Bombing of Darwin 1942*, New Holland Publishers (Australia), 2005. First published as *Australia's Pearl Harbour*, Cassell Australia, 1966

Mulholland, Jack, *Darwin Bombed: An A/A Gunner's Reflections*, Bookbound Publishing, Ourimbah, 2006

Pearce, Howard and Bob Alford, *A Wartime Journey: Stuart Highway Heritage Guide*, Northern Territory Tourist Commission, 2006

Powell, Alan, *The Shadow's Edge: Australia's Northern War*, Melbourne University Press, Melbourne, 1988, revised and reprinted NT University Press, Darwin, 2007

Ruwoldt, Rex, *Darwin's Battle for Australia*, Darwin Defenders 1942–45 Inc., Clifton Springs, 2005

Some Of The Boys, *Soldiering On*, Australian War Memorial, Canberra, 1942

Williamson, Kristin, *The Last Battalion*, Lansdowne Press, Melbourne, 1984

Index